More Lost
Massey Lectures

More LOST MASSEY LECTURES

Recovered Classics from Five Great Thinkers

BARBARA WARD

FRANK H. UNDERHILL

GEORGE GRANT

CLAUDE LÉVI-STRAUSS

WILLY BRANDT

ANANSI

This edition published in 2008 by
House of Anansi Press Inc.
110 Spadina Avenue, Suite 801,
Toronto, ON, M5V 2K4
Tel. 416-363-4343
Fax 416-363-1017
www.anansi.ca

Distributed in Canada by
HarperCollins Canada Ltd.
1995 Markham Road
Scarborough, ON, M1B 5M8
Toll free tel. 1-800-387-0117

Distributed in the United States by
Publishers Group West
1700 Fourth Street
Berkeley, CA 94710
Toll free tel. 1-800-788-3123

House of Anansi Press is committed to protecting our natural environment.
As part of our efforts, this book is printed on paper that contains 100%
post-consumer recycled fibres, is acid-free, and is processed chlorine-free.

12 11 10 09 08   1 2 3 4 5

LIBRARY AND ARCHIVES CANADA CATALOGUING IN PUBLICATION DATA

More lost Massey lectures : recovered classics from five great thinkers /
by Willy Brandt . . . [et al.].

(CBC Massey lectures series)
Contents: Dangers and options / Willy Brandt — Time as history / George Grant —
Myth and meaning / Claude Lévi-Strauss — Image of confederation / Frank H.
Underhill — The rich nations and the poor nations / Barbara Ward.

ISBN 978-0-88784-801-8

I. Brandt, Willy, 1913–1992. II. Series.

JZ1242.L6753 2008   081   C2008-901760-9

Library of Congress Control Number: 2008924730

Cover design: Bill Douglas
Text design and typesetting: Laura Brady, Brady Typesetting & Design

Canada Council
for the Arts

Conseil des Arts
du Canada

ONTARIO ARTS COUNCIL
CONSEIL DES ARTS DE L'ONTARIO

*We acknowledge for their financial support of our publishing program the Canada Council
for the Arts, the Ontario Arts Council, and the Government of Canada through the
Book Publishing Industry Development Program (BPIDP).*

Printed and bound in Canada

Contents

Introduction

The Massey Lectures were born in the winter of 1961. They were unveiled in late February by the vice-president and general manager of English networks at the Canadian Broadcasting Corporation (CBC), H. G. Walker. "Each year," he said in the press release announcing the series, "the CBC will invite a noted scholar to undertake study or original research in his field and present the results in a series of half-hour radio broadcasts." He continued, saying that he hoped the lectures would "make significant contributions to public awareness and understanding and . . . further development of the art of broadcasting."

The lectures were named for the Right Honourable Vincent Massey, who had recently completed a seven-year term as governor general of Canada. Massey is notable as the first Canadian-born person to hold the post, but it was work he did before becoming governor general that inspired the CBC to name the new lecture series after him.

In 1949, Vincent Massey had been appointed by the government of Prime Minister Louis St. Laurent to head a royal commission mandated to carry out a sweeping study of "the entire field of letters, the arts and sciences within the jurisdiction of the federal state." Grandly named the Royal Commission on National Development in the Arts, Letters and Sciences, it came to be known more simply as the Massey Commission. Its scope included science, literature, the arts, music, drama, film, and broadcasting. The commission held hearings across the country. It listened to testimony from more than a thousand witnesses and received 462 written submissions. It took two years to do its work and issued its final report in 1951.

The Massey Report was enormously influential. It led to, among other things, the establishment of the National Library of Canada and the Canada Council. But more broadly, the report was instrumental in modernizing the role of the federal government in cultural activity. Naming a prestigious lecture series after Vincent Massey was the CBC's way of giving him special recognition for the work he had done to promote culture and the humanities in Canada.

The first set of Massey Lectures was broadcast in the spring of 1961. It consisted of six half-hour talks by Barbara Ward, a British expert in economics and international affairs. Her lectures were called *The Rich Nations and the Poor Nations*, and in them she examined the causes of poverty in what were then known as the "underdeveloped nations." The lectures were broadcast once a week, on Thursday nights at 8:30. Vincent Massey himself introduced the first broadcast. The CBC later published the lectures as a book, and so began a tradition in public broadcasting and publishing that has continued for forty-seven years, a tradition that has evolved and expanded with the times.

Most, but not all, of the Massey Lectures are still in print. The lectures today are the product of a happy collaboration of three partners — CBC Radio, House of Anansi Press, and Massey College in the University of Toronto. For most of their history, the Massey Lectures were recorded within the austere confines of a CBC radio studio in Toronto. But since 2002, they have been delivered each fall before large audiences on university campuses in cities across Canada. The recorded public lectures are then broadcast to listeners in Canada on CBC Radio One, and to all of North America on Sirius Satellite radio. They are also streamed worldwide on the Internet and available as podcasts. Simultaneously with the broadcasts, the lectures are published as a trade paperback that garners international attention and usually makes the bestseller lists. The Massey Lectures have established their place as a truly Canadian institution and are an annual highlight of our national intellectual life.

The Massey Lectures have been graced by some of the finest minds in the world — writers, scholars, statesmen, activists — men and women from every field of human endeavour who shaped the thought of their times. In 2007, House of Anansi Press and the CBC reached back into the Massey archive to re-issue a set of early classics under the title, *The Lost Massey Lectures*. These lectures had been out of print for decades, and their appearance in the book marked the first time they again became publicly available.

Now comes a new collection of recovered classics, *More Lost Massey Lectures*, a selection of lectures from the '60s, '70s and '80s, a period of breathtaking cultural and political upheaval worldwide. Included are Barbara Ward's inaugural Massey Lectures, as well as lectures by the Canadian historian and social critic, Frank Underhill; the prominent Canadian political and religious philosopher,

George Grant; the father of structural anthropology, Claude Lévi-Strauss; and Willy Brandt, the former chancellor of West Germany and winner of the Nobel Peace Prize in 1971 for his work in fostering détente between eastern and western Europe during the worst years of the Cold War.

When Barbara Ward delivered her Massey Lectures, *The Rich Nations and the Poor Nations*, in 1961, much of the world was undergoing a wave of de-colonization that had begun after World War II. New countries, former European colonies, were emerging in Asia and Africa and beginning to assert their place on the world stage. She began her lectures by noting that, "we live in the most catastrophically revolutionary age that men have ever faced." It was an age of multiple revolutions, she said, that were rapidly changing everything about our way of life beyond recognition. Ward singled out four revolutions for particular attention: two "revolutionary" ideas — the idea of equality and the idea of progress; a biological revolution — the earth's rapidly increasing population; and a scientific revolution — the unprecedented application of science to almost every facet of life. Through these revolutions, the nations of the North Atlantic — the United Kingdom, Western Europe, and North America — had become the wealthiest societies in human history. In contrast were the emerging, developing nations, "traditional" societies, where these revolutions had not yet taken hold. The distinction between rich and poor nations would become, Ward predicted with a prescience that still holds true nearly fifty years later, "one of the great dominant political and international themes of our century."

Frank Underhill was the third Massey Lecturer. A political scientist and historian, Underhill had taught at the University of Saskatchewan, the University of Toronto, and Carleton University. He had fought as an infantry officer in World War I. Underhill was a leader of progressive thought in Canada and had been one of the founding members of the Co-operative Common-wealth Federation (CCF), the forerunner of today's NDP. His Massey Lectures, entitled *The Image of Confederation*, were given in 1963.

That year, Canada had gone through a searing debate over a proposal to station American nuclear weapons on Canadian soil. The Conservative government of Prime Minister John Diefenbaker had refused and was defeated on the issue in a general election that spring. The Liberals, under Lester Pearson, came to power, and the new government reluctantly agreed to accept the weapons. Pearson faced another major challenge: the threat to the unity of the country from rising Quebec nationalism. In 1960, Jean Lesage had been elected premier of Quebec, ending the long grip on politics held by Maurice Duplessis' conservative Union Nationale party. Lesage ushered in the Quiet Revolution and adopted the phrase *Maîtres chez nous* — Masters in Our Home — to express Quebec's aspirations. There was also a darker side to the issue. In 1963, a new and violent nationalist group appeared on the scene, the Front de libération du Québec (FLQ). It launched a campaign of more than two hundred bombings that were to continue until the end of the decade. In his Massey Lectures, Underhill hearkened back to the newly formed Canada of 1867, a bold experiment that brought together English- and French-speaking Canadians, "divided though they were in race, language, and religion." A nation that had been founded in optimism, Underhill thought, now seemed dispirited. He sensed "a feeling of defeatism in the air." The lectures provided a good opportunity, he wrote, "to review what Canadians, from time to time, since 1867, have thought about their nationhood, its purpose and significance."

The iconic Canadian philosopher George Grant delivered his Massey Lectures, *Time as History*, in 1969. They were a meditation on "what it means to conceive the world as an historical process, to conceive time as history and man as an historical being." History, he explained, is a word with ambiguous meanings. On the one hand, it is a scholarly discipline — the study of the past; on the other, it is the course of human existence itself. The modern social sciences, Grant thought, believed they could understand human beings by observing their behaviour and using the observations to predict the future. They were not interested in what he called, "the animating source from which those behaviours spring forth." He spoke of the idea of "will," both as an expression of determination and an orientation toward the future. It was important to be able to imagine a future in order to create a better world. Meaning, he wrote, is not found in what is, but in what we can bring into being. Grant remarked on a paradox between thought and action, between "deliberation" and "will": "what seems required among human beings for the greatest thought is opposite to what is required for the greatest doing . . . Certainty in closing down issues by decision is necessary for great deeds."

The theme of the 1977 Massey Lectures, by the French anthropologist Claude Lévi-Strauss, was *Myth and Meaning*. In a unique approach, never taken before or since, the audio recordings with Lévi-Strauss were done as a series of extended interviews, conducted in Paris over a number of days, then edited in Toronto into a seamless "lecture" presentation. The edited audio was later transcribed for publication.

What can mythology tell us about the world? Are myths "true"? Mythical stories, Lévi-Strauss said, can seem meaningless, absurd, and chaotic. If they were simply fanciful creations of the mind, you would expect them to be unique. Yet the same stories — or similar stories — appear in different guises all over the world. Beneath apparent disorder is order, without which meaning would not be possible. "What does 'to mean' mean?" he asked. The only answer "is that 'to mean' means the ability of any kind of data to be translated in a different language. I do not mean a different language like French or German, but different words on a different level."

Lévi-Strauss addressed the relationship between mythology and science. There had been a divorce between the two in the seventeenth and eighteenth centuries, when science was trying to establish itself. It could only do this by distancing itself from centuries of mythological and mystical thought. Science regarded data from the world of the senses — sight, sound, smell, taste, and touch — as unreliable. The real world could be captured only in mathematical relationships and abstractions, and apprehended only by the intellect. This, Lévi-Strauss thought, was changing; science was re-integrating sense data into its methods. The divorce, he thought, could be reversed.

The final lecture series in this collection is by Willy Brandt. A former leader of the German Social Democratic party (SPD) and chancellor of West Germany between 1969 and 1974, Brandt delivered his 1981 Massey Lectures, *Dangers & Options*, at a time of worldwide crisis. The lectures followed an economic conference of the world's seven leading industrialized countries, held in July 1981 in Cancun, Mexico. Economic growth was slowing. Inflation and unemployment were high. Food and energy were expensive. There were tensions between East and West, and a dangerous arms race. The disparity between North and South was growing ever greater. Brandt described the changes taking place in the world as "a series of wide-ranging upheavals." We would continue to face radical change well into the future, and would need imagination and commitment to confront it. He issued a warning and an appeal. "The shaping of our common future is much too important to be left to experts and governments alone," he said. He called upon young people, women's and labour movements, political and religious leaders, scientists, intellectuals, business leaders, and farmers to work together on the new challenges of global survival. "We must open our minds to the difficult problems of others in all parts of the world," he wrote. "And we must realize that together we might survive — or we will not survive at all."

In concluding my introduction to *The Lost Massey Lectures* in 2007, I wrote the paragraph you are about to read at the end of this introduction. If the themes of this new collection of recovered classics, *More Lost Massey Lectures*, seem familiar, it's because they are. I have always been struck by the continuity between past and present, by the fact that though we encounter radically different circumstances in different eras, the underlying themes of our lives are remarkably similar. I want to repeat here what I said then.

We live in an age that is said to be ahistorical. It is difficult to remember the past — or even acknowledge it — living as we do, focused on an "eternal present," driven by busy schedules and information overload, and wrapped up in anxieties about careers, family, health, the environment, terrorism, the future of the world. It can be both comforting and discouraging to know that many of the issues we confront today have been with us in different forms for a long time; people have thought about them and grappled with them for generations. I hope you find that these lost Massey Lectures are both a useful mirror of the times in which they were written and an insightful context for some of our most pressing current dilemmas.

BERNIE LUCHT
Toronto
June 2008

THE RICH NATIONS AND THE POOR NATIONS

by
BARBARA WARD

I

ORIGINATIONS

I suppose we are all aware of the fact that we live in the most catastrophically revolutionary age that men have ever faced. Usually one thinks of a revolution as one event or at least as one interconnected series of events. But we are in fact living with ten or twenty such revolutions — all changing our ways of life, our ways of looking at things, changing everything out of recognition and changing it fast.

What I want to do here is to trace some of these revolutions in their effect on our environment and on the way we live. And since I cannot deal with all of them, I have chosen four which seem to me to weave their way in and out of our lives at every point.

Now, the first and perhaps the most pervasive of these revolutions begins in the field of ideas. This is hardly surprising since ideas are the prime movers of history. Revolutions usually begin with ideas and it is by our ideas that we change the way we live, the way we organize society, the way we manipulate material things. So let us begin with a revolutionary idea now at work from one end of the world to the other: the revolution of equality — equality of men and equality of nations. This is a bald statement. It cannot be treated exhaustively. There is simply not time to explore all the implications of man's equality with man. For one thing, no society yet knows fully what it means by such equality. Is it to be only a levelling? Does it imply indifference to excellence? Can it be combined with reasonable lines of command and control? And, since someone must rule, if all supposedly extraneous obstacles to equality were removed — birth, land, wealth, inheritance — would rule by brain and ability alone create a "meritocracy," a "Mandarinate" of refined intelligence, finally more unequal than a system demanding less rigorous and inflexible methods of recruiting the governing group? These are all fascinating questions to pursue and many of them are strictly relevant to the great international questions of our day. For instance, the recruitment of leaders among the dispossessed in the name of equality is a great strength for Communism, since in all developing nations the dispossessed make up the vast majority. But there must be limits set to our discussion and here we are concerned primarily with equality as a force making for social, economic, and national change.

We know that the passionate desire for men to see themselves as the equals of other human beings without distinctions of class or sex or race or nationhood is one of the driving forces of our day. And I believe it is a tap root of modern nationalism. I do not, of course, minimize the other roots of nationalism: the sense of community, the common tongue, the shared history. But when nations look out on the international arena, much of the strength of their nationalism comes from the sense that they are as good as their neighbours and ought to have the same rights; in other words, equality. The whole United Nations with its "one state, one vote," reflects this egalitarian nationalism and "the right to self-determination," the most cutting edge of nationalism as old empires dissolve, is in essence the new peoples' claim to national equality with the older states. For this reason, nationalism today comes to us in great measure in the form of equality — the equality of nations one with each other, the equality of esteem and prestige which comes from not being run by other nations. This is one of the great drives of our world. And when we discuss nationalism, I think it is legitimate to unite it with the idea of equality.

The second revolution also concerns ideas: the idea of progress, of the possibility of material change leading to a better world, not hereafter, but here and now. This worldliness, if you like, this emphasis on the goods and opportunities of this world, is another radical force at work in our world.

The third revolution is a biological revolution: the sudden vast increase in the rate at which the human race is multiplying upon the face of the earth.

The fourth and perhaps the most pervasive of all the revolutions of our day is the application of science and saving — or capital — to all the economic processes of our life. In fact, the application is much wider. We have begun to apply science and reason to nearly all our forms of living, to administration, to office management, to politics, to sociology, even to culture and to art.

These four revolutions — of equality, of this-worldliness, of rising birth-rates, and of driving scientific change — all started in the North Atlantic arena, in those nations which lie around the North Atlantic Ocean. Britain, Western Europe, and North America have, by working and expanding together, created a quite new kind of human society. A sort of mutation has occurred and we in the Atlantic area no longer share a continuous way of life with under-developed and emerging peoples, because in their societies none of the revolutions has been fully at work. They have had little idea of equality. There was in the past no great urge for general material progress. The pressure of population followed a strict rotation of famine and feast and had little of the explosive burst that we have seen in our day. Above all, traditional societies did very little saving and had virtually no science. By the same token, these changes which cut us off from all earlier forms of social organization have created in the Atlantic world what can only be called a new kind of human community.

I do not know whether one would say of this new society that it is demonstrably happier. Sometimes I think people wonder whether it can be claimed to be more civilized. But there is one thing which is absolutely certain. It is sensationally richer. What has happened around the North Atlantic is that a ring of societies has come into being with more wealth, more economic resources at its disposal, than has ever before been known in human history. This is the profoundly revolutionary change to which all the subsidiary revolutions have contributed. And, since all nations have not yet come within the scope of this revolution, or rather this series of revolutions, and since all of them without exception desire to do so, the distinction between rich nations and poor nations is one of the great dominant political and international themes of our century.

How have these four revolutions, working together, produced the mutation of a quite new kind of society: the wealthy or affluent society? How is it that, remoulding the traditional forms of social order, they have developed a form of society so different from any that went before? Let us begin with the revolution of equality. It has its roots in two profound traditions of Western society: the Greek view of law and the Judeo-Christian vision of souls all equal in the sight of God. For the Greek, the essence of citizenship, what distinguished the *polis* — the city-state — from the barbarians outside, was that men lived in the Greek city according to laws which they themselves had helped to frame. This was not a full vision of equality; slaves and women were excluded. But the citizen enjoyed equality with his fellows before the law, and the law was the final shield of his integrity and equality against the threat of tyranny — either the tyranny of a single leader or the possibly more dangerous threat of an arbitrary majority. Here in its first emergence in history could be found a definition of the "rights of man" in terms of his rights against a dangerously sovereign government.

The other mood of equality is expressed in Christian metaphysics, in the vision of souls standing equal in the sight of God. During the Middle Ages, cathedral and church were the educators of the common man and a favourite theme in those days was the "Doom," or Last Judgement, carved above the portals of cathedrals or painted on the humbler walls of parish churches. From these panoramas of bliss and misery men received with vivid emotional force the sense of human equality. Among those called to bliss would be the shepherd, the peasant, the woodman, the carpenter, while those descending with tortured faces to everlasting misery were all too often kings, princes, dukes, and bishops as well. Here, expressed with the most dramatic sense of contrast, is the profound root of equality: the belief that souls are equal before God and that, therefore, their equality is innate, metaphysical, and independent of the vanities of class, race, or culture. Clearly, once you implant an idea as revolutionary as this in the soil of society, you can have no conception of the luxuriance and diversity of the growth that may follow. And one consequence in our Western civilization is especially worth examining. It is the emergence to a dominant position in society of men and groups who have never achieved a political "break-through" in any other civilization.

Since the beginning of history, you can say in shorthand that the dominant rulers have been the kings and the priests. They were flanked by the warriors, and often, as in the early Middle Ages in Europe, warriors were rewarded for their services with fiefs of land. Or, as in India, land revenue was allotted to court officials and advisers as a source of income. Thus the political leadership of the community came to be monopolized by the court and by landed men. In such societies — and most traditional societies resemble this pattern — the merchant was of necessity a marginal figure. To this day, in parts of Latin America and Asia, this old, more or less feudal pattern persists. But as the Middle Ages unfolded in Europe a different picture began to appear. Owing to the division of power between Pope and Emperor at the head of society, the possibility of a plurality of powers opened up for the whole social order. Subsidiary groups — nations, cities, communes, corporations — grasped the power needed for their operations, defined it in terms of law, and defended it in the name of equal rights. In such a society the merchant was able to exercise real power and to enjoy real security for his work, his trade, and his savings. The charters given to cities defined his rights of self-government and, as early as the fourteenth century, the sovereign called him into consultation — through parliament — before trying to tax his wealth for national purposes.

These developments gave the cities with their merchants and bankers and rising middle classes an independence they enjoyed nowhere else. There was never any figure in Delhi or Canton who had the status, influence, and rights, of the Lord Mayor of London or the Burgomaster of Ghent. And without the self-confidence and security of the merchant class the later evolution of capitalist society would have been inconceivable.

But of course the leaven of equality did not cease to operate once it had raised the middle classes to effective influence. It worked right on through the rest of society and it works on to this day. In England's Civil War it was John Lilburne, a soldier on the more extreme wing in Cromwell's Army, who gave classic expression to the drive which would dominate politics for the next four hundred years. "The poorest he that is in England has a life to live as the richest he." This was Lilburne's phrase and ever since it has been the motive power of revolutions beyond number. It underlies the growth of socialism, the cutting edge of trade union organization, the emancipation of the workers in the wake of the middle classes, the whole concept of the modern welfare state. We do not see the end of the process for, as I suggested earlier, we do not know what the ultimate stage of equality may be. Is it level equalness? Is it equal chance and opportunity? Is it conceivably a society ruled by love, not force?

We do not know. But we *do* know that the leaven of equality has worked through every stratum of our society, emancipating new classes and letting loose new political forces onto the great stage of history. Now we have to ask the question: What in the main have these new classes asked for in claiming their emancipation? At this point we meet the second of our revolutionary ideas: the idea of what one might call this-worldliness, of immense interest in *this* world, in its processes, in its laws and construction, in the ways in which it can be set to work and made over according to human ends and purposes — in a word the world as an arena of work and effort where needs and dreams can be satisfied.

These ideas spring essentially from our triple inheritance: Greek thought, Judaism, and Christianity. It was in the Greek vision of law that science acquired its fundamental confidence in a material universe predictable and orderly enough to be explored. From the Judeo-Christian religious inheritance came the idea that the whole of creation is God's work, and as such must be of immense interest and value. "Call thou no thing unclean" was the divine instruction to Peter and, in spite of the temptations of religious pessimism, Christianity has never dismissed as "illusion" what comes from the hand of God. Other societies have lacked this essential insight into the value of created things. In Hindu culture, for instance, the world is *Maya*, illusion, a fevered dance of fleeting appearances which mask the pure reality of uncreated being.

But perhaps the sharpest break in Western tradition from the basic ideas of other civilizations lies in its vision of reality as an unfolding drama, as an immense dialogue between God and man crowned at some inconceivable end in an outcome of fulfillment and bliss. All archaic societies feel themselves bound to a "melancholy wheel" of endless recurrence. Seasons, the life cycle, planetary order, all revealed the return of things to their origins and life swung round in the orbit fixed by destiny. Marcus Aurelius, wisest of Roman emperors, believed that at forty a man had experienced all there was to experience. No vision of reality as progressing forward to new possibilities, no sense of the future as better and fuller than the present, tempered the underlying fatalism of ancient civilization. It is only in the Jewish and Christian faith that a Messianic hope first breaks upon mankind. In Christianity, the hope is expressed in religious terms of deliverance and salvation. But over the centuries the idea became transmuted into this-worldly terms, in fact into the dominant idea of progress, of getting forward, of being able to see hope ahead, and of working for a better future, not hereafter, but here and now.

Now let us examine the effect of this respect for material things, coupled with a Messianic hope of the future, upon one aspect of Western society — upon its economic system. As the Middle Ages ended and the merchants felt their status and their opportunities increase, they found in the Christian tradition those elements which best suited their outlook and condition. Opposing the luxuries of the courts and the loudly alleged idleness of monastic living, they preached a gospel of work, praising the religious value of what men did in the counting house, in the workshop, in farm and field, and looking forward to the coming of the Kingdom in terms of work, effort, and material success. No one can doubt that, as a result, an immense charge of energy was added to the urge to work and produce at the beginning of the capitalist era.

But there were still limits to the merchant's materialism. As workers, they stood out against an idle and luxurious world. To acquire wealth was one thing; to spend it in riotous living quite another. So, instead, they accumulated capital and set it working further. This restraint was one of the roots of saving on a large scale without which sufficient capital might never have been accumulated for the modern economic system. Work, austerity, and an increasingly secularized version of the Messianic hope were thus the ferments of a new society, the portents of a revolutionary age when the desire for better things and "the revolution of using expectations" — to use Mr. Adlai Stevenson's phrase — would engulf the whole world.

Before we leave these mutations in the Western idea, we should also examine the extent to which equality and material progress have enlarged the concept of the nation. Undoubtedly today the main drives behind the idea of nationhood, especially in the emergent territories, are equality and material progress. Nevertheless nationalism as such is so deeply rooted in human affairs that we must make a brief detour to examine it in its own terms. It begins with the tribe. The tribe is the oldest of human associations, a total community bound by links of kinship and blood all too often propelled into action by the sense of having competing interests with other tribes, which it fights for hunting fields and grazing areas and, when conflict becomes insoluble, involves in tragic wars of extermination.

In large parts of Africa, this original organization of mankind remains and, as the collapse of the Congo has shown, easily reverts to violence and destruction. But in other continents wider forms of political organization have developed. We move on from the tribe to congeries of tribes and to the union of different tribes under conquering dynasties or empires. In these wider states the sense of blood kinship is lessened. Wars of imperial conquest take the place of wars of tribal extermination. Professional armies arise in place of a people armed *en masse*. In large parts of Asia and for long years under the Roman Empire in Europe, wars changed the leadership of the state and the distribution of power, but the life of the peasants and villages and country towns continued with relatively little disturbance. Throughout northern India, for instance, after the collapse of organized imperial rule, Rajput princes fought each other continuously while the villagers took virtually no part in the wars.

This relative discontinuity between rulers and ruled began to end when, toward the end of the Middle Ages, a new sense of blood brotherhood and cohesion was restored to the political community in Western Europe. At that time Europe began to reacquire an almost tribal sense of the state. It had been dynastic. The Plantagenets, the Capets, were symbols and leaders of their peoples but, owing to the coincidence of language and frontiers in Western Europe, people began to discover again a sense of kinship based upon what they came to feel was almost common blood, an organic family unity. So the nation-state has in it some element of the tribe, operating at a more elaborate and a more organized level.

Now this almost tribal concept of the nation had extremely important effects both in the development of the modern economy and in the development of the West's relations with the rest of the world. Modern capitalist society needs a certain scale of market if it is to gain anything from the division of labour and the diversification of work and product. The nation-state provided a framework cohesive enough to act as an enlarged market. Merchants felt that they had a common unit in which to work. They moved on from the highly restricted market of the village, the estate, or the river valley to the larger market of the nation. And they moved on with all the more vigour and all the more drive because they were competing with other nations who were developing their own markets in the same sense: British merchants competing with French merchants, French with Dutch, Dutch with Portuguese, and so forth. The nation defined the market and then, reciprocally, the interests of the market helped to underline the exclusiveness of nationhood.

The effect was not limited to Western Europe. Out of the intense rivalry came the great thrust which led to the colonial control of most of the world by these same Western nations. Arabs, after all, had been out trading in Asia for generations before the Westerners arrived. But the trade was peaceful and did not impinge much on local politics. What the Westerners brought with them was a fierce competitive determination to cut other nations off from the profits of the new oriental trade. This led to the struggle for the control of the seas. And, if one follows the process closely in such areas as Indonesia or India, one can see how the determination of the Dutch to throw everybody else out, or the determination of the British not to allow the French to maintain a foothold, afterwards led to the kind of jockeying and manoeuvering and backing of local rulers that, little by little, brought about the extension of Western colonial control to the whole area.

At this point it should be easier to understand why modern nationalism has such deep roots in the ideas of equality and material progress. The Western traders-turned-rulers in Asia took their fierce exclusive nationalism into societies still loosely united as dynastic or imperial states. There they settled down to make money, to trade, to build up export industries, and to set in motion some of the economic processes which underpin the modern economy. They carried with them a concern for progress, for material well-being, for this-worldliness, all unknown in Eastern lands. They began to spur local peoples to think in this same sense.

At the same time, they created a nationalist reaction against their own nationalist pretensions. By ruling other groups in the name of their own national interests, they taught these groups to see themselves as nations and to claim equality for their own rights. There was no "nationalism" in India until Britain aroused it by teaching Indians the ideals of nationhood and at the same time denying them the rights of national self-determination. Material progress and equality have been the great spurs to nationalism throughout the colonial world, and the reason is simply that it was in the mood of national self-assertion and economic advantage that Westerners established and maintained their rule.

Now let us turn to the third of the revolutions that have created the metamorphosis of Western society. From the eighteenth century onwards new medical sciences and steady advances in public sanitation, coupled with the crowding of more and more people into the new cities, lengthened life and set in process an explosion of the birth-rate. In the West, on the whole, this explosion has proved a boost to growth, a boost to wealth, a boost to economic development. The reason is, in the main, that the creation and expansion of the modern economic system came into being while the explosion of population was still in its early stages. In fact, as population grew the economy could grow with it. There was a time in the eighteenth century when it looked as though a shortage of manpower would set a definite limit to the growth of economy. In nineteenth-century America massive immigration was one of the great spurs to economic growth. In the nineteen-twenties and -thirties, the Depression coincided, earlier in Britain and later in America, with a considerable falling off in the birthrate. Today, once again, it seems certain that some aspects of American growth are greatly stimulated by its spurt in population. So, on the whole, economic growth and growth in population have gone together in the West. That they have not done so in the East is one of the world's great problems. But in the West the dilemma of population outstripping resources has not occurred. On the contrary, an expanding manpower, absorbed into an expanding economic system, has provided labour for the production of goods and a consumers' market for their sale.

Now we come to the last of our revolutions, the most pervasive of all, that of capital and science, and the application of both to our economic processes.

Now, capital is saving; and saving means not consuming. But there is no point in delaying or cutting back consumption unless, at some point, the saving made will result in more consumption later on. For example, it takes more effort, time, and input to produce a better seed or to develop a better plough. But in the end you are rewarded with a better harvest; in other words, consumption can go up as a result of the extra effort.

The trouble with traditional society is quite simply this: man's knowledge of how material things behave is still very limited. He has not yet developed the habits and tools of science and experiment to explore all the ways in which matter can be changed and manipulated. There are few ways known of making better seeds; not very much has been tried in the way of constructing better ploughs; better ploughs have to wait on more refined techniques for dealing with iron ore; and experiments with iron ore have in turn to wait on finding a substitute for charcoal. In short, the heat of wood, the energy of wind and water, the speed of a horse, the skill of the land still represent the outer limits of a very restricted technology.

The great change that occurred in the eighteenth century was above all an enormous expansion in the techniques and technologies to which savings could be devoted. This change came about because of the revolutionary change we have already discussed: the West's steadily increasing interest in material things, in this-worldliness, and in the purposive exploration of physical reality.

We take this attitude so entirely for granted that it is easy to forget how recent it is and how entirely its origins lie in our Western society. The scientific spirit, drawing on the Greek sense of law and the Judeo-Christian respect for the handiwork of God, is perhaps the most profoundly distinguishing feature of our civilization. Science could hardly arise in Hindu society since one does not devote a lifetime to exploring an illusion. It did not arise in China, for in spite of orderly government, rational rule, and intense intellectual interest stretching back through millennia into the past, the dominant Confucian class turned its back on science and preferred instead the consideration of human relations and urbane life.

But in the West, the aftermath of the Wars of Religion was to turn educated opinion to the examination of material things in which, it was hoped, the clash of dogma could be left behind. As a result, in the seventeenth and eighteenth centuries, all over Western Europe, especially in Britain, the inventors and experimenters set to work to explore matter and improve technology. They revolutionized the use of iron. They transformed textile machinery. They invented the steam engine. The age of the railways and the factory system opened up ahead.

An emancipated and self-confident merchant class, with a strongly developed credit system, had savings to pour into these new technologies. They were joined by enlightened gentleman farmers and by sturdy self reliant artisans, all ready to experiment and back the experiments with their own — and other people's — savings. This combination of new technology and expanded saving made possible great increases in productivity. Much more could be produced by each pair of hands in each working hour. The surplus could be reinvested in further expansion. This process depended on keeping general consumption low. The mass of workers did not at first profit from the new system. Herded into the towns, ignorant, unorganized, they contributed the massive new saving by working for wages which were much lower than their true productivity. But the savings were made by entrepreneurs who reinvested them to expand the whole scale of the economy.

Out of this massive "primitive accumulation" came what one might call a "break-through" to a new type of economy where, with fresh capital applied to all the processes of production, the expansion of each helped the expansion of all with a sort of internal momentum which finally put the economy into orbit as the new type of advanced, capitalized, industrialized, technological society that we see around us in the West today.

These then, are the four revolutions that have transformed traditional society to give us the modern world. It is above all in the North Atlantic community that all of them have in fact started, grown, interacted upon each other, and come together to create a quite new kind of society. First, the "break-through" came in Britain. Then it followed in countries resembling Britain in basic social pre-conditions: the dominance of the merchant class, the relative openness of society, the pressure upwards of new social groups — merchants, workers, and farmers — and the basic attitudes of scientific interest and material ambition. Especially in empty lands settled by Europeans overseas, and above all in the United States, there occurred a mutual flow of capital, a mutual interdependence of trade which meant that all these lands helped to draw each other up the spiral of expanding production: Britain sparking growth in Europe; British and European investment spurring expansion in the United States. As early as the 1870s, the North Atlantic countries were providing over 60 percent of the foreign capital loaned in these areas and were together engrossing something like 70 percent of world trade.

The degree to which this interdependence stimulated the expansion of new wealth can, I think, be shown perhaps better by our failures than by our successes. This Atlantic society can still be wealthier than any known to man, in spite of the fact that it has contrived in the seventy to a hundred years of its interdependence to fight two wars of such appalling, such drastic, such monstrous destruction that one might have conceived that no people on earth could have recovered their wealth after such an outpouring of waste and carnage. But no; this interdependent community, even interdependent when fighting within itself, has been able to drag itself out of these holocausts and to achieve levels of wealth and well-being even greater than anything that went before. This, I think, is the most startling measure of the effectiveness of the new methods of science, the new methods of technology, the whole new field of saving applied to the production of wealth.

Nor is the story finished. On the contrary; at the present moment this group of wealthy countries — Great Britain, the white Dominions of the British Commonwealth, the United States, and Western Europe — represent a capacity, not only for present wealth but for future wealth of which we really have no very clear sense. Changes in technology are becoming more frequent and drastic. New frontiers open up in energy, in chemicals, in ever wider applications of science to production. Above all, we do not produce at full stretch. The scale of our reserves is illustrated by the fact that we only put our productive machine fully to work when, in war, we are all vowed to destruction. Our most productive periods are those in which we are destroying most fully what we make. And from this folly, we are not yet released, owing to the fabulous weight of our armament programs.

So this enormously wealthy community of nations is growing wealthier and could grow wealthier still. But at the same time it is not now having a comparable effect on the rest of the world. In the nineteenth century, a portion of the capital that went out in search of profits from this growing wealthy community did go out to the colonies, to India, to the Far East, to Latin America; and part of the growth of the Atlantic world was in some measure sparked by buying the raw materials of less developed countries overseas. But in the twentieth century, this kind of interdependence between an industrial centre and the producers of raw materials on the fringe has tended to weaken. In the last twenty or thirty years, the West has grown much more rapidly in internal production than it has in its need for imports. We are no longer, in the hopeful nineteenth-century sense, necessarily dragging up the rest of the world in our wake. The automatic stimulus we give to growth overseas is now much less than it was even seventy years ago; and this is because of a very profound change in our industrial processes. We apply science so much more freely through changed technology that the art of the substitute has come to a quite new effectiveness. Very often the imported raw materials on which we used to depend can now be produced within our own frontiers. One thinks of artificial rubber, new fabrics for textiles, petro-chemicals, conceivably even *ersatz* chocolate. And so, we no longer automatically exercise the same pull of development on the outside world as we did in our early days of growth and wealth. We have been filling the gap with extraordinary economic assistance. But we do not look on this "job" as a settled commitment. It is still a precarious expedient; and in any case it is too small.

Then there is another big change which alters the relationship.

It is quite simply that the West has completed its "break-through" to modernization and the emergent countries have not. Above all, they have not completed the first, hard, even merciless, phase of early saving.

To begin the whole process of saving is a massive task. A sort of momentum has to be achieved. All parts of the economy have to be affected if the economic pattern as a whole is to change. A little modification here, a little development there, may transform parts of the economy, but it is only when the flood of change begins to run right through society that you get that actual "break-through" to a new type of productive economy which has occurred in the West. But naturally, this "break-through" occurring in a traditional society, demands an immense amount of capital. You have to begin to modify almost everything; education, farming, transport, power, industry — all have to change. This means that capital is required not in little amounts, but on a massive scale. And yet society, being under-developed, is still too poor for savings on such a scale. This is the paradox of the phase which Marx called "primitive accumulation" — the first great effort of saving which has to be achieved if the new momentum is to begin. The Western colonial impact on the rest of the world did not create such a momentum. It created partial modernization: the beginnings of modern education and industry, some cash farming directed to export markets, some ports, some transport, some beginnings of modern administration. But all this did not amount to the full momentum of sustained growth.

The result is that the gap between those Western lands that are already "in orbit" in their economic life, and those that are not yet off the ground, is tending at the moment to grow wider, not narrower. We in the West have long completed our first phase of primitive accumulation; we have a machine in being to use for further expansion; and, incidentally, we contrived to acquire that machine while our population was still at a relatively low level. Now that we are "in orbit," our own wealth can multiply by compound interest because we are already wealthy. This, after all, is a cycle we recognize very well in family life. It is very much easier for a rich man to invest and grow richer than for the poor man to begin investing at all. And this is also true of nations. Nations that are not yet through the "sound barrier" of saving are tending to get poorer with the added complication that their populations are meanwhile going steadily up.

So our world today is dominated by a complex and tragic division. One part of mankind has undergone the revolutions of modernization and has emerged on the other side to a pattern of great and increasing wealth. But most of the rest of mankind has yet to achieve any of the revolutions; they are caught off balance before the great movement of economic and social momentum can be launched. Their old traditional world is dying. The new radical world is not yet born. This being so, the gap between the rich and the poor has become inevitably the most tragic and urgent problem of our day.

II

THE POOR NATIONS

How are we to define the "poor" nations? The phrase "under-developed" is not very satisfactory for it groups together very different types of under-development. India and Pakistan, for instance, are heirs of a great and ancient civilization and have many of the other attributes — in art, literature, and administration — of developed states, even though they are also very poor. Other areas — one thinks of the Congo — are developed in virtually no sense at all. I think, therefore, that perhaps the most satisfactory method of defining poverty at this stage is to discuss the question simply in terms of per-capita income — the average income available to citizens in the various countries. If you fix the level of wealth of "wealthy" communities at a per-capita income of about $500 a year, then 80 percent of mankind lives below it. It is chiefly among the privileged nations living round the North Atlantic that we find levels of annual income above the 500-dollar mark. Indeed, in the United States or Canada, it is three and four times above the minimum. Australia and New Zealand also belong to this group. In the Communist bloc, Czechoslovakia is moving up into it, and so is Russia. In fact, it is a marginal question whether they should not now be included among the rich. But what is certain is that the mass of mankind live well below the income level of $500 per head a year; and in some countries — one thinks particularly of India — per-capita income may be as low as $60. Yet between 400 and 500 million people live in India — something like two-fifths of all the poor people in the uncommitted world. So the gap between rich and poor is tremendous and, as we have already noticed, it is tending to widen further.

What is the cause of this? Why is there this great blanket of poverty stretched across the face of the globe? Before we attempt an answer, we should, I think, remember that ours is the first century in which such a question can even be put. Poverty has been the universal lot of man until our own day. No one asked fundamental questions about a state of affairs which everyone took for granted. The idea that the majority could have access to a little modest affluence is wholly new, the break-through of whole communities to national wealth totally unprecedented.

To return to our question: the contrast between the wealth of the West and the poverty of nearly everybody else does have some puzzling features. For centuries, for millenniums, the East had been the region of known and admired wealth. It was to the Orient that men looked when they spoke of traditional forms of riches: gold and diamonds, precious ointments, rare spices, extravagant brocades and silks. In fact, for over a thousand years, one of the great drives in the Western economy was to open trade with the wealthier East. And one of the problems facing that trade — as far in the past as in the days of imperial Rome — was the West's inability to provide very much in return. It is hard to sell bear rugs to merchants at Madras, especially during the monsoon. Nor is the contrast between the East's endowment and the relative poverty of the West simply a matter of history. Today, for instance, Indonesia seems obviously better endowed in a whole range of ways than are some European countries — one might perhaps pick Norway.

In spite of these puzzles, there are some underlying physical causes which explain why some countries have been left behind in the world's present thrust toward greater wealth. Many of the tropical soils have been submitted to millenniums of leaching under the downpour of heavy rains and are precarious soils for agriculture. Nor is the climate of tropical regions precisely designed for work. When the temperature rises to ninety degrees and the humidity to 90 percent, you do not feel like rushing out and solving one of the first problems in Euclid. Even less do you want to cut a tree — favourite occupation of Victorian gentlemen — or dig a ditch.

Wherever monsoon is the rain-bringing force, there is an underlying element of instability in farming. The concentration of rain in a few months creates expensive problems of control and storage. Rivers vary from raging torrents to dry beds. And if the monsoons fail in India or South-east Asia, then there is quite simply no agriculture because there is no water.

Another fact making for poverty is that the great tropical belt stretching round the world has only limited sources of energy: no coal and not too much oil outside the Middle East, Venezuela, and Indonesia. One must conclude, therefore, that certain original differences exist in the actual endowment of resources in the advancing Northern Hemisphere and the relatively stagnant South. Nonetheless, I think the profound reason for the contrast of wealth and poverty lies in the fact that the various revolutions which have swept over the face of the Western world in the last hundred years exist at only a chaotic or embryonic stage among the poorer states.

The biological revolution of more rapid growth in population is on the way in these areas. But the other vast changes — an intellectual revolution of materialism and this-worldliness, the political revolution of equality, and above all the scientific and technological revolution which comes from the application of savings and the sciences to the whole business of daily life — are only beginning the process of transforming every idea and institution in the emergent lands. The revolution of modernization has not yet driven these states into the contemporary world. The greatest drama of our time is that they will be swept onwards. But we are still uncertain over the form these revolutions will finally take. Everywhere they have started; nowhere are they yet complete; but the trend cannot be reversed. The modernizing of the whole world is under way.

Millenniums ago, hunting and food-gathering began to give way before the advance of settled agriculture. So today the transformation of society by the application of reason, science, and technology is thrusting the old static subsistence economies to the backwaters of the world. The world is, in fact, involved in a single revolutionary process of which our four dominant themes are all a part. In the wealthier lands, the first stage of this transformation has been completed in the emergence of the modern, wealthy, reasonably stable, technologically adept capitalist state. In the poorer lands, the first stage only has opened. The contrast between world wealth and world poverty largely turns upon this lag in time.

Now we must examine the impact of the four changes upon emergent lands — and we should remember again the distinction between poorer lands such as India which are at the same time rich in culture, history, and tradition, and tribal lands, whether in Africa, Australia, or Latin America, which lack even the rudiments of a developed tradition. The biological revolution brought about by a sudden acceleration of the birth-rate could not take place in these countries until colonial rule abolished local wars and modern medical science and modern sanitation began to save babies and lengthen life. That these changes were introduced *before* the establishment of a modern economy is one of the most fateful differences between East and West, and one to which we will return. But until the second half of the nineteenth century most of these lands still followed the old millennial pattern of a population rising to the limits of production and then falling back into violence, struggle, and death where the limits were surpassed. In tribal life, for instance, when the tribe had eaten up the resources available in its hunting-grounds, it had no alternative but to reduce its numbers by malnutrition and starvation or break out and conquer the lands of other tribes, thereby diminishing the numbers on both sides. This cycle was one of the perennial causes of tribal war.

Even in a great settled civilization like China, history has given us a kind of physical representation of the "melancholy wheel" of fate in the pressure of population rising to the limit of resources, and there precipitating violence, despair, banditry, civil war, and invasion. Then, under tribulations of all kinds, the population falls back again to numbers which the food supply can carry, only to rise once more as peace is restored — a kind of self-perpetuating cycle in which the wheel of fate is driven by pressure of population into a constant alternation of peaceful growth and violent diminution. This, until the day before yesterday, seemed to be the fundamental fatality of man's existence.

Now let us turn to the second force: the new revolutionary emphasis on work and effort devoted to the things of *this* world, the drive of interest devoted to changing and bettering man's physical environment. In traditional or tribal societies, this force is, in the main, lacking. Very largely, the material organization of life and, above all, the natural sequence of birth and death, of the seasons, of planetary change, have been taken as given: they were not the subject of speculative activity. In primitive tribal society one can say that nature is very largely accepted as impenetrable by reason. It can be propitiated. It can be worked on by human will through magic. A flood may be diverted by drowning a male child. But no one connects the precipitation of rain at the head of the watershed with the expected annual flow and devises earthworks to avert disaster. Life is lived in the midst of mystery which cannot be manipulated, beyond very narrow limits, in answer to human needs.

In the great archaic societies — of Babylon, of Egypt, of the Indus Valley, or of the Yellow River — both the exploration of reality and the use of technology registered a formidable advance. Irrigation works such as those of ancient Egypt demanded elaborate scientific calculation, accurate observation of nature, and efficient, large-scale administration. And societies which evolved astronomy and the mathematical sciences to the levels achieved by the Persians or the Greeks achieved a penetration of matter by the human intellect unequalled until our own day. But the dynamism of our modern interest in created things was lacking. In some societies, as we shall see, the lack followed from a certain scientific indifference; in others, from a dissociation between the understanding of natural law and any idea of using the laws as tools for experimental work; and in all societies from a static concept of life in which the chief means of subsistence — agriculture — provided daily bread for the many and magnificence for the few, but was not a capital resource to be steadily extended by further investment. And, in truth, once the limits of land and water were, reached, lack of scientific experiment inhibited further expansion.

In short, the chief aims of these societies were not this-worldly in our modern sense. Take, for instance, that significant Victorian phrase "making good." We understand it in terms of making money, of achieving material success in the broadest sense. In premodern society no such meaning could possibly have been attached to any activity thought of as being "good." In tribal society, approved behaviour implies strict observance of tribal laws and customs. In archaic civilization, the good man, the man of wisdom, is the man who observes the rules and duties of his way of life: the rich man, in magnificence, affability, and alms-giving; the poor man, in work and respect. No group, except the despised merchant, devotes his life to accumulation. And even the merchant tends, as he did in China, to turn his wealth into land and leave the life of capital-formation behind as soon as his fortune permits the change. Such societies incline of their very nature to be backward-looking, to preserve rather than to create, and to see the highest wisdom in the effort to keep things as they are. Under these conditions no underlying psychological drive impels people to work and accumulate for the future. Wisdom is to wait on Providence and follow in the ways of your forefathers, ways of life compatible with great serenity, great dignity, profound religious experience, and great art, but not with the accumulation of material wealth for society as a whole.

The lack of the third revolution — equality — has worked in the same sense. There was no concept of equality in traditional society. As one knows from still-existing tribal societies, leadership lies with the old men of the tribe. There is no way for the "young men" to claim equality. They simply have to wait for the years to pass. Seniority (as in the American Senate) also ensures that the leaders are men who respect the backward-looking traditions of the group and have a vested interest in the unequal prestige conferred by advancing years. It is the inescapable recipe for extreme conservatism.

When tribal society is left behind, the values supported by the leaders are still conservative. They are fixed by an inviolate upper order. Save in times of immense upheaval, the peasant does not reach the throne. King, warrior, landlord form a closed order to which recruitment is in the main by birth. In India the fixedness of the pattern extended to everyone. A man is born to his caste and to no other. The very idea of equality is almost meaningless since you are what you are and you cannot measure yourself against other men who are entirely different by birth and by caste. Caste thus reinforced the inability of the merchant class to achieve greater influence and status. The merchant remained a Vaishya — the merchant caste — and money-making was not considered a valuable enough occupation to warrant any increase in status or esteem. Thus the Indian merchant did not achieve the political break-through which launched the rising power of the middle classes in Western Europe.

Another facet of equality — a vital facet for economic growth — was lacking: since there was no national community as we understand it, competitive drives based on national equality were also absent. The tribe is a sort of tiny nation, a nation in embryo, but it cannot exercise the same economic influence as the modern nation because it is too small to be a significant market. In any case, tribal agriculture is devoted to subsistence, not to exchange.

The larger post-tribal political units were, in the main, dynastic or imperial units — one thinks of such loose structures as the India of the Guptas or of China's gigantic bureaucracy — in which there was little interconnection between the scattered cities and the great mass of people living their isolated, subsistence village lives. Certainly there was not enough economic and social coherence to define a market in such terms that a merchant would feel himself in competition with other vigorous national markets and could operate with driving energy to defend national interests against the rival national interests of others. The competitive "equality" of Western Europe's commerce was wholly absent. As one sees again and again in human history — or in daily life — people do not begin to act in new ways until they have formulated the ideas of them in their minds. The idea of the nation was immensely reinforced — but also in part created — by the rivalry of commercial interests in Western Europe.

Now we turn to the last and most pervasive of the revolutions, the crucial revolution of science and saving. There is virtually no science in tribal society. There is a good deal of practical experience, skilled work, and early technique. It seems possible, for instance, that primitive farming developed as a result of close observation of nature's cycle of seed and harvest and its imitation in fertility rites and religious festivals. But the idea of controlling material things by grasping the inner law of their construction is absent. An underlying sense of the mysteriousness of things explains, as we have noticed, the use of magic. But magic depends on the force of a man's will, not upon the nature of the things upon which he tries to exercise his will. And since the human will is a very potent force, one occasionally encounters some very strange and unaccountable results which seem inexplicable in ordinary terms. Few travellers return from Africa without some sense of having brushed the uncanny fringes of a world where some of the ordinary rules do not apply. Nonetheless, primitive society lacks the sustained and purposive manipulation of matter for human ends which becomes possible once you grasp the laws to which matter responds.

In great traditional civilizations such as India and China, there certainly was enough intellectual ferment for a vast scientific break-through to be theoretically possible. Many of the most acute minds in those societies devoted themselves to systematic thought for generations. In the Eastern Mediterranean, among the Chaldeans and the Egyptians, some of the basic mathematical tools of science had been forged long before the Christian era. Yet the break-through never came. In India, there could be no obsessive research into material things since many of the finest spirits thought of the natural world as in some sense an illusion with no fundamental significance for human beings. In China, for a rather different reason, science failed to achieve the pre-eminence one might have expected in one of the most brilliantly intellectual societies of all time; and one in which printing — and gunpowder — were invented far ahead of the West. The reason is one more illustration of the degree to which revolutions begin — or fail to begin — in the minds of men. The Confucian gentle-man who dominated the official thinking of Chinese society thought science an occupation for charlatans and fools and, therefore, not really respectable. One need hardly add that if the best brains do not think a pursuit respectable, the best brains do not devote their time to it.

The Confucians had an excuse for their prejudice. In Europe, the medieval alchemists spent much of their time and energy trying to discover the "philosopher's stone" — the catalyst which would turn base metals into gold. In the course of their futile search they made many sound experimental discoveries about the properties of metals and some people regard them as precursors of the inductive and experimental methods upon which modern science is based.

In China the "philosopher's stone" took another form — the "elixir of life." China's emperors did not want gold. They wanted immortality and at their courts the Taoists, followers of a mystical and metaphysical religious "way," conducted practical experi-ments with plants and chemicals to see if the elixir could be produced in a test-tube. To the Confucian, the folly of the aim overshadowed the potential value of the means. They turned their backs on experiment and, in doing so, on science as well. So in China, for all the ancient glory of its culture, for all the force and vitality of its intellectual tradition, the scientific breakthrough could not occur.

Primitive and archaic societies match their lack of scientific *élan* by an equal lack of sustained saving. Every society saves something. Saving is, after all, not consuming. If everything were consumed, men would be reduced to hunting and fishing — and even these occupations require rods and spears. But in settled agricultural societies, seed-corn is set aside for the next harvest and men do the hedging and ditching and field-levelling needed to carry production forward year by year. Probably such saving for maintenance and repair — and more occasionally by land-clearing and irrigation, for expansion — does not surpass 4 or 5 percent of national income in any year.

The savings which make possible a general change in the techniques of productivity — more roads, more ports, more power, more education, more output on the farms, new machines in the factories — must rise dramatically above the 5-percent level. Economists fix a level of about 12 to 15 percent of national income as the range needed to cover all possible increases in population, some increase in consumption, and a high, expanding level of investment. And no traditional society ever reached this level.

One reason for this fact takes us back to the revolution of equality. The merchant in the Orient never achieved decisive political influence. There were no city corporations, no charters based on autonomous rights. As a result, the merchant never achieved full security either. The government of kings and emperors was a government above the law, depending upon the monarch's whim. There is a brilliant phrase used by one of the young gentlemen of the East India Company to describe the uncertainties of the commercial calling in India. He describes the monarch and his tax-gatherers as bird's-nesters who leave a merchant to accumulate a nestful of eggs and then come to raid them all. One can well understand that under such conditions the stimulus to sustained capital accumulation is fairly marginal. On the contrary, the tendency is to put money that is earned from trade — and a great deal of money was earned — either into hoards of currency that can be hidden or else into jewels which are easily transportable and easily hid. But neither of these reserves makes for the expansion of productive enterprise.

In short, the chief point that distinguishes tribal and traditional society is that all the internal impulses to modernization have been largely lacking. And yet today these societies are everywhere in a ferment of change. How has this come about? Where did the external stimulus come from? There is only one answer. It came, largely uninvited, from the restless, changing, rampaging West. In the last 300 years, the world's ancient societies, the great traditional civilizations of the East, together with the pre-Columbian civilizations of Latin America and the tribal societies of Africa, have all, in one way or another, been stirred up from outside by the new, bounding, uncontrollable energies of the Western powers which, during those same years, were undergoing concurrently all the revolutions — of equality, of nationalism, of rising population, and of scientific change — which make up the mutation of modernization.

The great world-wide transmitter of the modernizing tendency has been without doubt — for good and evil — Western colonialism. It is typical I think, of the way in which the changes have come about that, again and again, Western merchants were the forerunners of upheaval. They went out to bring back the spices and silks and sophistications of the Orient to cold and uncomfortable Europe. At first, they had no intentions of conquering anything. They simply tried to establish monopoly positions for themselves — hardly surprising when you could earn a 5,000-percent profit on a shipload of nutmeg making landfall in Europe — and to drive the traders of other nations away. They fought each other ferociously at sea but on land controlled only "factories" — clusters of warehouses, port installations, and dwelling houses held on sufferance from the local ruler. And so the position might have remained. But Dutch pressure was too great for the frail political structure of Java in the seventeenth century and little by little, by backing compliant sultans and deposing sullen ones, the Dutch became political masters of all the rich "spice islands."

In the following century, the Mogul superstructure collapsed in India and in their manoeuvring to destroy French influence the British found themselves assuming power by a similar route, first backing local contenders, then, saddled with them as puppets or incompetents, gradually assuming the power which slipped from their enfeebled grip. The Europeans had come out to trade. Imperial control was a by-product — and an increasingly ruinous one in commercial terms — yet as late as 1850 the nominal ruler in India was still a merchant corporation — John Company, the East India Company.

Colonial control, developing from its origins in trade, began to set the whole revolution of modernization into motion. It launched the radical changes brought about by a rapidly increasing growth in population. Western control introduced the beginnings of medical science. It ended internal disorder. A crowding into the big cities began. There were some attempts at more modern sanitation.

Toward the close of the nineteenth century a spurt of population began throughout India and the Far East. But this spurt had a different consequence from the comparable increase in the West. Western lands were relatively underpopulated — North America absolutely so — when the processes of modernization began. The growth in numbers was a positive spur to economic growth; it brought labourers into the market and widened the market. At the same time the new machines, the new developing economy based on rising productivity, expanded the possibilities of creating wealth in a way that more than outstripped the growth in population. But in the Far East, in India, where population was already dense, the effect of the colonial impact was to increase the rate of the population's growth without launching a total transformation of the economy. More births, longer lives, sent population far beyond the capabilities of a stumbling economy. Today the grim dilemma has appeared that population is so far ahead of the means of satisfying it that each new wave of births threatens in each generation to wipe out the margin of savings necessary to sustain added numbers. The West, where growth in population acted as a spur to further expansion, has not faced this dilemma, and in the East it is not yet clear how so grave a dilemma *can* be faced.

Colonial rule brought in the sense of a this-worldly concern for the advantages of material advance by the simplest and most direct route — the "demonstration effect." The new merchants, the new administrators, lived better, lived longer, had demonstrably more materially satisfying lives. The local people saw that this was so and they began to wonder why and whether others might not live so too. Above all, the local leaders saw vividly that the new scientific, industrial, and technological society enjoyed almost irresistible power. This, too, they naturally coveted.

At the same time, the colonial system did set in motion some definite beginnings in the processes of technical change and economic growth. There was some education of local people in the new techniques of Western life. Some merchants in the old societies, the Compradors in China, for instance, or the Gujaratis in India, began to exercise their talents as entrepreneurs in a new, settled, commercial society. Some of the preliminaries of industrialization — railways, ports, roads, some power — the preliminaries we call "infra-structure" — were introduced to the benefit of the new colonial economy. Some export industries expanded to provide raw materials for the West. Virtually nothing was done about basic agriculture; but plantation systems did develop agricultural products — tea, pepper, ground-nuts, jute — for the growing markets of Europe.

Above all, the new political ideas streamed in. Western education gave an *élite* a first look at Magna Charta. In their school-books in India the sons of Indians could read Edmund Burke denouncing the depradations of Englishmen in India. The new sense of equality, inculcated by Western education, was reinforced by the daily contrast between the local inhabitants and the colonial representatives who claimed to rule them. Personal equality fused with the idea of national equality, with the revolt educated men increasingly felt at being run by another nation. The whole national movement of anti-colonialism was stirred up by Western ideas of national rights and national independence, and by the perpetual evidence that the rights were being denied.

Everywhere there was ferment; everywhere there was the beginning of change; everywhere a profound sense that the old ways were becoming inadequate, were in some way no longer valid or viable for modern man. And this feeling stirred up an equally violent reaction. Men rose up to say that the old ways were better and that the new-fangled fashions would destroy all that was valuable and profound in indigenous civilization. Between the modernizers and the traditionalists, between the young men who wanted to accept everything and the old men who wanted to reject everything, the local community threatened to be distracted by contradictory leadership. A crisis of loyalty and comprehension superimposed itself on all the other crises. It was rare for a country to achieve the national coherence that was achieved in India under the leadership of Gandhi in whom ancient vision and the modern idea of equality could coexist, and around whom old and new were thus able to unite.

The important point to remember, however, if one wishes to grasp the present contrast between the rich nations and the poor, is that all these changes, introduced pell-mell by colonialism, did not really produce a new and coherent form of society, as they had done in the West; there was no "take-off," to use Professor Rostow's phrase, into a new kind of society. The colonial impact introduced problems that seemed too large to be solved, or, at least, problems that offered immense difficulty to any solution. Take, for instance, the problem of population. You could not deny medicine; you could not resist sanitation; yet all the time life lengthened, the birth-rate went on going up, and you could almost watch population beginning to outstrip resources that were not growing in proportion because saving and capital formation were still inadequate. Yet the rising population continuously made saving more difficult.

This small level of saving meant that all economic developments under colonialism — or semi-colonialism — were on too small a scale to lead to a general momentum. China is a good example. After the Opium Wars the British compelled the crumbling Manchu Empire to open its ports to Western trade. In the so-called treaty ports, quite a rapid rate of economic and industrial expansion took place. Europeans brought in capital. Some Chinese entrepreneurs joined them. International trade soared. The customs, also under European control, grew to be an important source of revenue. Plans for building railways were prepared. Meanwhile, however, the desperate, over-crowded countryside where the bulk of the people lived slipped steadily down into deeper ruin. Little economic activity could spread beyond the Westernized areas; for there were no markets, no savings, no initiative; only the dead weight of rural bankruptcy.

Similarly, in India the only areas where anything like a sustained "take-off" began to occur were in the neighbourhood of Bombay with its shrewd merchants and great port, among the Scottish jute-growers round Calcutta, and with the lively, adaptable farmers of the Punjab. Elsewhere, the countryside was largely unaffected by the new economic forces.

The same patchiness affected social life and education. All over Asia the educational system began to produce an *élite* who believed in Western ideas of law, Western ideas of liberty, of constitutional government. But behind them there was little general change among the people at large and, above all, no trace of change in the vast number — 80 or more percent of the population — who lived on the land where the old, unchanged, subsistence agriculture went on as before. And so there came about what one can only call a kind of dual society, in which the scattered growing-points of a modern way of life were restrained almost to the pitch of immobility by enormous forces of inertia inherent in the old framework of society.

When, for instance, one reads of the attempts made by small groups of Chinese merchants in the late nineteenth century to transform their economy in such a way that they could withstand the commercial and political pressure of the West, one confronts again and again the fact that the real society simply had not changed enough to go along with them. The Court was backward-looking. The Confucian bureaucracy was still utterly unchanged. Worse still, the merchants themselves were still divided in their own minds. They still hankered for the days when a successful merchant naturally put all his capital into land and became a member of the landed gentry. At every point, there were psychological blocks in men's minds when it came to completing the changes they had been ready to start. In a very real sense societies like China or India in the last century were caught between a world that had died and a new world that could not yet be born — and this is, of course, the perfect recipe for maximum psychological and social strain.

Perhaps one can best judge the extent of the inhibitions by examining the opposite example of Japan. There, an extraordinarily efficient and ruthless ruling class determined, after the forced opening of their ports by the Western Powers, to transform their country completely on the modern Western model. They decided that nothing short of almost total technical transformation would give them power to resist the West. So they forced through the reform of agriculture, the imposition of savings on the people, the absolute liquidation of all forms of the feudal economy. They introduced industry, sent many men to train abroad, and set in motion a drive for universal literacy. Although, unhappily, they also borrowed from the contemporary West a spirit of imperialism also present in their own traditions, they were able to transform their society radically in about thirty years and eliminated the social blocks and psychic inhibitions which held the other societies miserably suspended between contradictory worlds.

But elsewhere throughout the uncommitted world, in the traditional societies of China and India, in large parts of Latin America, and in the primitive emergent countries of Africa, old and new remained locked in a kind of battle, stuck fast in an apparently unbreakable deadlock. And how to break out of it; how to get the forces of modernization flowing through all of society; how to change leadership; how to get the new cadres in education; how to stimulate massive saving; how to get agriculture transformed: all these urgent and irresistible problems of the new society still wait to be answered.

This is a fact which the West cannot ignore. Most of the dilemmas of the under-developed areas have been stirred up by Western impact. Yet I think it is not entirely untrue to say that the Western powers are not looking very hard to find answers to these dilemmas. And this, I think, is for a very good reason. They have largely forgotten about their own transition. They are not conscious of the fact that a hundred years ago, even fifty years ago, many of them were struggling with just these problems of changing leadership, of developing new social groups, giving rights to new classes, finding methods of achieving greater saving, and securing a technological break-through on a massive scale. We take our development so much for granted that we hardly understand the dilemmas of those who have not yet travelled so far.

Another reason for our relative indifference is that owing to the relative under-population of our part of the world and owing to the scale of latent resources waiting to be developed in the Atlantic world, we in the West had not too difficult a passage to modernity; certainly nothing compared with the really appalling dilemmas that are faced by the under-developed world today. So, although we are perhaps beginning to see that they face almost insurmountable problems, I do not think that we have worked out our response or even perhaps fully measured our responsibility. Yet there is no human failure greater than to launch a profoundly important endeavour and then leave it half done. This is what the West has done with its colonial system. It shook all the societies in the world loose from their old moorings. But it seems indifferent whether or not they reach safe harbour in the end.

This is one difficulty; but there is another, a greater one. While we face these dilemmas, another set of answers to them has been formulated — also in the West. It claims to go to the heart of all these revolutions and offer a surer route to equality, to material well-being, to the achievement of technology, science, and capital. Communism claims to be the pattern of the future and to hold the secret of the next phase of history for mankind. In one sense, the claim is serious. Communism *is* a sort of résumé of the revolutions that make up modernization and it offers a method of applying them speedily to societies caught fast in the dilemmas of transition. We must, therefore, admit that, at the present moment, the poor nations, the uncommitted nations, face a double challenge. They face an enormous challenge of change. But, in addition, they face an equally vast challenge of choice.

III

COMMUNISM'S BLUEPRINT

Today about one-third of mankind lives under the political control of Communism, and already I think we can ask the question whether a variety of different kinds of Communism may not be beginning to appear in the world and whether a picture of one vast monolithic Communist bloc may not be disintegrating a little. There is not only the deviant strain of Titoism in Yugoslavia. Even among "orthodox" Communists the emphasis put on different problems varies. Different methods of dealing with the basic problems of agriculture, for instance, have appeared, varying from the private farms of Poland through the collectivization of Russia to the more extreme communal system of farming in China.

There is, again, a different approach to the problems of war, and of the Cold War. It seems possible that China, at an earlier stage of its revolution, is more anxious to stir up trouble abroad than is Russia where forty years' painful construction is at stake. And there may be an even more fundamental divergence. Although we do not yet know what its consequences will be, there is surely a clear distinction between the Communism of the relatively rich in such countries as Russia or Czechoslovakia, and the Communism of the desperately poor that we find in China. When the Chinese Communist revolution exploded, it was against a background of gross over-population in a land where the per-capita income was probably below $60 a year. It seems quite clear to me that the kind of society that can develop in Russia on the basis of relatively low population and extraordinarily rich resources may well move steadily away from the forms of a society struggling, as in China, with gross poverty and an extreme pressure of population.

Bearing these differences in mind, we must nevertheless try to define Communism and one way would be to say that it is an attempt to put all the revolutions of our day into one coherent system. But before following up this approach we have to see that one of our revolutions is missing — the biological revolution of explosively rising population. So far as this crisis is concerned, official Communism neglects it, disregards it, and in fact claims that it is no problem.

For the Russians, Malthus might never have written. His basic thesis — that the growth of population would tend at some point to outstrip resources — is simply dismissed as a reflection of a basic inability to understand the inadequacies of capitalism and as a fundamental defeatism before the bright prospects of the future.

Nor is this simply a theoretical attitude. In China, for a time in 1957, some effort was made to persuade people to limit the size of their families. But the campaign came to an abrupt end, in spite of an annual growth in population of some twelve million souls. Thereafter the general line seems to have been that the problem of over-population or of potential over-population is bound up, not with basic biological facts, but simply with the inadequacy of capitalism to cope with it.

But all the other revolutions of our times are absorbed into Marxism, probably reaching there a pitch of coherence, of drive, and of unity unique in human history. Take, first of all, our revolution of materialism. In the West, materialism has taken the form certainly of an enormous interest in the natural order and of a determined attempt to penetrate its secrets by means of science. It has taken, too, the form of a strong commitment to the possibility of better conditions on earth and a belief that man has the right, the privilege, even the duty, to better material conditions, both for himself and for his fellow men. But it has certainly not led to a total disbelief in, and rejection of, any other order of reality. Our societies are plural in thought, plural in their ideals, plural in their ways of approaching reality.

Communism attempts, on the contrary, to make materialism the measure of all things. The basic physical techniques, economic forms, and property relations of society are held to be the determinant factors in fixing all other aspects of human reality — art, philosophy, religion. This anchoring of all phenomena in a supposedly definable and explorable material base is what, in Marxist claims, gives the system alone the right to be called scientific; and it enables Marxism to predict "objectively" the course of history by examining the material forces which will compel it to behave as it does. This, incidentally, is why to this day all anti-social behaviour in Russia tends to be attributed to the remaining traces of capitalism. The blame could not lie with Socialist institutions which are, by definition, incapable of projecting evil results.

Nonetheless, the materialist base supports a Messianic hope. This Marx achieves by attributing all the faults and errors of society to the institution of private property. The jealousies, the envies, the obstructions to which it gives rise drive society forward on an ever-renewed cycle of discontent, in which once-dominant classes are succeeded by new groups thrusting upwards until at last the workers, rejecting private property, take over and set up a classless society where the lion will lie down with the lamb and all the evils of the world will pass away.

This is, I think, all highly theoretical and it is my impression that in Communist education these days much of the dogma is accepted unthinkingly and slips very much to the back of people's minds. What is left is perhaps not so much an elaborate ideology as a general attitude of mind which regards the achievements of the kingdoms of this world as the most important issue for man and which looks on Communism as the key to the future. It includes considerable distrust of other forms of society since, by definition, capitalism is wicked and obsolete. Perhaps above all, it conveys the feeling of moving forward to a vision of world-order, to a final consummation of history which gives a Messianic turn to life and a sense of excitement to the road ahead. I do not suggest all Communists share the hope. Indeed, there is evidence that a certain boredom with the high imperatives seems to be fairly widespread among young people. As with religion in the West, the appeal may be intense only to an *élite*. One can also doubt whether this strange transformation of materialism into a kind of religion is as crucial as other aspects of Communism. Yet dreams are dreams and men cannot live without them. We would be unwise to underestimate the potency of Communism's dream of a world made one and equal and rich.

When we turn to the revolution of equality we see that it is, of course, central to Communism. It claims to provide the consummation of all equality. Men and nations alike will be organized on the principle: "from each according to his capacities, to each according to his needs." This principle, it will be noticed, not only eliminates all class differences; it tries to establish a fundamental norm of "need" which applies to every human being and should, in theory, do away with all differences in reward and status based on performance or special talent. Such a "norm" has been tried successfully in human history. It is the basis of monasticism, Christian or Eastern, and is rooted in the rejection of personal possessions of any kind. But Communism assumes that the intense religious dedication which makes monastic communalism possible can be spread to the whole civil community.

At first, a violent cataclysm will bring down the mighty from their seat and exalt them of low degree — the old Biblical phrase is strictly relevant. Thereafter, however, the course is less clear. What we have seen of Communist society so far suggests the force of George Orwell's warning that whereas "all animals are equal, some animals are more equal than others." Certainly, we have seen in actual Communist societies that those who control power — the bureaucrats, the organization men — secure for themselves social differences, both in wealth and in opportunity, which are at least equivalent to the kind of class distinctions we have in the West. Indeed, they may in some areas be wider since the base of society is still so desperately low. To have command of a car in a society where there are virtually no cars confers greater privilege than does the manager's Cadillac in the West. The gap between top executive and floor-cleaner is almost certainly larger in Soviet society because the whole community has not yet reached the affluence of mass consumption. Milan Djilas, the dissident Yugoslav leader and writer, goes farther and suggests that "the new class" of bureaucrats will be self-perpetuating since its children will be born to privileges denied to others and start as an *élite* enjoying all the unequal advantages wealthy children enjoy in the West.

However, Communism as an order of society is not yet fifty years old. Its future rigidities and encrustations can be guessed at but not confirmed. What is certain is that its primary appeal *before*

it takes power is to those whom the existing social order disap-
points or oppresses. Rising young sons of the middle class who see
power remain with traditional feudal leaders; workers herding
miserably into cities in the first "push" of primary capital accumulation; above all, the dispossessed on the land: these make up the
cadres and the mass following of the Communist upsurge.

When, however, we come to the question of *national* equality
under Communism, the situation is not so clear. In theory,
certainly all nations are equal and none may oppress or control
another. One of the most striking first gestures of the Bolshevik
revolution in Russia was to announce the liberation of all
central-Asian subject peoples brought into the Russian empire
by the Tsarist régime: Kazakhs, Uzbeks, Armenians, Kirghiz.
But then the ambivalence begins. Communism also teaches that
nationalism is simply a projection of the capitalist *bourgeois* phase
of human development; and, as we have seen, there *is* some link
between the definition of market and the definition of the
nation. When, therefore, Communists argue, mankind passes
beyond capitalist economics, it will leave nationalism behind as
well. Nationalism, as a restrictive and dividing device, will come
to an end in the classless, nationless world order which Communism will bring about. This change need not suppress national
culture; and indeed, national differences of culture and language
must be respected. Yet nationalism should be understood as a
passing phase.

This, in shorthand, is the theory. When it comes to practice, the
outlook is much more complex. Even if in strict theory nationalism
is primarily a projection of the *bourgeois* phase of development,
the Communists have been quick to see how intense nationalism
can become in under-developed and pre-*bourgeois* communities,
provided they have come under colonial control. Societies at
very varied stages of growth can catch the nationalistic epidemic,

since nationalism is the driving force behind the movement to end Western colonial control — what the Communists call "the old imperialist order." They are ready to support local nationalists in Africa or Latin America — men such as Castro or Sekou Touré — if by that means they can hasten the end of Western influence. Such local leaders do not have to be Communist. They may, like Nasser, keep their own Communists under lock and key. The Communists are not perturbed. End Western influence first, they argue, and then we can adopt new tactics. Meanwhile, we say "Yes" to local nationalism as a means of ending the old Western forms of rule and influence.

Communists would also, whatever the theory, admit the usefulness of nationalism as a means of rallying the people to support an accomplished Communist revolution. In Russia, devotion to the Russian image, in China dedication to Chinese strength, is obviously used in the effort to win people to the revolutionary régime. Particularly during the devastating impact of Hitler's attack upon Russia, the sense of Holy Russia, of Great Russia, of all its history, all its glory, all its resistances and victories was drawn on fully to rally its citizens to the defence of the Soviet Union.

So far, then, nationalism, whatever the underlying stages of economic development, can be legitimate in Communist eyes. But now comes the paradox. One of the basic facts in world Communism today is that the doctrine has taken root in two immensely powerful and imperialist states — states which have, over the centuries, absorbed millions of citizens of other tribes and races. What of the nationalism of these groups? Suppose it does not wither away as a result of economic development under Communist discipline? Can it be fostered and supported? Clearly not; for, on the analogy of self-determination elsewhere, it might weaken Soviet or Chinese control. So we reach the ambivalence that nationalism is good in Ghana or Cuba or Iraq, but bad in Hungary or Kirghizia or Tibet. Nationalisms may, like men, all be equal; but some, clearly, are "more equal" than others; none more so than in Russia or China. The Russians dismiss the stirrings inside their own frontiers as "*bourgeois* vestiges." Yet in 1932, as the horrors of collectivization drew on, it proved necessary to shoot most of the cabinet of the Ukraine for these same "vestiges." And in all our memories the tragedy of Hungary is still vivid: the desire of a perfectly coherent self-conscious European nation to throw off Russian control led first to an uprising of the whole people and then to its brutal suppression by the Russians. There could be no more striking illustration of the fundamental inequality between national groups within the Soviet sphere. Nor do I think that we have yet seen the end of the possible permutations and combinations of this ambivalence.

Where the Communists incorporate the revolutions of our day into their system with least equivocation is in the sphere of science, savings, and technology. Science is welcomed as the basic secret of successful existence. Marx, as we have remarked, always claimed that his Communism, unlike the visionary Socialism of his contemporaries, was the truly scientific Communism. Only Communism uncovered the inner laws that explain the workings of human society and human classes, just as such laws as those of thermodynamics explain the workings of solids and masses. In a sense, this is simply a variant of nineteenth-century rationalism — indeed of some types of philosophy today — which accepts only one form of meaning and validity: the form which can be checked by the measuring and calculating techniques of science. Western thought today is perhaps more inclined to accept the limits of this approach, while giving full value to the astonishing results it can give in its appropriate field. In the Soviet Union, one can imagine that the uninhibited acceptance of science as the key to everything gives an extra edge of energy to its pursuit of scientific objectives. Certainly, a nation that has produced the Sputnik and photographed the dark side of the moon possesses an incomparable thrust of scientific energy; and in Soviet education, emphasis on science has already produced a society capable of mobilizing more scientific and technical skills than perhaps any other — certainly at a comparable stage of development.

But this scientific break-through in Russia would have been impossible if the Soviet Union had not also directly developed into a highly capitalist state — state-capitalism, but capitalism nonetheless. The vast accumulation of savings in the decades of the Plans permitted the equally vast expansion of education. Without capital, schools and universities could not have multiplied; without the trained minds the economic system could not have expanded. In fact, as we see now, Communism's present strength depends more on its educational thrust than on any other single early development.

Nevertheless it is worth looking for a moment to the pendant development, the forceful accumulation of capital, for it goes to the roots of Marxism. Marx believed fundamentally that the Capitalists would first create an industrial society and that the Communists would then take it over as a going concern. And he had a reason for seeing this as an historically inevitable process. He derived it quite simply from his direct observation of the first stages of the first industrial break-through in Britain. Private capitalists, private merchants, private entrepreneurs invented the capitalist system; they did not know they were doing so; they thought they were making profits. But it was their desire for profits that drove the whole system forward and was, in the context of Britain's new unified national market, a most effective method of promoting economic expansion. The man who makes profits is the man who organizes the production of some goods or service in such a way that people are prepared to give up more resources to procure it than he put into it in the first place. And the better he organizes his resources, the larger the margin between costs and the price people are ready to pay for the goods. This margin is his profit-margin and it is then available for further investment, for creating new tools in the economy, for making experiments in new goods and in new types of technology. Moreover, at a time when labour is plentiful, unorganized, and weak, the cost element of wages can be held down and profits will be proportionately greater. As we have already noticed, in the early nineteenth century British workers were in this condition. Their wages were subsistence wages. The extra surplus was available for even more capital investment. The "big push" in investment was helped by the failure of the workers' consumption to rise in the first decades of industrialization.

This was the condition that chiefly impressed Marx. He regarded all profits as exploitation; he did not deny their role in releasing further resources for further investment; such was the historic task of the *bourgeoisie*. But he believed the process could not last because of an essential contradiction. Although the new machines were able to pour out more and more goods, wages would remain low and people's purchasing power would not grow to meet the output of the machines. There would be crises of over-production — which were really crises of under-consumption — and this would involve the system in ever deepening instability and contradiction. Further, Marx believed — for reasons sufficiently fantastic for us not to go into them here — that wages would actually fall and that people would get poorer. And as the mass of the people grew poorer, a shrinking number of "monopolists" — the organizers, the profit-makers — would grow richer, and in the end the whole society would relapse into a revolutionary conflict in which the vast mass of the poor would cast out the small body of the rich, take over the industrial machine which the monopolists had built, and establish a classless, profitless society

— which would be Communism.

As we know, the snag to Marx's theory lay in the fact that as the nineteenth century advanced, the workers began to share more adequately in the new society's wealth. Far from going down, their real wages went up. They began to organize, to exploit their position as voters, and to agitate for what we now call the welfare state. They began to have a stake in the new kind of society which Marx had not foreseen and which contradicted his basic assumptions. He died with the contradiction unresolved. Lenin took it up and discovered — at least to his own satisfaction — that the reason why there had been a greater sharing of wealth in the West, even with the workers, was that the wealth had been filched from the Western colonies. The colonial workers were now bearing the full brunt of the industrial revolution and carrying on their sweated backs not only Western "monopolists" but Western trade unionists. One consequence of this discovery was that Lenin put very much greater emphasis on the revolt of the colonies against Western imperial supremacy and came to believe that the way to the West would lie through Peking and Delhi.

Another aspect of his theory also deserves notice. He believed that Western capitalists had to invest abroad since the failure of internal consumption to increase limited the scope for further profitable investment at home. Seeking hungrily for profits, they would entrench themselves in foreign lands, either directly or through local puppets, then fight to keep everybody else out of their preserves. This was the essential link between capitalism, colonialism, and war; and the twist Lenin's interpretation gave to men's thinking about colonies survives to this day. In ex-colonial lands it is not unusual to find leaders who are highly suspicious of all forms of private foreign investment on the grounds that it must entail foreign control and could even involve the territory in war. This old preconceived idea is stronger than the new fact that the

Western economy, having translated itself to a new base of high consumption, no longer has capital to spare and the danger is not "exploitation" but that capital will simply not be forthcoming for overseas development.

Establishing why Western workers were no longer revolutionary still left Lenin with the problem of what to do about a proletariat no longer ready to act as the vanguard of revolt. He met the problem by evolving the idea of the party as a small secret core with total discipline dedicated to cajoling or compelling the majority to accept its revolutionary leadership. In the conditions of the early twentieth century, Lenin's instrument has proved more potent than any mass movement. Even after the agonies of war, Western workers remained fundamentally un-revolutionary. But in Russia the war went like a steam-roller over the beginnings of modernization. And it was in this disintegrating society that the small, highly restricted conspiratorial group of Bolsheviks took over power and set up the first government in history to be based upon Communism.

At this point the inadequacies of the Marxist analysis became apparent. The Communists were in control. But what they controlled was not a highly evolved industrial society; it was a nation flattened by war and barely emerged from the Middle Ages. In 1917, in 1921, and for years after, the great problem in Russia was how to build Communism in a society for which capitalists had not obligingly built the industrial structure in advance. Lenin died with the dilemma unresolved and it was the lot of Stalin to take the formidable and unprecedented decision to achieve a fully developed Western type of industrial community; not by taking it over from the capitalists, but by building it himself — in short, to use the state to do the job which the capitalists had done in the West.

Fortunately for Stalin it was by this time fairly clear how the government could undertake such a task. During the First World War, the massive mobilization of men and material by central government for specific tasks had occurred in Britain, Germany, and France; and the West's war economy was in all probability the great model for the first Five Year Plan. As in war, the planners expand the great metal-using industries, which pour out further machines — as the war economy pours out munitions. Total mobilization is achieved by compelling men and materials to fit into the over-all plan of industrial expansion. And savings are produced by seeing to it that only a very small part of what the workers produce ever goes back to them in terms of consumption. Wartime rationing and wartime inflation provided this discipline between 1914 and 1918. Resources were released massively for war. The "saving" was probably greater than even in the heroic days of primitive accumulation in Britain. But whereas the early capitalist system in Britain may have saved the classical 12 to 15 percent of national income, the harsh disciplines of the Russian Plans drove the figure up to 25 and 30 percent of the national income. Massive savings derived from the work of the people poured into the new industries, into the new developments beyond the Urals, into the vast expansion of mines, of transport, of education and research.

The saving had to come from the people since it could come from no other source. It came, above all — as it does in all stages of primitive accumulation — from the vast mass of the people living on the land. And here the sufferings which were imposed upon the peasants, by the effort to draw out of the farms every last margin of resources that could be transferred to the cities, culminated in the agonies of collectivization. And to this day I think we can say that Soviet agriculture has never fully recovered from the enormous impact of forced saving imposed on it in the early days.

Let us now examine the full paradox of the first Communist

revolution. Communism which should have come into being by the ineluctable forces of history, by the revolt of the large working class in a fully developed industrial economy, was in fact forced through by a small conspiratorial group in a vast country in which nearly 80 percent of the people still lived in a pre-industrial society. Moreover, the revolution, which was to have liberated the workers and peasants, submitted them to a discipline of forced saving more rugged than anything imposed in the unplanned West. And the system which was to be most truly the people's government took for its first model not so much the developed economy of the West in its peacetime semblance, but the rigidly organized, centrally controlled economy developed in total war.

Thus, in its first incarnation, the revolution had little resemblance to Communism as Marx had foreseen it. What it did was to create one of the most formidable concentrations of power, both economic and political, that human history has ever seen. And to this extent it accorded well with the traditions of Russian society; a society in which there had been virtually no older forms of constitutional government, no older forms of plural power, and in which autocracy had always centred in a single man — the Tsar.

As if to reinforce the authoritarian stamp imposed on Communism by the nature of Russian society and the scale of the collapse in 1917, the next great break-through of Communism — in China — repeated something of the same pattern. China, too, had received only very partial modernization; and what it had of a modern structure — in industry, in communications — had been ravaged by almost continuous war for fifty years. It was in this broken-down, despairing country on the margins of chaos that the Communists, as a small disciplined group, took over power and then imposed upon it the disciplines of total mobilization. And once again, the pattern fitted the traditions and the history of the country. All through China's millennial record — and no country in the world has so long, so continuous, and so sustained an historical tradition as China — two master institutions preserved the unity of the vast empire: the autocratic emperor and the tough, powerful, efficient, imperial bureaucracy of the Mandarins — the first civil service in the world to be recruited by competitive examination. There are other resemblances. In previous dynasties, the incoming rulers frequently experimented with massive policies of social change such as reorganizing the basis of landholding and nationalizing industry. It can even be argued that Confucianism was to a very real degree a state ideology. However, the chief point of resemblance lies in the degree to which the levers of effective power in China have always remained in the hands of the bureaucrats.

This, then, is the basic paradox of Communism. It does not achieve power by the route foreseen by Marx; nor does it establish a society much resembling his blueprint — in so far as he had one. Marx was in fact extremely vague about the shape of his classless utopia. Communism has succeeded in taking over power by the forceful action of a dedicated minority in two great societies of traditionally autocratic stamp which were undergoing the collapse and chaos of disastrous war. After the takeover, the Communists' first task has been not — as Marx expected — to run a working system, but on the contrary, to create it, bringing the nation back from the very verge of chaos and mobilizing it into an effective system of modern power.

How is this actual, practical form of Marxism likely to appeal to the emergent, uncommitted nations? How does this pattern of forced growth, achieved through the central planning power of an autocratic state, appeal to countries caught in the twilight zone between the need for change and the capacity to change in fact? We have to realize that its possibilities of attraction are considerable. We have to remember first that in all the uncommitted lands — in Asia, in Latin America, in large parts of Africa — the processes of change have begun. This is the legacy of colonialism and of the impact of Western trade and expansion. A few local leaders are educated in the new ways. Some industries — usually for export and under foreign ownership — have been established. There are new means of transport and communication. Above all, there is a change in the air. The winds blow in from the world bringing the hint of larger opportunities and better things. As a first step, colonial rule must be ended or has been ended. So much is clear. But what then? How can the bright promises of independence be achieved when, all around, the institutions and inhibitions of the old static society seem to remain more or less intact?

It is to the mood of psychological frustration that Communism can speak. It attacks the traditional leaders of the old society — the old rulers and princes, the old landlords, the entrenched groups in commerce and industry, the men who seem to stand in the way of the emergence of the new forces of modernism. And uncommitted peoples need to be fairly sophisticated to wonder whether the old landlord and the new bureaucrat may not share some of the same vices of absolute power. Communism attacks foreign control; it denounces imperialism. And once again you need a certain sophistication to wonder whether Soviet control over its satellites in Eastern Europe may not itself be a new form of imperialism.

In the economic field, Communism offers an intense discipline of saving. By compelling people to postpone consumption, it attacks head-on the most difficult task in any society where people live so near the margin of absolute poverty that saving must be an agonizing choice. By removing choice and compelling accumulation, Communism offers a pattern of quick growth. When growth-rates are compared between the United States and the Soviet Union — to the advantage of the Soviets — the Communists can claim that they alone know how to give poor societies that kind of boost to saving without which no economy has any hope of moving forward into the "take-off" into sustained momentum.

This fundamental strategic claim is enhanced by other advantages. Communism has been shown to be a method of seizing power and of developing a society through the work of a small *élite*, a small group of people. In most of the really under-developed areas, the number of men and women who feel themselves able, educated, and dedicated enough to undertake the making of the new society is necessarily small. There is, therefore, an innate appeal in the idea that a small group acting cohesively can accomplish so much. This attraction is reinforced by a certain bold simplicity in the Marxist determination to explain everything in terms of its revolution. When you struggle between a dying world and a world that will not be born; when everything comes to you bearing the face of confusion; when your old ideals and your new ambitions cannot be made to coincide; when the old is fading and you are not sure that you want it to go; and the new must come but is a long time acoming; when you wander in a twilight zone between ideas and ways of life which seem inherently contradictory — then the appeal of the firm simple explanation is intense and you listen with fascination when men come to you and say: "We have the prescription for the future; we have the total answer; we can tell you what to do; because, look, we have already done it." It may be that this simplicity, this bold claim to solve everything, is Communism's greatest attraction; and it is one which we in the West would be very unwise to underestimate.

This, of course, is not the whole story. If we are to measure the appeal of Communism soberly and judge where it is most likely to influence policy-makers in emergent territories, we shall have to look much more closely at the dilemmas and possibilities of development itself, at the actual process of growth through which the developing countries have to pass. The dilemmas are becoming clearer, the questions are now more specifically formulated than they were a decade ago. For instance, how can under-developed countries save upwards of 15 percent of their national income when per-capita income is as low as $60 a year? How can the whole field of agriculture, where entrenched ways and ancient methods are most firmly set in popular imagination, be set on a new way of growth? How can farmers be brought to produce more, not only for themselves but for the market as well? Where can capital be found for all the "infra-structure" of industry, for the pre-conditions of growth itself in the shape of roads and power, transportation and harbours? How can manpower and saving be found for the most decisive element of all in infra-structure: the building up of educated manpower? In the field of industrial expansion, given the fact that resources are always limited, which industries should be developed and which should be neglected? Where is it folly to invest? Where is it wisdom to go forward? Should the aim be a high return on capital immediately? Or is there a case for slower returns aiming ultimately at more balanced growth? All these are perfectly concrete questions which are forced upon the leaders of the under-developed areas the moment independence has been achieved and the unity and enthusiasm of the nationalist struggle begins to fade.

At this point we encounter one more advantage enjoyed by the Communists. They say they have the answers. We in the West may very rightly be dubious about a number of the answers. We do not care to be dogmatic — least of all in the daunting but essential field of agriculture. We cannot, therefore, emulate the confidence of the Communist who comes and says, "Listen to me and I can tell you what to do." Now, in so far as this hesitation springs from genuine uncertainty about methods, it is honest and can be met by greater efforts to discover what the answers are. But if it simply reflects the fact that we have little sense of urgency about the developing areas and have not given them the hard thought they deserve, then we can take no credit for our "pragmatism." It is simply another name for indifference.

Today, for whatever reason, I think we must admit that many of our answers are not formulated, our general policies are not worked out. And sometimes when I look at this whole emerging group of countries coming out of their struggle for independence and facing realities of economic choice and political decision, I wonder if we realize how fast time is running out, how quickly some of these decisions have to be taken, and how urgent it is for us, in our turn, to formulate our own policies for the poor nations of the world. If we do not have the sense of urgency now, can we be certain it may not be too late?

IV

The Economics of Development

We have seen how the great revolutions of our time have worked to create a group of wealthy nations in the North Atlantic arena. Now we must look at their impact upon the economies of the developing nations. In this context, only three of the revolutions come into question: the materialist revolution by which people become concerned with this-worldly affairs; the biological revolution by which population has begun to grow in an unprecedented way; and, last but most important of the great changes, the application of capital and science to all the processes of earning man's daily bread. The fourth of our revolutions — the revolution of equality — is more concerned with the problems of statecraft and of political development. This we will discuss later.

I do not think there is much need to stress the impact of the revolution of materialism and this-worldliness on the prospects of development. It is simply a fact of human nature that you do not get what you do not want, and you do not work for what you cannot imagine. Whether this drive for material betterment takes the form of the profit motive in the minds of business men or a politician's determination to see his country strong and economically developed, it is an essential spur to the modernization of the economy. The point is obvious enough not to need much underlining. Yet it is a useful reminder that some societies still lack this drive toward material advance and change. Wherever men and women still prefer status to economic development and set more store by traditional privilege and custom than by the risks and rigours of economic change, capital and science cannot act as full instruments of development since the leaders will not only be ignorant of how to apply them. They will also have no wish to do so. The example of Chinese business men toward the end of the nineteenth century has already been cited. In the first stages of a developing business system, one finds again and again a pull between the desire to use the new wealth for old forms of privilege — investing in land, adopting feudal habits — and the opposite desire for more adventurous ways of further investment to widen the economic base of the whole society. Where the identification of new business with old privilege occurs, it creates a formidable block to further change and creates social frictions which easily lead to widespread popular discontent. Communist propaganda in France between the wars was constantly directed against *les deux cent familles*: the two hundred families who owned the bulk of French industry in interlocking alliance with a small section of the earlier aristocracy. In Latin America, today, the business-feudal pattern is a potent cause of unrest and it seems clear that unless the next corner of development can be turned — to the wider spread of consuming power, the growth of a strong, independent middle class and the systematic construction of a market based on mass demand — such a society is likely to be swept away in a tide of radical left-wing or right-wing revolt.

These blocks occur even though a society has already set in motion the processes of modern development. It can be argued that the chief obstacles lie in a much earlier phase: in primitive tribal societies where development has yet to begin. In Africa, for instance, most of the peoples are still organized on tribal lines. In such communal societies, rights to the fruits of the land can be shared by a very large number of strictly non-working members of the kinship group. Why then should an individual farmer work harder if a flock of his "sisters and his cousins and his aunts" — and they can really be numbered in dozens in polygamous Africa — may come in and eat up his supplies? The "extended family" acts as a sort of private welfare state. No man need starve if his kin can maintain him. But equally, if there are more to maintain every time a man's income goes up, his incentives to greater effort finally reach zero.

For these reasons, some observers doubt whether modernization can come quickly in Africa. The leaders want it. This first step toward change has been taken. But the pre-conditions of actively seeking change do not exist among the people at large. This view is almost certainly exaggerated. The peasant farmers of Ghana became the largest cocoa-producers in the world on the simple incentive of cash. The Chagga tribe in Tanganyika have used their communal system to build up a highly effective coffee-producing co-operative. In Kenya, Kikuyu farmers, resettled on viable farms, are producing crops equal to those on white farms. Change is possible. Material incentives do work. But clearly the task is a much longer and more expensive one than in countries of good soil and a progressive farming tradition.

Now we come to what I have called the biological revolution: the enormous acceleration in the rate of growth of the world's population and its possible disproportion to the world's available resources. Many people regard this as the gravest of all mankind's problems and look forward with apprehension to the day, still some centuries ahead, when "standing-room only" may be the terrestrial rule. I confess that this more distant prospect seems to me somewhat too uncertain for immediate concern. Who knows what changes, maladies, cataclysms, or openings into outer space may not come to modify the strict geometrical progression of population growth? What I want to discuss here is the immediate problem. The increase in population in such areas as Latin America or the Indian subcontinent is such that new mouths threaten to gobble up the margin of fresh savings which alone permits enough capital accumulation for sustained development to become possible. The dilemma is very real. The whole of our modern economy depends upon saving, upon not consuming. But if year after year the population goes on increasing, the number of new mouths coming in to consume can quickly eat up the fresh savings which should have been available for the transformation of the economy. So the question can be restated: Is the rate of population-growth so great that in fact economic development cannot take place?

So far, the answers of history are ambiguous. In Western countries where modernization and rising population went hand in hand, the enormous spurt in population in fact spurred expansion by producing sufficient workers for the new industries and a mass market without which the output of the economy would certainly have been checked.

On the other hand, in tribal or traditional society — for instance, in the great traditional civilization of China — the opposite tendency has been at work. As we have seen, in times of peace the trend is that population climbs to the limits of production. These cannot be further expanded, for science and technology have not yet brought about such astonishing phenomena as the American farmer constantly producing more food from a smaller acreage. At this point, therefore, a melancholy cycle sets in: rising births first eat up the means of living; then starvation and its accompanying disorders set in motion a downward trend. Once population is again below the possible levels of production, there is a restoration of peace and stability which, unhappily for humanity, also brings the return of rising population. This vast, hopeless alternation between the fat years and the lean years can be all too fully documented from the records of Chinese history.

In our own day, which of these two patterns is likely to prevail? One has to remember that the new technology is based on saving. The means of ending the disproportion between people and resources is to apply capital massively to the resources. The difficulty is to secure this massive saving when rising population forces up the levels of consumption. If the rate of increase is 2 percent a year — as it is in India, or even 3 percent as in parts of Latin America — can people really save on anything like an adequate scale?

By a rough rule of thumb, economists reckon that to secure one unit of income you have to invest three times as much capital. So, even to keep pace with a 3-percent increase in population, a nation has, roughly speaking, to invest 9 percent of its national income each year. This is well beyond the 4 to 5 percent of traditional society. To get *ahead* of such a birth-rate, the rate ought to go up to between 12 and 15 percent of national income devoted to productive capital. This is thought to be the central point in achieving a break-through to sustained growth. But can you push savings up to that level, given the original poverty of society? And can you have any hope of doing so if the tide of babies rises faster still?

Communist societies hope to do so by the iron discipline of forced saving. Russia undoubtedly achieved its break-through by this rule; but Russia had no excess population in relation to resources. Scarcity of man-power was the trouble in the early days. China claims to have reached a level of saving in excess of 20 percent of national income. But we do not yet know whether it has moved decisively ahead. In democratic India, where people are being asked for the first time in history to vote themselves through the tough period of primitive accumulation, savings are lower. Domestic saving is probably not yet 10 percent of national income, although it is rising. But outside capital assistance has raised the proportion to over 13 percent. As a result, in spite of a 2 percent increase in population, India is just keeping ahead. Savings are growing, consumption is a little higher, the vast majority of the people can work and eat. Clearly, however, material progress might have been more rapid if some eighty million more people had not been added to India in the last decade. It is for this reason that Asian governments tend to put increasing emphasis on birth control as one of the pre-conditions of development.

However, here we have something of a "hen-and-egg" puzzle. It seems to be an historical fact that nations tend to have the birthrates they want. For example, in the nineteenth century the French, confronted by new laws on the inheritance of property, opted for smaller families. The Japanese first went through a cycle of very rapid expansion of their population. Now, however, as a result of both personal choice and government legislation, the expansion has ceased and the population seems to be stabilizing. We have to stress the point of choice because we are certainly not suggesting, I take it, that governments should decree what size of families people should have. Their choice will be decisive. And in this context of choice one thing seems clear: that it is when people see more opportunities for better education that they begin to consider whether a smaller family might not be better for themselves and for their children. In other words, I doubt whether one can disentangle the issues of economic development and rising population by any flat argument that stabilization of the population must come first. Lower births are more likely to be a consequence than a cause of economic expansion. It is above all by the thrust of development and literacy in the modernizing economy that conditions can be achieved in which parents begin to choose smaller families. Governments may assist the choice by encouraging family planning. There will doubtless continue to be considerable moral debate upon the means of limitation. But the decisive point is what millions of parents choose to do; and here, I think, history suggests strongly that a certain amount of modernization must occur before smaller families seem desirable.

This leaves unsolved the problem of securing the original thrust of investment. The Communist answer remains that of forced saving. The answer in the free world should, I believe, be a sustained and imaginative strategy of economic aid by the wealthy to the poor. This we shall discuss later. Here the point need only be stressed that modernization does appear to bring with it a corrective influence on high rates of expansion in the population. If, for instance, in the next twenty years there is a very large increase in the momentum of economic growth in India, there is nothing to suggest that the Japanese rhythm of expansion followed by stabilization may not occur. The basic point remains that without the thrust of growth there is no particular reason why people should want smaller families. Children may not die; they cannot be educated; meanwhile they work. A certain fatalism prevails. It is only when hope and expansion begin that the choice of a smaller family makes sense. So the revolution of scientific and capitalist change probably decides the biological revolution as well.

Saving and science are the keys to the revolution of economic growth. Technology is applied science and it results in a great increase in productivity; and productivity is a shorthand way of saying that with the same amount of work we can produce more results, or that we can produce the same results in shorter time and with less effort. Technology, in short, enables us to reinforce the workings of man's hand and brain so that the final output is much greater than could be produced by his own unaided efforts. This, I think, is fairly obvious, and the West has long been a society interested in technology. From the early Middle Ages windmills sailed over the landscape of Western Europe adding the energy of the wind to human efforts.

What is not always so obvious is that technology in all its forms is expensive. The cost of a fully developed technology is formidable. Let us take one example — the building of a large power station to open up a new region to electrification. The preliminaries — levelling the site, constructing roads to it, putting in possibly a branch line to bring in fuel, assembling materials, machines, and generators — are all expensive. Then follows the costly construction period. But if the electricity is to have its full effect, the consequences are more expensive still. Power-lines have to be built, consumer industries developed, trade schools are needed to train both electricians and skilled workers for the new factories. The magnet of more work draws in migrant workers needing housing and urban services. And so it goes on, every step swallowing up capital and setting in motion new demands for still more capital. In other words, if technology is the key to producing more output with less use of resources — productivity — then capital — or saving — is the only key to technology. Without saving, there is no economic growth. Moreover, as we have already remarked, the saving has to be on a fairly massive scale. Under Western colonial control, the poorer countries did see the beginnings of technology — the first roads and ports, some light industries, some development of production for export, a start in education; but the capital involved was not enough to change the whole nature of the economy.

To return to our economic rule of thumb — that when 12 to 15 percent of the national income is being devoted to saving, to capital formation, the economy grows — it is important to grasp that the reason for such a percentage is not simply that it allows a country to keep ahead of its growth of population and to set more aside each year for saving; it is also that without a certain momentum of saving, development can remain patchy and the growth of each sector fails to assist the growth of all the rest, railways helping the ports, the ports helping the growing cities, the cities promoting markets for the farms, and factories providing external economies to each other. When the spiral of growth runs right through the economy it begins to be within sight of the break-through to sustained growth. But if capital formation remains below the level needed to create a sort of contagion of development, the result is what you see throughout the developing world where small segments of modernization coexist with stagnant traditional areas and no full momentum of growth develops. So the problem in the first instance is how to achieve the accelerated rate of savings which will ensure a break-through to sustained growth.

Where is the massive injection of capital to come from? We have to remember that developing countries are, by definition, poor. The process of saving, therefore, will be rugged. Under any conditions, it is very difficult to make the man who is living on the margin of subsistence see that only by consuming less now can he in the future consume more. The saving, after all, is coming out of his work and effort. It is only human to want that work to result in some fairly immediate satisfactions, especially the satisfaction of actually getting enough to eat. The first phase of rugged saving may be mitigated by importing other people's savings from elsewhere. We shall return to that point. But the first reliance has to be on domestic saving, however tough the process may be.

We can say, broadly speaking, that there are two chief ways in which capital can be coaxed or induced to leave the circle of consumption and be drawn into the creation of more capital goods. It can be done by the operation of private enterprise in which the profits which are made by enterprise are then available for further investment. In conditions of reasonably open competition, the entrepreneur who does the best job in satisfying consumers at least cost to himself earns the biggest margin for further investment in other undertakings; and he will use his skill to find out the enterprises which, once again, maximize profits and hence release more resources for further investment. This was how the first cycle of development occurred in Britain and it is still dominant throughout the Western world.

But of course this is not the only method of diverting resources from consumption to capital development. In the West as in the East, the state intervenes by taxation — directly through income taxes, indirectly through sales taxes, and so forth. And where public corporations make profits, then, again indirectly, the state can withdraw resources from consumption and devote them to more capital development. Sales taxes and public profits are the main sources of capital in Soviet Russia.

At this point one limiting factor in the effectiveness of *local* capital should perhaps be mentioned. Quite obviously, local savings are in local currency. They do not automatically buy goods in other lands. Yet just because developing countries are still poor and still lack so much of the technology that they need, they have to find means of bringing in goods and services from abroad; otherwise, they will quite simply not be available. It is for this reason that nearly every break-through to sustained growth has been linked either with the import of capital from abroad or the creation of an export industry which could secure foreign exchange by its sales abroad. The Swedes, for example, sold their lumber overseas and bought the technology of the more developed nations. American growth received a boost from railway-building financed by British capital.

But what happens when the countries have few effective lines of export — when they have few openings for foreign investment or do not command a great deal of confidence in the minds of foreign investors? These are frequent conditions in developing countries. In India, for instance, any increase in national exports will be very arduous. Political insecurity unsettles investment in large parts of Africa. We will return later to this problem when we consider what the wealthy nations might be able to do in the way of a sustained strategy for boosting the revolution of economic growth in poorer countries. Here it is only necessary to underline the point that developing nations not only need capital, they also need a particular kind of capital — foreign exchange.

At this stage of development among the poorer communities it is virtually certain that the state will play a major part in raising more capital for development. This is because in these early days of growth, a large, confident business class is simply not available. Few countries had the long years of merchant dominance such as evolved in Western Europe. Only North America, Australia, and New Zealand began from scratch in a post-feudal age. Everywhere else, leadership has not been with the merchants but with courtiers and landlords — neither of them entrepreneurial types. Even in a country like Japan, which is now what we would call a free-enterprise country, government, not private interests, set in motion all the major industrial projects of the first break-through. Only later were these sold back to the clans and the merchants. By then, they were already going concerns. Throughout most of Africa today, you can count the number of effective African business men on two hands. In parts of Latin America, business has still to disentangle itself from feudal links and limitations. Clearly an almost non-existent entrepreneurial class can hardly launch the revolution of sustained growth. The men are quite simply not there to do it. This is the primary reason why we find a much greater emphasis upon government activity in raising the necessary savings today. In addition, one has to remember the political factor that the accumulation of large profits by a small group of business men is not popular in our modern days of social equality, and there is, therefore, a fairly widespread inhibition against relying massively upon private enterprise.

The more likely pattern is of a good deal of state initiative in the primary stages of growth. However, such a trend does not rule out vigorous private enterprise as well. On the contrary, one of the discoveries of our Western "mixed economy" in recent years has been the degree to which well planned programs of public investment act as a stimulus to private enterprise. The Monnet Plan remade the base of the French economy and sparked a quite new spirit of recovery in France's private sector. And it, in turn, was launched as a result of the Marshall Plan which, beginning with generous American public grants to Europe, ended by remaking the whole pattern of a dynamic market economy in Western Europe.

A similar process is at work in India today where the very large programs of public investment under the Plans — combined with very strict control over imports — has given Indian private enterprise the best decade in its history. This is not to say that friction and uneasiness between the public and private sectors do not persist. But it is growing less; and there appears to be more comprehension as each side gains in experience and self-confidence.

When it comes to the exact proportions between public and private enterprise, the problem cannot be solved by any rule of thumb; and — except by the Communists — it cannot be solved by any dogmatic statement either. In every country the mix between public and private enterprise is likely to be different, because it will in each case reflect local political pressures, local opportunities, the local scale of developed private enterprise, and the capacity of the country itself to find resources within its own borders. Given such varying opportunities and pre-conditions, it is quite impossible to make an absolute rule, once one leaves behind the ideology of total state control. There is, of course, the opposite ideology of total private enterprise. But this exists nowhere.

The fluctuating role of public and private enterprise does not end the uncertainties. All economics is a matter of choice — of allocating scarce resources to alternative and competing needs. There would be no economics if there were no scarcities. If everything were as available as the air around us or the sky above us, then "the gloomy science" would not exist. Choice must enter in because there is not enough to go round. And in this field of development it is very easy to make the wrong choices — choices which, in spite of a vast expenditure of money, do not lead to sustained growth, to an upward spiral of interdependent expansion. Getting the "mix" right is the great factual problem of economic development, and it must vary from economy to economy according to local conditions and endowment.

However, experience suggests some general points. One can say, for instance, that in our day most of the "infra-structure" — that is the preliminary capital overheads needed for growth — will be provided in the main by government. Everywhere, the state finances a very large part of the essential investment in human capital — in other words, in education. Transport systems are not often financed by private enterprise these days because returns on them are low and it takes a long time to recover the initial investment. Large power projects also tend to belong, these days, to the public sector. I think one can go further and say that this is a field in which the government's competence to plan and act effectively is fairly widely recognized. To give only one instance: it is very difficult to plan to have too much electric power because the experience of developing economies is that they always need more than they can get. But, of course, some aspects of "infra-structure" create special economic problems. Housing and schooling do not give a quick return in economic terms, essential as they may be. Their contribution to the economy in better skills, health, and habits of work takes time to mature. Meanwhile, if too much current capital has gone into such social services, government may find itself with no money left to finance immediate-income earners in other fields. It is a difficult question of balance, and false calculations are all too easy.

Government also tends to be more active these days in the field of heavy industry. This was formerly the preserve, in the West, of private enterprise, though government backing and even government subsidies have often played a part in building and sustaining this sector. The reasons for government intervention these days are partly economic, partly political. In developing countries, there may not be entrepreneurs with the confidence or capital to put up a whole steel works; moreover, many new governments are unwilling to entrust anything as crucial and influential as heavy industry entirely to private enterprise. "The commanding heights of the economy" should, as the Indians argue, be under public control. The result in India has been the creation of a very large public steel industry combined with a doubling in the capacity of private steel-making.

One consequence of sheer scale in this sector is that if errors of calculation are made they tend to be very costly. One of the causes of the under-spread unrest in Eastern Europe in 1956 was the misplanning of resources in the first days of Communist euphoria. Heavy industry was lavishly planned, and then the units were found to be without adequate raw materials and hence with little hope of economic production. Half-finished steel-mills were symbols of planning that had miscalculated in the most expensive way. The recent cancelling of a whole aircraft industry in East Germany offers another example of costly misplanning. It is said of Mayor LaGuardia that he once said: "I make very few mistakes, but when I do make a mistake, it's a beaut'." I think you can say that the same is true of governments. They do not necessarily make mistakes in the development of heavy industry. But if they do make a mistake, it tends to be a very large one — in short, a "beaut'."

In the rest of the industrial structure where scale and need vary enormously, there is a strong case for the effectiveness of private enterprise simply because of the variety of demand and the differences in size of enterprise appropriate to various forms of output. Where consumer demand is highly unpredictable and the need for flexibility in the product is highest, very large industrial organizations are not necessarily the most efficient. To give only one instance, a large bureaucracy is not likely to plan successfully the infinite varieties of feminine clothes. May there not be some inner fatality underlying the fact that, at present, countries of total state control do appear to be singularly ill-dressed?

The desirability of widespread and diversified enterprise does not, however, answer the question whether there are enough entrepreneurs to undertake the expansion. And where they are lacking, as in large parts of Africa, government must inescapably play a part in helping the entrepreneur to begin. Small-scale private enterprise will have to be fostered carefully. This is in part a matter of loans from government and the establishment of such facilities as properly equipped trading estates. But perhaps even more important is training in managerial techniques and accountancy. Industrial extension services can in fact be even more important than finance, especially if the finance is not properly supervised. The effort is well worth while. Widespread entrepreneurial talent is one of the most effective forces in the production of greater wealth. In Kenya, for instance, where resources are certainly lower than in some other African countries — say, Ghana — the presence of European and Asian businessmen has given the country a much more rapid rate of industrial growth. But private enterprise cannot grow without encouragement in countries where hitherto the entrepreneurial tradition has been lacking.

This shortage explains why developing countries are anxious that foreign firms should come in to invest, and to establish the new entrepreneurial patterns. In fact, pace-setting private industry can be a valuable legacy of the colonial period. But the legacy gives its full effect only if the foreign companies draw local interests into partnership, encouraging local stockholders to invest, and training local managers and technicians. This has not always been done in the past and this is one reason why foreign enterprise in newly independent countries is often unpopular and governments are torn between the desire to encourage more foreign investment and the fear of having too much.

Now we must turn to what is in some ways the most crucial and difficult problem of all: the transformation of agriculture. Farming, I think, has been the Cinderella of developing economies. So much emphasis has been placed upon the new techniques of industry that it is sometimes forgotten that if farming cannot be transformed there can be no genuine revolution of economic growth. The first reason is that most of the capital has to come from the countryside, because the bulk of the population lives on the land and the bulk of the wealth comes from agriculture in the early days. If farm productivity goes up, a surplus can be transferred to other growing sectors and the farmer will still be better off than he was. This gives him an incentive to produce more food. Prosperity also enables the farming population to provide a growing market for industrial goods. If the countryside is stagnant, the farmers cannot buy the new goods and the beneficent cycle of interdependent upward growth in both industry and agriculture cannot go forward. If you do not change agriculture, you will not change the economy: this is, I think, one of the safe rules one can lay down for developing communities. At the same time, agriculture is the most difficult sector to change for the simple reason that agricultural methods are thousands of years old and people prefer on the whole to go on in the ways of their fathers. To coax the traditional farmer still at work in his old setting into new patterns of agriculture is infinitely more difficult than to persuade people to undertake new techniques in a wholly new, industrial urban environment. In the city, all is new; change is part of the landscape. On the land, everything seems the same; this makes change so much more difficult.

To transform farming solely by means of private enterprise offers some formidable difficulties. The chief instrument of change is the development of the market, the incentive to production which market prices offer. But will the farmers come into the market? Private landowners in under-developed areas are very rarely enterprising. Whether it is a question of the Zamindars in India, the tribal leaders of Africa, or the feudal landlords of Latin America, they are not, as a group, intent on transforming their lands and their techniques. They still live for subsistence and display. The peasants have no incentive to change since any gain could go to swell the landlord's rent. Tribal farmers face comparable inhibitions because sharing the fruits of work with the clan discourages intensive effort.

The first answer to these obstacles is, of course, ambitious land reform. The peasant must own his land. Where he does not, modernization is unlikely. But this does not end the problem. In many lands, the pressure of population is such that no farmer can receive an effective economic unit once the land has been split up.

Uneconomic, fragmented holdings push production further down. Once again, there is an answer; but it is not a cheap or easy one. A massive development of co-operative societies for credit, processing, and marketing can give the small farmer the advantages of scale and the inducements of private ownership. This has been done triumphantly in Japan where a five-acre farm can give a decent living because it is backed by co-operatives organized and run by the farmers themselves. But such a development takes time, patience, and a great deal of capital.

I doubt, however, whether there are any short cuts. It is very tempting for the state to believe that there are: collectivize the land, employ the peasants as so many day-labourers, and in this way repeat in agriculture what is in fact the basic pattern in industry. But agriculture is not industry. Peasants in developing countries feel for their land and for their beasts and for the rhythms and satisfactions of their farming life in ways which are quite different from the reactions of men to machines and factories. The mood may change, of course. Western farmers increasingly regard farming as simply a business. But the need to change agriculture is not a future problem. It is urgent and immediate. If the state steps in too aggressively, the result seems to be a profound underground opposition to the whole idea of transforming agriculture under state direction. Even after forty years, Russian agriculture is still the chief trouble-spot of the régime. In China, the desperate move of transforming the whole of agriculture according to a communal system — in which in essence people work on the industrial pattern — has, at least in some measure, broken down as a result of the peasants' resistance and apathy. In fact, no state-run agriculture today reflects anything like the productivity of Japanese or American agriculture. In Yugoslavia, where output is going up most sharply among public systems of farming, the emphasis is heavily on decentralization and workers' control.

Perhaps the failure can best be illustrated by a remark made at an agronomists' conference held a short time ago at Bangalore. Agricultural scientists had gathered there from all over the world. At the end of the discussion, the Yugoslav delegate was asked to sum up. This is what he said: "There are two main agricultural problems in the world: American agriculture produces too much; Russian agriculture produces too little. But we have the solution, gentlemen. If Russia will use American methods and America will use Russian methods, there will be no further problem." This is perhaps an apt summary of the degree to which massive state intervention in agriculture has so far failed to produce results.

And yet the problem remains. The transformation of agriculture cannot be secured without massive investment. In fact, one reason for the Russian effort to enlarge the scale of farms is to produce economic units substantial enough to absorb large inputs of capital. Yet the capital must also in the early stages come largely from rural savings and be deployed in fierce competition from other driving needs — education, transport, power, industry. In this competition, the tendency has been to overlook the essential demands of farming. In India's Second Plan, for instance, or in Pakistan's First, agricultural priorities were too low. The new Plans correct this bias; for the realization is growing that without capital the land cannot progress. All the methods of transforming agriculture are expensive. Farmers need more skills, more fertilizers, more credit. There is no hope of a productive agriculture if saving is squeezed out of the country and nothing is put back.

Perhaps this is just another way of saying that all the methods of economic transformation are expensive. There are none that can be accomplished without some capital, and many of the most crucial ones demand great sums of capital. The scale of capital raises, therefore, the crucial political problem. Can you persuade people to undertake this degree of saving voluntarily? May it not be an essential short cut to allow the state to step in and say to the citizen: "You must save; you will save; and it is good for you even if you object." Such a short cut is not easy under a democratic government. Voters may will the end of development. They do not relish the means — higher taxes, higher savings. So the question must be asked: does dictatorial government enjoy a built-in advantage in developing lands? At this point, however, the economic problem fuses into the political problem which must be examined next.

V

The Politics of Development

The time has now come to look at the fourth of the great revolutions of our day: the revolution of political equality. It is everywhere at work in the under-developed and uncommitted nations and everywhere, too, it complicates and even exacerbates relations between the rich nations and the poor. It is an all-embracing concept of equality: equality of the nation, of the race, of the class; above all, the equality of man with man in the new world-society that is beginning to emerge.

Most of the poor and uncommitted lands have acquired this vast, almost cosmic vision of equality as a result of their colonial contact with Western societies. The ambition to modernize, to pull level with the more developed societies, has been implanted in them by their experiences as part of a Western imperial pattern. Western merchants, Western educators, Western administrators, brought the ferment of the new ideas and the new sense of the need for, and the right to, equality.

But these Western contacts brought in the new ideas by different routes. There have been positive, constructive, and creative methods of transmission; and the work of great imperial administrators — one thinks of a Monroe or an Elphinstone in India, a Lugard or a Guggisberg in West Africa — undoubtedly created a framework of order and opportunities of advance unequalled for centuries. It is in this sense that empire has proved one of the great civilizing forces in human history. But these were not the only methods by which the sense of equality was fostered. We must not forget the dark ways of dislike, exclusion, fear, and prejudice, which make imperialism one of the catastrophic forces of mankind as well.

During the West's impact on the surrounding world — an impact which has lasted three hundred years — there is evidence enough of both forms of transmission. We have already spoken of the great administrators who laid the foundations upon which such services as the Indian Civil Service came to be not only efficient and selfless, but even a nation-building force. Today, with the collapse of the Congo before us, we are less likely to underestimate the supreme contribution orderly administration can make to the arts of civilization.

To the administrators we must add the missionaries and the scholars. Not all missionaries came out in the spirit in which fruitful cultural contact can flourish. Too much contempt for the "heathen," too much ignorance of alien cultures diminished the effectiveness of what was done. Had more gone with the sympathy and understanding displayed by Father Matteo Ricci, the great Jesuit missionary to China, who knows what new insights might not have been achieved? Yet the influence of Christianity on great Indian reformers such as Sir Ram Mohan Roy or great leaders like Gandhi should not be forgotten. In Africa, the figure of David Livingstone, working with fortitude to end the slave-trade, towers above the greedy mob of adventurers and profiteers looking to Africa, like Pistol, for its "golden joys." And throughout West Africa, unknown heroes of the Protestant missions risked almost certain death by yellow fever to bring religion, education, and the first beginnings of modern health to the Africans. Nor should one forget the work of Western scholars who have played so great a role in piecing together from the records of monuments, temple scrolls, and archaeology the history of Asian peoples who might otherwise have lost their history, and their identity as well.

Another essential element in a developing society — a modern managerial class — was also introduced through the Western impact. There would have been no quick development of a modern middle class with effective commercial and entrepreneurial energies if colonial rule had not created a new atmosphere of peace and fostered, in great countries such as India, the development of modern commercial law, the notion of contract, a new sense of security for property, a new belief that if the merchant sets to work to develop, accumulate, and invest, his wealth should be secure.

Nor is the role of the army negligible. Elements of discipline and service were injected into traditional communities as a result of modern army training. In fact, one could argue that in some countries the officer corps had qualities of loyalty and patriotism free from any tincture of self-interest not found too generally in the community at large. To have such cadres is a positive achievement upon which much can be built.

Yet it would be a grave mistake if we in the West thought only of the constructive efforts and forgot the darker side of the record. Take first of all the most resented aspect of Western rule, particularly of British rule: we took with us in our colonial dealings an ignorant and almost irremovable racial prejudice. Now I know that most nations have had their racial prejudices; in fact,

I am reminded of a Chinese proverb to the effect that God first made the African and overbaked him black, and then God made the European and underbaked him white, but then God made the Chinese and baked them exactly right — which is yellow of course. And it is an irony of history that in the nineteenth century, the Chinese called Westerners "red" barbarians; perhaps because there were so many Scotsmen among them. Prejudice, the sense of separateness and superiority, are certainly not confined to the West.

But for three hundred years the white race has enjoyed a dominant position in the world. Its members were able to stamp their prejudices across the face of the globe because they were, in fact, on top. And there can be no doubt that many white men, particularly Anglo-Saxon white men, cannot overcome a straightforward colour prejudice. And this belief that coloured people are inferior has left its mark all over the world. Perhaps one realizes how deep the wounds are only when one has lived in ex-colonial lands. Occasionally in confidential talks, late at night, when there is no longer an official front to be kept up, one hears of the insults at the hands of London boarding-house keepers or of careless wounding words from educated people: trivial incidents, perhaps, but ones which leave a mark on people's consciousness that can never be effaced.

Another whole set of problems is concerned not so much with race as with class. It seems to be a fact of life that in the early days of industrial development, the merchant, in process of turning himself into an entrepreneur, often demonstrates facets of greed and rapacity which make him a not too attractive figure to the society he raids and exploits. This of course is not a problem confined to the newly developing areas. If you read the pages of Dickens, you will meet the Mr. Merdles and the Mr. Veneerings who pursue wealth with a passion and irresponsibility that leads them to ruin others and finally themselves. Yet such men are influential. Money talks. And in a poor but developing economy it is much more likely that such men will have contacts with the colonial rulers, be consulted by them, and entertain them. There is probably no very great identification of interests. British colonial administrators tended to think of business men as the Victorians thought of trade. It was not quite "the thing." But there was enough contact to create some identification between colonial rule and the local magnates, and to give a social edge to nationalist criticism.

It was reinforced wherever — as was usual — the landlord system remained intact. The administrators arriving from overseas to take up their imperial appointments would not refuse the offered tiger-hunt. Again, some identification was possible between colonial rule and the local social hierarchy.

The educated groups in the new sense — the new lawyers, the new technicians, the men and women who had access to modern forms of knowledge — remained a very small group in relation to the people at large. A sense of isolation tended to weaken them and undermine their political confidence. Moreover, the environment confused them further. After a number of small hopeful beginnings, colonial economies failed to move forward to sustained momentum. The economic picture was patchy, with bits of development here and bits of development there, while social changes went forward in one sector and were quite absent in others. Young people had the feeling of belonging to a discontinuous society — a mood which increased their unease. And to all this we must add the stagnation of the twenties and the thirties.

After the First World War, the colonial powers of Western Europe entered upon a period of relative economic decline. It was followed by the appalling depression of 1929 and the chaotic conditions of the thirties. Local stagnation increased the social discontents of the colonial world and coupled rising political consciousness with social protest and economic frustration. It was no longer only the tiny educated middle class who felt the pressure. More unsophisticated people began to ask questions about the foreigner who came and lived in the big house at the top of the hill, the colonial officials with all the influential administrative jobs, the big foreign merchant and banker with something of an economic monopoly. And round these foreigners tended to cluster the few members of the local society who were doing well out of the system: the large landowner, the local merchant, the new industrialist whose wealth — old or new — cut them off more and more from their frustrated fellow countrymen.

It is therefore not surprising that the revolution of independence and national equality which has been gathering strength round the world for the last fifty years has more than one political and social overtone. There is the ambition for economic change sparked by the example of what Western society can do with its new technology. To it must be added the social unrest stirred up by the contrast between the small rich *élite*, comfortably profiting from the *status quo*, and the vast mass of the people who are beginning to resent their desperate poverty. This, in turn, fuses with anti-colonial sentiment, with the feeling that the subject nation has the right to self-government and independence. In fact, the two are often barely distinguishable; for local opinion tends more and more to see "colonial servitude" as the chief obstacle to social rights and economic development. These were the days when students like Chou En-lai or Ho Chi-minh went to Europe for their education and found that only Leninism really seemed to describe their predicament. A stirring, uncertain, chaotic time of social, political, and economic change, all woven together — this, I think, is how we must regard the struggle of the poorer nations to get through all the sound-barriers of their life at once: the economic barrier, the social barrier, the political barrier. And if one sees the struggle in this perspective, surely it is not surprising that our days are tense. The remarkable thing is how much stability still remains in the midst of these whirling passions and ambitions for total change.

At one time, it must have seemed that the whole colonial order, battered by such pressures, would end in a violent explosion of hatred and violence. Some experiments have ended in bloodshed. The Dutch left Indonesia after war had decided the issue. The French withdrew from Indo-China under the same tragic star of conflict. Britain had to fight an ugly little war in Cyprus before a settlement could be reached. Certainly Lenin foresaw such a consummation and even suggested that the revolt of the colonial masses might be a quicker route to world Communism than the milder resentments of Western workers.

But in fact, the transfer of power from the old colonial governments to the new independent states since the war has, I think, proved easier than we might have feared. We can now see that, at least in these first decades of independence, the transfer of power by Britain to India and Pakistan — the first great voluntary transfers of government — was accomplished with such restraint and generosity that a new pattern of compelling force appeared on the human scene. It was, of course, an achievement toward which British political thought had long been directed. As early as the 1820s, great British proconsuls in India had said that there could be no justification for British rule in India save to build up the conditions under which Indians would govern themselves. The evolving Commonwealth in which the white Dominions — Canada, Australia — had already found an independent place provided a structure of friendship and co-operation within which the new nations could fit without any diminution of their newly established sovereignty. But equally, the transfer was made possible by the political vision and immense personal generosity of men like Gandhi and Nehru who were ready, when the day came, to treat their former gaolers as trusted friends. For this mutual respect and conciliation there was no place in the Marxist canon, and it has had a dominant influence ever since.

Transfers of power have continued to take place with similar grace and dignity in other parts of the world — in the rest of the British Commonwealth, in French West Africa. In fact, one can say that there are perhaps only two types of ex-colonial community in which it is excessively difficult to achieve a transfer of power with anything like the goodwill that is needed to make it effective and peaceful. One type is the country where a settler problem complicates the issue — as in Algeria, in the Rhodesias, or in Kenya. In such communities, the lines of cleavage between groups — the political, social, and economic lines we have already discussed — are strengthened and exacerbated by the greatest dividers of all, the dividers of culture and race. Settlers from the metropolitan country come in and root themselves in the local community. They take the best land. Being better educated, they produce more wealth from it. They hold the best posts. They often control the administration. At the same time, internal peace and the beginnings of modernization can set in motion a violent explosion of the birth-rate among the more primitive peoples whose chief means of subsistence — the land — has nonetheless been taken away. Two societies develop. In one, the white settlers build up a more or less wealthy modern community. Around and among them the dispossessed exist, multiply, and finally begin to revolt. This has been the pattern of Algeria. In Kenya, in the Rhodesias, in parts of the Congo, acute racial differences complete the picture of separatism and hostility. Here the transfer of power presents overwhelming difficulty. The long bitter Algerian war is testimony to the vast obstacles that must be overcome.

The second category is rather more ambiguous. In some countries the transfer of power is made, but conditions prevent it from convincing the local people that a genuine transfer has in fact occurred. Lenin had these cases in mind when he argued that metropolitan powers could still exercise a preponderant influence in ex-colonial territories, simply by keeping all the levers of economic power in their own hands. Any form of foreign investment, particularly investment from a dominant Western or ex-imperial government, had hidden in it, he suggested, the tentacles of continued control. One cannot underestimate the degree to which the Leninist myth of power by indirection, exercised through "the monopolists and the trusts," has sunk into the distrustful minds of developing peoples. Where in fact investment from abroad seems overwhelmingly dominant and the doubt can arise whether local interests have any chance against the big foreign firms, then the Leninist pattern is not too difficult to apply and people begin to ask whether their own supposedly independent government may not be the puppet of a foreign power. There was an element of this feeling in the Cuban reaction to Batista; and we do not yet know what sorrows have been brought upon the Congo by the decision of a separatist government to establish itself in the Katanga where Belgian mining interests are overwhelmingly strong.

Yet we are now realizing for the first time that, in spite of these difficulties, it is not in fact the moment of transfer of power that is most difficult in the emergence of the poorer nations to a sense of national equality in the modern world. After all, in the periods that lead up to the ending of the colonial régime, usually a considerable sense of common purpose unites the country. More and more people come to feel that colonial rule must be the chief target and that all differences of race or tribe or class can be subordinated to the greater struggle to achieve political equality and independence. This is the great unifying force behind such movements as India's Congress Party where the rich mill-owner and the simple peasant hand-weaver were united under the leadership of Gandhi and Nehru. This unifying force is enough to carry the country forward to the great effort of achieving independence. In fact, the greater the effort, the greater the unity. Where independence comes virtually without struggle — as in Burma or Ceylon or Nigeria — the advantages of national unity may well be lessened. It is after independence that the real troubles begin. With national equality and independence achieved, the problems of social and economic equality begin to take pride of place.

The first and obvious conflict to gather force is the fundamental conflict between rich and poor within the nation. Gone is the overriding unity of struggle. The contrasts between wealth and poverty are now all the more stark because, during the struggle, independence had been painted in millennial terms, with milk and honey for everybody.

If, as often happens, independence coincides with the early days of industrialization and economic modernization, then the conflict may take on even sharper social overtones. At this period the merchant-turned-entrepreneur is not necessarily an inspiring national leader, not often a man to whom the masses will turn with a sense that his integrity is unquestioned and his work unequivocally for the public good. A lot of the prejudice one meets in India — for example, against the Mawari trading-class — is based on the fact that the masses believe, not always without foundation, that these men will put profit before everything, even before the well-being of the community. The belief breeds acrimony, distrust, and class-hatred.

The new entrepreneur is an object of suspicion because he gets on too fast. Another dominant group — the landlords — are often disliked for the opposite reason: they do not change themselves and thus make change impossible for everyone else on the land. They are still so embedded in the past, still so set upon the old questions of status, the old attitude toward land as a way of life not as a way of development, that often it seems as though an immovable social and political lid had been clapped tightly down on the countryside, inhibiting any possibility of development and change. The unhandiness of unchanged feudal leadership for a modernizing economy can be illustrated from Japan after 1870 where the Meiji reformers found it necessary to begin their economic revolution by total land reform. In many parts of Latin America today, land reform is probably still the single most efficacious way of setting in motion the processes of economic growth.

The shortcomings of leadership based upon the old rural leaders and the up-and-coming entrepreneurs of the city are not overcome simply by introducing the formal machinery of parliamentary democracy. All too often, the present groups in power simply manipulate the democratic machine for their own purposes. They resemble in some measure the House of Commons in Britain before 1832 when the landed gentry had the margin of political strength. But Britain's parliamentary government became an efficacious instrument of social change only after several further modifications. It was widened first to include the rising middle classes including, of course, the entrepreneurs and then later, after a very considerable advance in literacy, the mass of the citizens as well.

These pre-conditions of parliamentary effectiveness often do not exist in developing economies on the morrow of independence. The entrepreneurial groups are still socially irresponsible; there are no Lord Shaftesburys, no Disraelis to express the conscience of the dominant class. In addition, the middle class is miserably small and has none of the self-confidence of the bustling Victorian world. And the mass of the people are wholly illiterate and are still overwhelmingly country folk at the mercy of local lords or bailiffs or, as in much of Africa, unaware of any leadership or change outside the tribal pattern. In such conditions the machinery of democracy is not enough to create its spirit. Parliament tends to remain an affair of cliques and manipulators. Pakistan before Ayub, Iran, the Egypt of Farouk — all are examples of systems, which though parliamentary in form, were and are in fact self-regarding, oligarchic, and to a considerable degree anti-social.

Since the old rural leaders and the new rich are so often unable to canalize the new ambitions of the people, they are often thrust aside in the years following independence. Again and again it is the army that steps in to provide new government: in the Sudan, in Egypt, in Iraq, in Pakistan. The representatives of the merchant and landlord groups are set aside, and military leaders, coming in with a tradition of service and a reputation of integrity, take over and attempt to pull the country together to face the truly daunting problems of development in the first stages of independence.

And I think we would do well to remember how daunting these problems are. The first and deepest is the dilemma we have already explored. In early days of economic development, there is no hope for expansion unless the people can be persuaded to undertake a large and expanding program of capital saving. Yet they are poor — poor by definition since the wealth-creating process has yet to begin. Saving for them entails lopping off a margin from current consumption when consumption is already so low that it is barely enough to sustain life. Even though the hope is that, five and ten years from now, conditions will be better, can the people be persuaded — least of all by free vote — to submit themselves to an even worse plight now? The dilemma, as we have seen, is absolutely inescapable because the need for saving is as unavoidable as the fact of poverty. It needs exceptional leadership, with very considerable administrative capacity and imaginative grasp, to ease the people out of this particular trap; and these qualities are not easily forthcoming in the traditional groups who make up the leadership in transitional societies.

The problem is made all the more involved by the fact that the coming of independence is precisely the hour when the hopes of the people are most acutely roused by the possibilities of achieving a modern form of society. The colonial struggle gave them political consciousness. They were told again and again during its course that only the wicked imperialists hold them back from a better life. Thus, when independence comes, they expect that better life and they expect it now. It is against this background that we should assess the pressures on their leaders.

To maintain themselves in power — the first commandment for politicians — they must be able to meet some of this rising popular pressure and to show some positive results. The chances are, however, that the turmoil of transition has lessened administrative efficiency, weakened disciplines of work, and possibly slowed down the entry of foreign capital. Economic conditions may well be worse. The pressures mount all the more rapidly as a result. These pressures are much greater than our stabler, wealthier world now finds easy to imagine. The only striking analogy that comes to mind is the pressure on any Western government if unemployment rises above a certain level. But to gauge the force of protest and discontent in the developing countries one would need to multiply the pressure a thousandfold. The issue is not simply one of being out of work for a time; it is all future possibility of work, all hope of a little wealth to come, the whole chance of moving on from stagnation and misery. Such pressure is political dynamite.

These conditions alone would be enough to tax the powers of leadership in the new state to the full and even to make the new rulers feel that they must take dictatorial powers in order to find the direction and discipline needed to face the nation's inescapable problems. But in addition to all these internal problems, they face an even more testing external difficulty. They have all come to power during the bitter international tensions of the Cold War.

They can neither change nor modify the broad struggle for power in the world in which the Great Powers manoeuvre to maintain their position, to extend their dominion and to achieve predominant influence. Smaller states may be able to play a part at the margin and, unhappily, as the pre-1914 crises in the Balkans showed, shifts of power at the margin can precipitate the general struggle. But the core of the fight is not theirs to influence. Dr. Nkrumah is never tired of quoting an old Swahili proverb which says that when the bull elephants fight, the grass is trampled down. In many parts of the world, the sense that the poorer, weaker nations are pawns in a bigger game, just grass to be trodden down in the struggle by the great ones, lends a tragic and, I think, moving edge to the search for neutralism. In the past, the Western Powers have often shown too little sympathetic understanding for the mood. The United States for years under the late Mr. John Foster Dulles condemned neutralism as a moral evil, forgetting its own early distaste for "entangling alliances." But the "morals" of resistance for very small states in the age of the megaton bomb are at least dubious and it is not certain, in any case, whether a neutrality prepared to defraud itself is not a much better safeguard than co-operation in alliances with the West.

The reason is very simple. Mass opinion still tends to become very easily anti-Western because colonial memories are so recent. To build alliances with the ex-colonial powers can easily be twisted to look like falling once again under their imperial control. This twist, it need hardly be said, is staple Communist propaganda. The royal government in Iraq fell in part because of its readiness to work with the West in a Middle-eastern military alliance.

The blame is not all on one side. Neutralists have also earned suspicion by the way in which they have interpreted neutrality. Unfortunately the Cold War not only scares smaller powers; it also offers them temptations which very often they are unable to resist. It is, after all, very tempting for a local leader to think that he can play the Great-Power game. It gives a great sense of importance to believe himself able to play off America against Russia. The advantages at first seem greater than the risks. That by riding the tiger one may end up inside is not too obvious in the early stages of the game. If, for instance, you are having trouble with the opposition, why not turn to the Communists and get a little help? The problem of getting the Communists to *stop* helping afterwards belongs to a future too distant to be taken into account. In other words, the danger offered to small governments is not only a direct risk of invasion or attack but also a permanent temptation to involve themselves far out of their depth in the rapids and shoals of world politics.

I do not myself think we should meet this situation by succumbing to irritation and denunciation. It is tempting to lose one's patience and exclaim against local leaders who seem so irresponsible. But could we not try sometimes to put ourselves in their position? Are they not like adolescents who leave their father's house only to be involved instantly in an enormous street fight; or like children who go out into the great school of the world only to find the faculties shooting it out in just those classrooms where they had hoped to get their education? One cannot, I think, underline too much the inexperience and the sense of uncertainty which must prevail among new leaders who enter the school of the world and find the faculty throwing everything, including their desks, at each other. I confess that my own feeling is not one of irritation but rather of intense sympathy for leaders who have to take the first steps of independence over ground which gives way at every step.

However, there is no escape from the fact that for the time being the Cold War forms the environment of the modern world. The Communists' attempt at world dominion is one of the great ideological strains in their faith; however much their tactics may vary, the underlying strategy has not yet changed. Equally, the Western powers will not abandon their desire to preserve a world in which plurality of power and capacity of choice are possible. The two aims are not compatible and all along the frontiers of the two worlds the struggle for influence and dominance cannot be evaded. We have therefore to assess the impact of the Cold War on the problems of developing states and to see how the rival ideologies influence local aspirations, particularly the great central driving aspiration to equal status and an equal chance.

We would, I think, be unwise to underestimate some of the immediate advantages which the Communists enjoy in this tough tussle for influence in the newly independent nations. For one thing, this is a time of chaotic change and hence of chaotic ideas. It is dangerously attractive to many minds to be offered a political and economic panacea as complete and apparently self-explanatory as Marxism-Leninism. It seems to tie up all their problems in a single order of explanation and to make sense of a world which they feel they do not understand and fear they never may. Another advantage enjoyed by Communism is that in Asia, in Africa, in Latin America, Russia does not bear the stigma of having been a colonial power. This is paradoxical when you consider how much of Central Asia's non-Russian peoples are under Soviet control. But Russia's extension across Central Asia and Siberia to embrace so many Turkoman and Mongol peoples within its empire has the same irresistible, irreversible, almost geological force as China's imperial extension southwards or the engulfing of most of North America by the United States.

Moreover, the subject peoples — Kazakhs, Kirghiz, Uzbeks —

have been drawn into the advantages of modern society as well as into its pains. The nomads from the steppes were thrown into the modernizing, industrializing process as ruthlessly as the Bantu of South Africa have been flung into the mines. But today such educational advance has accompanied the process that there are more graduates per head of population in Uzbekistan than in France. The Bantu of the Union of South Africa and the felleaga of Algeria have not fared so well. They have been left on the margins of the new modern society, unintegrated, unreconciled, the sullen proletariat of revolt. Add to this Russia's apparent freedom from racial prejudice, and its advantages in the minds of developing peoples should be clear. Then there are a number of reasons in practical politics to explain the Communists' relative advantage. When a new nation is faced with the enormous complexity and variety of economic and social problems that are inescapable after independence, the temptation to impose the rule of a single party and use hard discipline to solve them is obvious. And there stands the Communist Party ready-made, offering its pattern of total obedience. Nationalist leaders looking for policies in the post-revolutionary phase are caught by the deceptive directions and vigour of the Communist solution.

It can, I think, be argued that this availability of the Soviet pattern helps to explain the unfolding paradox of the Castro régime in Cuba — a régime brought in by widespread popular revolt against the dictatorship and corruption of Batista, promising elections and civil liberties; yet degenerating almost at once into another kind of police state. There is evidence to suggest that Castro chose a Marxist pattern not because he had drawn his support from embattled peasants and workers — in fact, middle-class disgust with Batista was his strongest suit — but because it was the only pattern he knew to help him to exercise the power he had unexpectedly achieved. Faced with the multitudinous uncertainties of responsibility, he grabbed the only pattern which seemed likely to preserve his leadership and deal with his difficulties. It was Cuba's tragedy that a nation so relatively advanced in development — to give only one instance, more than half its population already live in the cities — should be thrust back by totally inexperienced leadership to a repressive and brutal system usually associated with much earlier stages of break-through.

It is, of course, not only a question of Communism offering ready-made solutions. Many of them seem to fit the real dilemmas very closely. At a time when changing the old leadership and bringing the masses into the new dynamic economy are pre-conditions of development, there is no doubt where Communism stands. It is against the old landlord; it is against the new entrepreneur. It sides with the majority of the people whose aspirations are the motive force of change. The content of their policy also has its relevance. The Russians claim that such is their ability to achieve such large rates of growth in the last forty years, they can offer a pattern of rapid development and rapid capital accumulation in just those areas where the countries of the newly independent world most need help. They claim that their scale of capital formation has driven them forward at growth-rates of 6, 7, and 8 percent a year. Given such expansion, any new government, they argue, can quickly meet what Adlai Stevenson has called "the revolution of rising expectations." The massive Communist drive for capital and production will quickly outstrip anything that the West, with its bungling, experimental methods can hope to offer. All this is heady stuff to a young government looking round desperately for policies with which to cope with all the problems of its day, and not perhaps sophisticated enough to grasp what the cost of so much "discipline" may be.

Nor do the Communists simply leave their claimed achievements to talk for themselves. Propaganda underlines them incessantly and offers of capital assistance reinforce the picture of Soviet success. Again and again missions set off to Moscow from Africa or Asia or Latin America and there receive offers of help in buying up the surpluses the West will not buy and capital assistance at very low rates of interest for a long period of time. At times it is almost as though the projects themselves — an Assuan Dam, a Volta Dam, a steel-mill for India — had become small sectors in the general fluctuating battle-front of world assistance. The building and the competition are not necessarily bad. On the contrary, more capital may be flowing into the under-developed areas than would otherwise be the case. But the political overtones, the sense of rivalry and pressure with which so much of the aid is beset, adds enormously to the political dilemmas of the poor nations reaching out desperately for a new way of life.

Given this context of competition, what shall we say of Western policies? Before we consider our positive aims and policies, I think we should realize soberly that the world-wide struggle is not necessarily "going our way," that we have formidable difficulties to overcome. The fact remains that the Western powers have been the colonial masters until the day before yesterday. Although the grace of making the transfers of imperial power has helped lessen colonial resentments, we still carry the ugly stigma of racialism. We are still implicated in the dangerous, insoluble problem of apartheid in South Africa. We have our own Deep Souths and Notting Hills. We do not come with clean hands.

Again, the political pattern of multi-party democracy which we prefer, and often set up in colonies before we leave them, is not necessarily workable in the first turbulent days of independence. Crises at these times are not much less rigorous than our own crises of war, and we in the West usually meet such crises with governments of national union. So it is in most ex-colonies. Single-party government represents the clear-cut leadership needed when times are insanely complex and confused. Such government need not be Communist. But it is also unlikely to resemble the West's advanced political democracy. Nor is it simply a matter of crisis. A certain sophistication is also involved. If a leader has spent his life to achieve self-government from the foreigner, he cannot find it easy to give government up five years after independence because some newer leader has appeared on the scene.

Some of our economic patterns are difficult, too. Many Western governments put great emphasis on private investment as a chief instrument of economic development. But this runs into two opposite difficulties. Private capital on the scale needed to achieve "take-off" would need to be so great that it would arouse nationalist or Leninist suspicions locally — especially if Western companies pushed their customary policy of seeking local participation not very vigorously or not at all.

The opposite difficulty is that, in fact, so much private capital is not usually forthcoming in any case and to rely on it alone would delay development indefinitely.

Of course, this difficulty has in fact been met by the great extension of Western public assistance programs in the last decade — to which the United States has made by far the largest contribution. But two things are clear about public aid. The rest of the free world has made no contribution commensurate with America's or with their own post-Marshall wealth. Certainly few have given anything like the 1 percent of national income — which cannot surely be considered an excessive contribution to world development. The second point is that the aid programs have not been part of a general development strategy designed to bring the poor nations to "take-off" in the shortest time. Capital has been voted year by year in a haphazard way. Trade policies have even pulled in the other direction. There are thus new challenges to face, a new strategy to be worked out, new decisions to be taken.

Of one thing I am certain: if we continue with what is surely our greatest Western temptation, and think that in some way history owes us a solution, that we can, by pursuing our own most parochial self-interest, achieve in some miraculous way a consummation of world order, then we are heading not simply toward great disappointments, but toward disaster and tragedy as well. There has to be a new start, new places, a new approach. Otherwise we prepare for our defeat simply by default.

VI

NOT BY BREAD ALONE

All the great revolutions of our contemporary world had their origin round the North Atlantic. The revolution by which equality has become a driving force in political life, the new concern with material things, the absorption in scientific analysis, the spurt of growth in the world's population, the whole transformation of our economic system by the application of technology and capital: all these vast changes were launched in the North Atlantic arena. Yet if you look at these Atlantic nations today they make the strange impression of not being particularly concerned with the revolutions they have wrought. The changes have been unleashed on mankind. Blindly, blunderingly, with immense impact and immense confusion, they are remaking the face of the earth. But can one say that the Western powers follow their course with any intimate concern? Do they see them as direct projections of the Western way of life or accept responsibility for the fact that it was the Western colonial system that chiefly set in motion the present world-wide movement of revolutionary change?

I wonder why this is. After all, is it not strange to care so little for what we have launched; to lose interest in our inventions just when they are beginning to have their maximum impact? And if one asks why this is so, I suppose some of the answers are not entirely comfortable. It seems to be a law of life that when you become rich you tend to become complacent. What is the Biblical phrase? "They sat down to eat and they rose up to play." Since the post-war economic revival in the West, the feeling has become fairly general that things are not going too badly. Elections have been fought on the slogan: "You never had it so good"; great nations have been lulled with the promise of "peace and prosperity." The once militant working class substitutes "I'm all right, Jack" for "Workers of the world, unite." This mood of ease and complacency unsuitably limits our ability to understand the needs and hungers of the millions who have not yet found their way into the modern world. To be rich and to be complacent invites the nemesis of such a condition — which is by indifference and by a narrowing of the heart to lose contact with the urgent desires of the great mass of one's fellow men. This constriction of pity can happen to individual men and women. History has always shown it. Today perhaps we see a new phenomenon: rich communities succumbing to the same limitation of human understanding.

But there is another more subtle reason that helps to explain why we are not as interested as we might be in all the revolutions we have launched. We simply cannot, out of our own experience, measure their truly daunting difficulties. All of them happened in the Western world under the conditions of maximum convenience. The West was relatively under-populated; it was immensely well endowed with the resources that are needed for the new kind of economy. Iron ore and coal were plentiful for the launching of industry. The great plains of North America and Southern Russia quickly began to pour out food for the new industrial millions.

But perhaps the chief reason for our over-confidence is to be found in the mechanism by which, in the main, the Western break-through to sustained growth was accomplished. In the critical early stages of change, the profit motive proved to be an immensely powerful engine of growth. Its success implanted deeply in the minds of many of us the idea that the greatest good of the greatest number can be achieved provided each individual or company or even nation vigorously pursues its own self-interest. The strength of the case lies in the fact that, up to a point and under certain conditions, the premise may well be right. Competition in a free market has produced enormous gains in wealth and efficiency. In fact, we are living today through another such burst of growth as the tariff barriers go down inside the Common Market. But equally the conditions in Western Europe between the wars showed that if each nation pursued its own self-interest by a wrong route — in this case by constantly increasing its protective tariffs — the end result was not the good of all but the ruin of each. Nor has the Common Market come about by the unguided pressure of local interests. On the contrary, it has been an act of high statesmanship, pursued by dedicated political leaders and purposefully formulated by planners associated with M. Jean Monnet — surely one of the most quietly and effectively revolutionary groups the world has ever known.

In other words, there are conditions in which the unchecked pursuit of self-interest is an excellent guide to socially desirable action. There are also conditions when it is not. But the West still has a certain bias toward believing in its general efficacy, without regard to the framework within which it is to act. We tend to have a Micawberish attitude toward life, a feeling that so long as we do not get too excited something is certain to turn up. Yet if we look back over history I do not think the experience of other generations teaches us precisely this lesson. On the contrary, it suggests that not the Micawbers, but those who will, and want, and work, are more likely to see their plans and visions realized. It is, therefore a disturbing reflection that in our own day the amount of effort, interest, preparation, and sheer slogging hard work which the Communists tend to put into the task of building *their* version of world order very greatly exceeds what we are ready to do or the sacrifices we are prepared to make. Even more obviously, their vision of a world brotherhood made one by Communism, outstrips the scale of our imagination. The West thinks only marginally in terms of the whole world, the whole family of man. Each group tends to concentrate on its own parochial interests. There is apparently no energy comparable to the world-wide ambitions that set the Communists to work from one end of our planet to the other.

If we are to face the vast gap between the rich nations and the poor, between the nations round the Atlantic area which have been through their modernizing revolutions and the searching nations all around the world who seek desperately to make the same transition, perhaps the first decision we have to make is to abandon the fallacy that, somewhere, somehow, everything is going to turn out all right. We have to be ready to be as foresighted, as determined, as ready to work and to go on working, as are our busy Communist comrades. We must be prepared to match them, policy for policy, vision for vision, ideal for ideal.

I must confess that I can see no inherent reason why such a rededication of ourselves to great tasks should be impossible. We have the resources available; we have more resources at our disposal than any group of nations in the history of man. And it is hard to believe that we have run out of the moral energy needed to make the change. Looking at our society I certainly do not feel that it already presents such an image of the good life that we can afford to say that we have contributed all that we can to the vision of a transfigured humanity. Our uncontrollably sprawling cities, our shapeless suburbia, our trivial pursuits — quiz shows, TV, the golf games — hardly add up to the final end of man. We can do better than this. We also have the means to do better. If we do not feel the need there is only one explanation. We no longer have the vital imagination for the task.

Let us suppose, however, that we slough off our innate complacency. What ought we to try to do? What should be our aim in the challenging testing-period that lies ahead when the aspirations of the poor nations are going to become more and more urgent? For let us have no doubt about this. So far we have been living through the more comfortable phase of transformation in the under-developed areas; we have seen them during a time when their concentrated effort to get rid of colonialism gave them political unity and a sense of national purpose which they may well lack now that independence is achieved. Now that they are running their own affairs, all the grim problems of life face them in the raw: their bounding birth-rates, their lack of capital, their desperate poverty, and, above all, the rising expectations of their own people. Every leader who has led his nation to the overthrow of Western influence or colonial rule is now faced with the stark problem: "What next?" Whether he is a Nasser in Egypt, a Kasim in Iraq, an Azikiwe in Nigeria, a Nkrumah in Ghana, or even — in a more hopeful setting — a Nehru in India, he still must answer the question. There are no evasions now, no blaming it on the West — though that temptation continues — no looking for outside scapegoats. So, by a paradox, the post-colonial period is more tense, dangerous and uncertain than the colonial struggle itself.

What can we do? What sort of policies can help the develop-ing nations in the crucial years that lie ahead? And if I give you something of a shorthand answer, it is because we have already discussed a number of the crucial changes that must be made. Let us be clear first of all over the general aim. During the next twenty to thirty years we hope to see a majority of the developing nations pass through the sound-barrier of sustained growth. Moreover, we want these societies to have political elbow-room with a measure of autonomy for different groups and political power organized on a plural basis. We do not specify institutions or ideologies; but we hope for open societies in an open world. How shall we set about it?

The first point to make is that some general strategy is needed. And strategy is inseparable from a sustained effort through time. The rhythm of growth is not the rhythm of annual budgeting appropriations. Unless the Western nations bring themselves to accept the need for five- and ten-year programs, they will even waste what they do spend, for it will not be geared into a genuine strategy of growth.

The next point is that the scale of aid must be adequate. Patchy development, a little here, a little there, does not lead to sustained growth. In every developing economy, there comes a time when, for perhaps two decades, a "big push" is needed to get the economy off the launching-pad and into orbit.

Not all nations come to that point at the same time. There seems to be a certain pattern of progress and expansion, and different economies are ranged at different points along the line. First there is a phase that one might call the "pre-investment" phase. Nearly everything needed for a "big push" in investment is still lacking. Educated people are not available, training is minimal, capital overheads or infra-structure — power, transport, harbours, housing — have still to be built. At this stage, the country must be prepared for a later plunge into investment and help with education and training, investment in infra-structure, surveys of resources, and some preliminary planning, are the great needs.

But at the next stage — where such countries as India or Brazil or Mexico now stand — the big investments begin to pay off. The ground is laid, rapid growth can be secured. It is at this point that large-scale capital aid from abroad can offset local poverty and lack of capital, thereby sparing governments the cruel choice of using totalitarian methods to compel people to save. Of all the countries at this stage of growth, I would say that India is the most important. The framework of a functioning economy is already built. But its ambitious capital plans are gravely endangered by a critical shortage of foreign exchange. In any Western development-strategy for the next decade, I myself would hope to see something like a billion dollars a year reserved for India's foreign exchange bill. If India can achieve its break-through, it is not only a question of India's preparedness. Nearly half the people living in the under-developed areas will be on their way to the modern world. If one adds Pakistan, more than half the problem of under-development could be met there in the Indian sub-continent.

Given that we accept the philosophy of a "big push" in aid and investment, once the pre-conditions of growth have been realized, where should the capital be directed? It is quite impossible to define a general strategy since each country varies so much in its capacities, in its endowment of resources, in the scale of its internal market, and its export prospects. But perhaps one or two general points are worth making here. The first is that investment in education must continue to receive strong emphasis. Recent studies suggest that between 60 and 50 percent of the gains in productivity made in the West in the last half-century spring from better trained minds, from more research, and more systematic use of the economy's brain-power. At present, most of the developing economies are only in the very first stages of the needed advance in education. Africa is strewn with societies where not more than 10 percent of the people are literate, where perhaps only 1 percent ever reach secondary levels of schooling. The final tragic consequence of these standards can be seen in the Congo which became independent with perhaps not more than a dozen people with university degrees. No modern economy can be built on this basis.

A second critical area is that of farming. Modernized agriculture is, as we have seen, indispensable to the creation of general momentum in the economy. There are two separate needs: to encourage the structural changes which modern agriculture demands — the land reforms, the consolidation of holdings, the building of an influential co-operative movement; and to ensure a sufficient flow of capital into farming. The great variety of modern techniques; new fertilizers, new seed, new methods in planting and tilling, are nearly all costly. So is the scale of credit needed to launch a successful co-operative system. So last of all are the agricultural extension systems without which the farmer cannot learn what new opportunities are open to him. In the past, agriculture has been all too often the last on the government's priority list. Modern experience suggests it should be moved to the top.

The third area of expansion — industry — shows such universal variety that most generalizations have little value. However, one or two comments have some validity. One can say that industrialization will proceed more rapidly if a mistaken sense of national prestige does not precipitate large and costly mistakes in planning, such as investing in an integrated steel-works where there is neither iron ore nor coking-coal. Programs will lead to a better use of resources if capital is recognized for what it is in all developing economies: extremely scarce. Its price should be high, even if this idea upsets the more usual concept that basic services should be kept cheap in order to stimulate growth.

Another aspect of the same problem is that since foreign exchange is the scarcest of all forms of capital, it may be necessary, by high import duties or by auctioning import licences, or by other measures, to ensure that the entrepreneur who gets his hands on foreign exchange pays for its full value. This approach may contradict another tendency — to overvalue a developing nation's currency so that its exports will buy a maximum amount of foreign supplies. But, then, the way to development is, as Professor Higgens once remarked, "paved with vicious circles."

A developing government should aim its policies at ensuring the quickest rate of capital accumulation. Profits should be strongly encouraged, in public as in private enterprise, and tax systems arranged so that all the incentives are toward their re-investment. This again does not always arouse much enthusiasm among planners brought up to believe in the inherent immorality of profits and ready to run essential public services on a "no profit, no loss" basis. But profits are one of the chief means by which resources can be put at the disposal of the investors in society and, as we have seen, are a major source of investment in Soviet Russia.

When it comes to the actual content of industrial policy, it must fit local conditions. Most countries can begin to produce locally some of the goods they import, provided protection is given. The "beer, boots, and bricks" stage of consumer industry only awaits a determined government and some local entrepreneurial talent. But large-scale industry depends upon the availability of crucial raw materials. And it depends, too, upon the scale of the internal market. Five large steel-plants in India, where over four hundred million people make up the market and where iron ore and coking-coal are available, make perfect sense. East Europe's prolif-eration of steel-mills after 1948 did not. Clearly, developing governments would be well advised to look round and see whether by customs unions or common markets with their neighbours they may not increase the size and efficiency of their industrial units without risk of over-production.

To all these changes — in education, in farming, in industry —

there are more than economic consequences. Investment in men, investment in new techniques, investment in new forms of activity, all widen and strengthen the managerial and professional class and increase the training and scope of the manual worker. That gradual extension of the middle class to cover more and more of the nation's citizens is set in motion. With it goes a brighter hope of rational politics and civil rights.

These, then, are some of the elements in a broad strategy of modernization. But I think we have to realize that we in the Western world are not now organized to accomplish anything of the kind. It may be true that for nearly a hundred years we have been a kind of interconnected economy, taking some 70 percent of each other's foreign investment, engrossing nearly 70 percent of world trade, and affecting each other radically by the shifts and changes in our economic policy. But here Mr. Micawber has reigned; here, above all, we have assumed that if everybody pursues his own national interest to the limit the outcome will somehow be to the advantage of everybody else. But this is very far from being generally true. Everyone's decision in 1929 — as the recession deepened — to cut imports and push exports reduced world trade by three-quarters in nine months. The recession itself had been in some measure sparked by the fact that between 1925 and 1929 Britain did not dare reflate its economy for fear of losing its foreign reserves and America dared not deflate its wild boom for fear of attracting even more of the world's gold. Now if we think that this unreconciled opposite pull between domestic and foreign interest is a thing of the past, let us remember that all through 1960 we saw comparable pressures between the German mark and the dollar. In short, we have not yet worked out the policies and institutions needed to overcome the conflicting interests in our interdependent Atlantic world. In fact, only once did we have such a policy: during the Marshall Plan when for a time, owing to

America's generosity and leadership, the nations of the Atlantic area walked in step toward common goals.

Today, I believe we have to revive the Marshall spirit if we are to have any hope of dealing — and dealing in time — with the problem of our obligations to the under-developed areas. Once again, I can suggest only in shorthand terms some of the policies we should undertake if we were a genuine community of rich nations dedicated to the task of creating the prosperity and the well-being of the developing world. And perhaps I should add, in parenthesis, that in doing so we should expand our own well-being as well. To me, one of the most vivid proofs that there is a moral governance in the universe is the fact that when men or governments work intelligently and far-sightedly for the good of others, they achieve their own prosperity too. Take our Western experience with the welfare state. We did not plan to do it as a good stroke of business. It was a moral decision going back to John Lilburne: it gave "the poorest he a life to live with the richest he." Yet one of the consequences has been to reduce business risks. Mass consumption, secured by social security, enables the economy to avoid the booms and collapses of the old economy.

I believe we should see the same outcome if in world economy we could determine to build up the purchasing power of the poorer nations. We should find that, once again, our own prosperity had been helped by the underpinning of world consumption and by the creation of a world economy free from the ups and downs, the uncertainties and incoherences, of the system as we know it today.

"Honesty is the best policy" used to be said in Victorian times. I would go further. I would say that generosity is the best policy and that expansion of opportunity sought for the sake of others ends by bringing well-being and expansion to oneself. The dice are not hopelessly loaded against us. Our morals and our interests

— seen in true perspective — do not pull apart. Only the narrowness of our own interests, whether personal or national, blinds us to this moral truth.

What then should we do? Our first step must be a commitment. All the wealthy nations must accept a common obligation to provide capital and technical assistance to the under-developed areas. Britain, Canada, Australia, Western Europe: we must all begin to do our share. Let us be quite clear about one thing. The reason why there is trouble over the American balance of payments is nothing to do with the inherent strength of the American economy, which is vast. It is nothing to do with the American trade balance, which is favourable. It has something to do, admittedly, with the American export of capital. But, above all, it is created by the fact that America is carrying far more than its fair burden both of the defence of the free world and of aid to the developing nations. And before we can hope to have a functioning Atlantic economy the other member nations must play their part. A suggested 1 percent of national income is a fair criterion; and, incidentally, I consider that Germany, so generously rebuilt after the war and so generously forgiven the enormous destruction which Hitler created, might be in the forefront of those who accept this obligation.

This commitment is, however, only the beginning of the matter. Such a common purpose needs the proper institutional form. I believe we should attempt to build up in our Atlantic world some of the institutions which make it possible for us to co-operate *within* the national community. I think we should have an Atlantic Reserve Bank. I think we should develop common strategies for development and investment both inside and outside the Atlantic arena. I think we should take a long, hard look, at our trade policies, particularly the prices we pay for primary products. At present they do not, as they once did, pull up the rest of the world behind us. On the contrary, they tend to widen the gap. And for all this I think we need to expand our present Atlantic Organization for Economic Development into as many institutions — banks, development funds, trade groups, common markets, statistical services, and, above all, common policy-making organs — which might be needed to knit our interdependent economy into an integrated whole.

If we did this, I think we should do more than simply provide ourselves with the means to work out a strategy for the developing world; we should be creating the economic pre-conditions of a functioning world order. After all, we know that inside our domestic society we cannot survive in peace without law and welfare. It is upon these two pivots that the health of a community depends. Is our narrow interdependent world so different? Should we not be trying to create in the world at large the basic pre-conditions of a peaceful society?

We recognize the principles more or less inside our own domestic community. We do not have private wars. The rich do indeed contribute to the advancement of the poor. And while I am not concerned here with the whole great issue of world law and of disarmament, I am deeply concerned with the second aspect of good order: the ability of the rich to recognize their obligations and to see that in an interdependent world — and Heaven knows our interdependence cannot be denied when we all stand under the shadow of atomic destruction — the principles of the general welfare cannot stop at the limits of our frontiers. It has to go forward; it has to include the whole family of man.

And having said so much, I begin to wonder whether there are any forces inside our comfortable, cosy, complacent Western world that will make us accept this challenge and see that we now face thirty to forty years of world-building on a scale never known in human history, since all our forefathers lived without the

community of science, the speed of transport, the whole intercon-
nectedness of the modern globe. What will spur us to face this
kind of decision? Facts? The facts are there. We cannot wish away
the great revolution of modernization that is sweeping round the
world; we cannot say it would be easier or more pleasant if it had
not happened. Perhaps so; but we started the revolution and we
can hardly ignore the forces that we unleashed upon the world.

Should we be guided by fear? Fear can indeed be the beginning
of wisdom. Those who can live comfortably and without perturba-
tion under the hideous threat of atomic destruction do not seem to
me to be very wise. But blind fear is not a constructive force. Fear
will serve us only if it drives us on to find a way out of our fears.
And there is only one: to leave behind our present community of
potential annihilation and build a community of moral purpose in
its place. In such a world public law would take the place of private
violence and the general welfare would be accepted over and above
the particular interests of particular communities above all,
mankind would discover, beneath the clash of ideology, some minimum standards of trust rooted in the fact that we are all men, that
we all stand under the judgement of history, and that we all love
and seek to live and know that we must die.

It is just because the task before us is the positive task of building a peaceful home for the human family that I doubt whether
realism or fear is enough to set us to work. We need resources of
faith and vision as well. Do we have them? Or have the revolutions
of our day, while increasing our physical powers, damped down
the ardours of our spirit?

I do not believe it. Every one of the revolutions we have
discussed goes beyond our material concerns and offers a challenge to the quality of our mind and spirit. The equality of men
which is such a driving force all round the world sprang originally
from the Western sense that men, as souls of infinite metaphysical

value, stand equal before the throne of God. And if we feel this equality of man as a profound, moral fact, can we really be content to see men hungry, to see men die, to see men continue in starvation and ill-health when we have the means to help them? Is this our concept of equality? If it is, do we not betray our faith?

Then, again, our concern with worldly things is not mere materialism. It has in it an essential element of religious insight. God looked on his universe and found it good. The materials offered us in farm and factory can be set to work to create a community in which no one need starve or go naked and unhoused. We can "redeem the time" by setting matter to work for the greater good of all our brothers, who are all mankind. The Christian God who bade His followers feed the hungry and heal the sick and took His parables from the homely round of daily work gave material things His benediction. It has not faded because material things are more abundant now.

Science itself — this vision of an orderly world in which matter does not respond to chaotic promptings but to some vast harmony of universal law — is in no way incompatible with a vision of moral order in which it can be the tool of a better life for all mankind. Science has removed us from the heaviest bondage of the past: the fact that material resources were always too scarce to match even the greatest goodwill. Only a hundred years ago, if we had wished to give covering, food, shelter, and a simple education to the mass of mankind, we could not have done so because our material means were not equal to the task. What science has done has been to set us free. It has delivered us from the bondage of our material poverty and opened a great area of choice where vision and will can operate because they have the physical means at hand.

Science, understood in this sense, is indeed a means of liberty. Perhaps you have wondered why I have not mentioned freedom as the greatest revolution of our time. Quite frankly, the reason is that I am not sure whether it *is* one of the spreading revolutions of this century. There are times when I feel that, in our Western world, freedom rather resembles the Biblical talent that was put in a napkin and buried in the ground. We have it — but do we use it? On the issue of freedom, the revolutions of our day are all ambiguous. The revolution of equality does not necessarily imply freedom. All prisoners in a jail are equal. But they are not free. The revolution of science offers the means of freedom. But it can be used as well for making dictatorship more efficient and war more dire. And materialism, misunderstood as a false over-concern with the things of this world, a false worship of "the idols of the market and the idols of the tribe," can create the reverse of true freedom when men and women become more and more entangled in their own clamant and unassuagable wants. Our revolutions will not do our work for us. They can yield us freedom or its opposite. The outcome depends on us, and I sometimes wonder whether we have made any very fundamental attempt to interpret the revolutions of our time in the light of freedom. Have we measured the margin of choice given us by our new capital resources, our new technology, our new ability to create the means of wealth? Have we understood that this liberty of action must be used? It cannot, it must not be left to rust with us. And given our ability to assist in the process of modernization, have we really grasped its relevance to the grand question of our time: whether the developing world society will be closed or open, slave or free?

After all, constitutional liberty is a sophisticated concept. Between Magna Charta and our present-day democracy there lie eight hundred years of experience and feeling our way. I am not a determinist. I do not believe that economic forces necessarily create political forms. On the contrary, I believe freedom to have been one of the innate formative ideas of our Western way of life. But equally I observe that its incorporation in concrete institutions did presuppose some economic and social changes. The emergence of a strong middle class after the Middle Ages helped to secure rights and liberties to a larger and larger group of articulate and responsible citizens. In the nineteenth century, the growth of wealth and the spread of literacy encouraged the extension of democratic privileges even further, and complete adult suffrage and complete adult literacy arrived at about the same time.

I think it is probably a safe assumption that something of the same pattern must be expected in emergent societies; though they need not wait so long since models of change already exist. A strong expanding professional and managerial class, a strong thrust of literacy, and the expanding resources both presuppose are almost certainly pre-conditions of political development in freedom. We are, I think, irrational when we suddenly expect those who emerge from primitive societies to seize our concepts of liberty intact, forgetting the long intervening history of our own experiments. If we are not to be disappointed, I think we must seek with new energy and commitment to fill in the historical gap. We need to be far more active in the way of economic aid, capital investment, and educational assistance. We need to work with far more purpose to create the framework of general literacy and personal responsibility. We need to be far more imaginative in showing that we regard the right of nations to govern themselves as only the first, essential, but preliminary, step in creating the conditions in which nations can be truly free. But the next step is equally vital: to give concrete substance to the experience of national liberty and not permit it to become a time of lessening opportunity and hope.

But I have the impression that when we talk so confidently of liberty, we are unaware of the awful servitudes that are created by the ancient enemies of mankind: the servitude of poverty when

means are so small that there is literally no choice at all; the servitude of ignorance when there are no perspectives to which the
mind can open because there is no education on which the mind
can begin to work; the servitude of ill-health which means that the
expectation of life is almost too short to allow for any experiences
of freedom, and the years that *are* lived are dragged out without
the health and strength which are themselves a liberation.

Because we have interpreted freedom in too narrow a sense
and assumed that people will find the outer form of freedom
natural when none of its actual substantial content has been realized, there has been something empty about our advocacy of the
free way of life. What is the free way of life to a tribal society
which does not know whether it can eat next week? What is the
free way of life to an ancient society where illiteracy bars most
people from any of the benefits of freedom? What, above all, can
freedom be said to mean when the nations who talk of it most
incessantly seem to have so little awareness of its wider moral
dimensions? Am I free if my brother is bound by hopeless poverty
and ignorance? Am I a prophet of the free way of life if I reveal
perfect indifference to the plight of the man who has fallen
among thieves, the man whom the good Samaritan helped while
the others passed him by?

If we want to spread the revolution of liberty round the world
to complete and reconcile the other great revolutions of our day,
we have to re-examine its moral content and ask ourselves whether
we are not leaving liberty as a wasted talent and allowing other
forces, not friendly to liberty, to monopolize the great vision of
men working in brotherhood to create a world in which all can
live. But God is not mocked. We reap what we sow and if freedom
for us is no more than the right to pursue our own self-interest —
personal or national — then we can make no claim to the greatest
vision of our society: "the glorious liberty of the Sons of God."

Without vision we, like other peoples, will perish. But, if it is restored, it can be as it always has been the profoundest inspiration of our society, and can give our way of life its continuing strength.

THE IMAGE OF CONFEDERATION

by
FRANK H. UNDERHILL

I

THE NEW NATIONALITY

| *The Climate of Opinion in 1867* |

"I congratulate you on the legislative sanction which has been given by the Imperial Parliament to the Act of Union, under the provisions of which we are now assembled, and which has laid the foundation of a new nationality."

These words that I have just quoted are from the Speech from the Throne delivered by Lord Monck, the Governor General, at the opening of the first session of the first Parliament of the new Dominion of Canada in November, 1867. This phrase, "a new nationality", which was to be much quoted at the time, was put into the Governor General's mouth by his official advisers, a cabinet that consisted of both French-Canadian and English-Canadian public men and that included many of the Fathers who had been the architects of Confederation at the Charlottetown and Quebec conferences of 1864. The experiment of the new nationality that they thus proclaimed was of a nationality that should link together a variety of rather isolated, little colonial communities scattered across the northern half of the continent, and that, in particular, should include and transcend the two groups of English-speaking and French-speaking Canadians, divided though they were in race, language, and religion. That is, it was a complex nationality; and they were well aware of their own boldness in the initiation of this experiment.

A nation is a body of men who have done great things together in the past and who hope to do great things together in the future. What makes them into a nation is not necessarily community of race, language, and religion, though these are powerful forces when they are present; it is their common history and traditions, their experience of living together, their having done great things together in the past, and their determination to continue doing great things together in the future.

Our experiment of the new Canadian nationality has now been going on for almost a hundred years. It must be confessed that we approach the centenary year of 1967 in a state of mind that falls far short of the spirit of optimism and high adventure that marked the Fathers of Confederation. We seem to have lost their clear assurance of national purpose. We are not sure even that we are one nation. Our Canadian politics in the 1960s is leading many citizens to doubt whether it is worth trying to be a nation if this is the only kind of politics of which we are capable. One senses a feeling of defeatism in the air.

This is a good occasion, therefore, to review what Canadians, from time to time since 1867, have thought about their nationhood, its purpose and significance. Since my time in these lectures is limited, I propose to pick out certain periods and issues in our history from the 1860s on, and to pause over them, in order to indulge in some reflections about what Canadians at different periods have thought they were doing or ought to be doing. That is, I shall devote my attention not so much to the events in our history as to what Canadians were saying and writing about them. So I have given my series of lectures the title of *The Image of Confederation*.[1]

I propose to devote this first lecture to some general considerations about the intellectual climate in which Confederation came about.

Nationality was, of course, one of the great inspiring conceptions of the nineteenth century. But we must remember that the peoples of the different British-American colonies had hardly any experience of living and working together before they united in the Confederation of 1867. The lines of communication of each colony ran toward the centre of the Empire in London, not toward the other colonies. Contrast this with the experience that the thirteen American states had behind them when they changed their loose confederation of the 1780s into a close federation. The British colonists had not done great things together in the past. The Americans had fought a war of independence together.

Strikingly absent, also, in British America, were such figures as Hamilton, Jefferson, Madison, Franklin, Jay, Adams, and others like them, who combined a genius for hard practical politics with a capacity for philosophy and a habit of looking for the wider and deeper general implications of particular problems. This lack of the philosophic mind to give guidance to the thinking of ordinary citizens has been a weakness of our Canadian national experience throughout our history.

Lacking also in the new constitution was the element that is represented by the words with which the American Constitution begins: "We, the People". The British North America Act was, in form, the work of the British Imperial Parliament, and, in fact, the work of a small élite group of colonial politicians who were in advance of their people. In the days when education on national union would have been creative, *before* 1864, they had done little to educate their people up to wider conceptions of their future. After 1864, the Quebec Resolutions were not submitted to the voters for ratification by general election or referendum. And this lack of an effective popular basis for the new system of politics has remained a flaw in the foundations of our national structure ever since.

In New Brunswick, of course, there was an election in which the voters rejected the Quebec scheme; and it took much devious manoeuvring to get that negative decision reversed. In Canada, the government professed that sentiment was so generally favourable that no appeal to the people was needed; and this anti-democratic stand was taken most strongly by the most vocal democratic party, the Upper Canada Grits. It was true, no doubt, that, on the British model, Parliament did not need a mandate for everything that it did; but in the coming democratic century, popular mandates were to become the necessary basis of policy. In Nova Scotia, the people showed their real sentiments as soon as they got a chance; they voted strongly against the union in the election of 1867, *after* the union had been imposed on them. As late as the 1930s, when the Nova Scotia Royal Commission on the fiscal disabilities of the province under Confederation was holding its sittings, one of the briefs presented to it was entitled "The Rape of Nova Scotia."

Was all this sudden haste for British-American union in 1864–1867 necessary? Well, one of the myths of our Canadian history, which historians have been reluctant to probe, is that it was necessary in order to forestall the Americans who threatened to gobble us up if we did not act quickly. Somewhere on Parliament Hill in Ottawa, during our centenary celebrations in 1967, there should be erected a monument to this American ogre who has so often performed the function of saving us from drift and indecision.

The section of British America that had everything to gain and nothing to lose by union was Upper Canada. The Grits, in their convention called in June, 1867, to prepare for the coming federal and provincial elections, gave an incisive exposition of how they saw things:

> Resolved, that this Convention records its high gratification that the long and earnest contest of the Reform party for the great principles of Representation by Population, and local control over local affairs, has at last been crowned with triumphant success; and claims from the people of Upper Canada the meed of gratitude due from a just and generous people to those who, by years of self-sacrificing labour, have peaceably achieved great and valuable constitutional changes — the accomplishment of which in other countries has rarely been attained except through the sad scenes of armed revolution.

So ran the first resolution of the convention.

The Grits had been campaigning for "Rep by Pop" for a dozen years before 1864, and in the new constitution they rightly considered themselves victorious. In the new federal Parliament, Ontario, because of its population, would have the largest delegation, and could look forward to a dominant influence in the making of national policy. It had been a favourite occupation of the Toronto *Globe* before 1867 to indulge in elaborate statistical reports about the growth of Upper-Canadian population and wealth as compared with what was taking place in the other colonies, and to argue that its constituents could count on the day when Ontario, shortly after the census of 1871, would have a majority of the whole population of Canada. It was thoughts of this kind that overcame doubts about the division of powers between federal and provincial governments. What did this matter when the federal authority would be under the firm leadership of Ontario?

In addition, federation would at last guarantee to the people of Ontario the control of their own local affairs. They would no longer see measures imposed upon their part of the community by a Lower-Canada, French-Catholic majority, as had just happened in 1863 in the critical matter of separate schools. In 1859, at the Grit convention of that year, a more radical group in the party had wanted to break up the union with Lower Canada altogether, on the ground that French domination had become intolerable. George Brown had saved the day by appealing to the national sentiment of his followers. Now, in 1864, they were in a more contented mood. They could not only look forward to dominating the federal scene; but for local affairs at home in Upper Canada — if they had deigned to speak French — they could now also tell the French Canadians that they were going to be "*maîtres chez nous.*"

Almost as important as "Rep by Pop" and local control of local affairs, as an argument for Confederation to the Upper-Canadian mind, was the fact that Confederation included westward expansion. The nationalism to which George Brown appealed in 1859 meant continental expansion to match the expansion of the United States. *The Globe* never tired of preaching that there was no future for British America if she remained cooped up in the north-east corner of the continent. Expansion meant not only the preservation of British power in the western hemisphere; it meant also new farms on the western prairie for the sons of "the intelligent yeomanry of Upper Canada," and new markets for Ontario industrialists. Out on the prairie there would be established a second Upper Canada, with its happy, liberal, progressive political and social institutions. Wherever he looked the Upper-Canadian patriot saw in Confederation an alluring prospect of wider opportunities for the abounding energies and ambitions of the dynamic, forward-looking, English-speaking, Protestant people of Ontario.

The Maritime colonies could have no such rosy picture of their future in the new union. Inevitably, they would be a small minority subject to being outvoted by the greater numbers of central Canada. True, they would get the Intercolonial Railway; and railway promoters held out prospects to them of expanded markets at the western end of the Intercolonial. But most of the money to be spent on railways and canals by the new federation would be for the primary benefit of Ontario and Quebec. Tariffs as well as railways would be constructed mostly in the interests of the St. Lawrence and Great Lakes economy. For this was a continental nation that was being established, whereas the Maritimers looked out across the ocean toward old England and New England. And, unfortunately for their future attitude toward the new continental nationality, Confederation came at a transition period for them, just when the great era based on wind, wood, and water, was coming to an end. As Stephen Leacock was later to put it, "the shades of night were falling, and the night was called Confederation." The Canadian delegates to the Charlottetown Conference showed a real virtuosity in sweeping the Maritimers off their feet with enthusiasm for their gospel of a continental federal nation. Alas, Canadian statesmanship since then, when confronted by Maritime grievances, has shown little of the same virtuosity.

Lower Canada also had reasons for being sceptical about the larger union. The French-Canadians were in a very satisfactory position in the existing province of Canada. They could look back over the past century since the 1760s on a remarkable record of achievement. A small conquered people, they had won self-government, giving a lead in the colonial struggle for "Responsible

Government" to the English-Canadians of Upper Canada. They had defeated the Durham policy of assimilation into an English-speaking community. When the Union of 1840 was set up, English had been made the official language; but before the 1850s they had got their own language recognized as equally official. And they had succeeded in something even more remarkable. Upper and Lower Canada had been given equal representation in the legislature of the Union, though Lower Canada had the larger population. It was hoped by the British authorities that the English minority in Lower Canada would unite with the Upper-Canadians in imposing an English régime on the colony as a whole. But by 1851, when the census showed that Upper Canada had now a majority of the population, and when that majority was bound to increase with immigration, the French had established the position that government was carried on by a cabinet with a solid French-Canadian bloc in it, co-operating in a bi-racial party; first with Reformers and then with Conservatives in Upper Canada. As long as the French bloc remained fairly solid, government could not be carried on without their consent. By the 1860s, it was the English-Canadians of Upper Canada who were complaining of French-Canadian domination. It was the French-Canadians who always sat to the right of Mr. Speaker in the Assembly and who controlled the administration.

If the Upper-Canadian Grit demand for Representation by Population were conceded, this happy position would disappear. To the French-Canadians "Rep by Pop" meant a majoritarian, English-Protestant government that would threaten the security of their own peculiar institutions. Under Cartier's skilled and tough leadership they maintained that interests should be represented in the legislature rather than mere numbers — which was a good British doctrine at the time, whereas "Rep by Pop" was American. On one famous occasion, Cartier had told the Grits that the codfish of the Gulf of St. Lawrence must be represented as well as the farmers of Canada West. And Cartier had the support of the English business interests centring in Montreal, as well as of his fellow Frenchmen, against the restless agrarian Grit radicals of the Great Lakes peninsula west of Toronto.

The French were sitting pretty.

Listen to George Brown, speaking in the Canadian legislature in 1865 during the great debate on Confederation:

> One hundred years have passed since these provinces became by conquest part of the British Empire. Here sit today the descendants of the victors and the vanquished in the fight of 1759, with all the differences of language, religion, civil law and social habit nearly as distinctly marked as they were a century ago. Here we sit today seeking amicably to find a remedy for constitutional evils and injustice complained of — by the vanquished? No sir, but complained of by the conquerors! Here sit the representatives of the British population claiming justice — only justice; and here sit the representatives of the French population discussing in the French tongue whether we shall have it.[2]

These are interesting remarks today in the 1960s when the rhetorical roles of the two races have been reversed and it is the French who are demanding what they call justice.

In the 1860s, justice, to the Grits, meant primarily Representation by Population, i.e. majoritarian democracy. And it was becoming evident to the shrewder French-Canadians that sooner or later they would have to yield to this demand. What had Cartier to offer to his followers by this scheme of Confederation that would constitute some recompense for this concession, and that would promise to safeguard French-Canadian minoritarian interests against the English majority, which would now be larger than ever?

For one thing, French Canada now got her own autonomous province, *l'état de Québec*, with provincial control over the cultural interests she held dear — religion, language, education, civil institutions.

For another, the wider continental state held out great promise for the economic development of Quebec. Listen to Alexander Galt, Cartier's ally from the Montreal business interests, speaking to his constituents in Sherbrooke in the fall of 1864 (reported in the third person):

> The interests of the British population of Lower Canada were identical with those of the French Canadians; these peculiar interests being that the trade and commerce of the Western country should continue to flow through Lower Canada . . . It would be found that the effect of the combination of all the Provinces would be to benefit Lower Canada — not French Lower Canada or British Lower Canada — but the whole of Lower Canada — by giving it the position of being the commercial heart of the country . . . He thought our material interests would have to govern us in this respect . . . When we extended the boundaries of our Empire to the countries bordering on the Saskatchewan and the Rocky Mountains, the whole wealth of that great country must pour down the St. Lawrence and stimulate the industry of the cities of Lower Canada.[3]

To Galt, what was being brought about was a highly profitable business merger. And Cartier was one of the French-Canadians who understood the importance of business considerations. Certainly, their vision in this field has been abundantly realized.

But what of the protection of French cultural interests in this larger federal field? Some of Cartier's clerical allies among the bishops were doubtful; and the Rouge group claimed that the proposed highly centralized federal scheme was only a facade behind which an English majority would eventually achieve what was in effect a legislative union. Cartier's real reply, which he never quite formulated with blunt frankness so that everybody could see what he was driving at, was to tell his fellow Frenchmen that their safety in future depended on their remaining united in a strong communal political bloc, as they had been under his leadership; if they made sure that this bloc was always entrenched in the cabinet at Ottawa, they would have a veto on anything that the national government might propose. Their security and their safeguard, that is, was a political one rather than a constitutional one. Things did not quite work out as he had foreseen in his overconfident optimism.

For the new nationality had hardly got under way when there began a great imperialist struggle between Ontario and Quebec for the control of the prairie West. Quebec won the first round by securing a constitution for the new province of Manitoba that secured the French language and the Quebec system of denominational schools. But the movement of Ontario wheat-farmers rather than of Quebec habitants into the West, and the stream of overseas immigrants into Canada who were assimilated into the English-Canadian way of life rather than into the French-Canadian way, brought about the eventual victory of Ontario. And the great business enterprises of the country developed under English-Canadian and American management, with the French-Canadians taking small part. Hence our present discontents. French-Canadian spokesmen now repeat the language of George Brown about justice for their group, with some of them threatening, like some of Brown's more radical followers in the 1850s, to break up the union altogether.

There is one further point to be noted about what was done in this field of English-French relations in the years 1864–1867. The conferences at Charlottetown and Quebec were not conferences between an English-speaking group and a French-speaking one, resulting in a solemn compact between the two "races" or "nations." This interpretation is a modern Laurentian fantasy, which can only be fitted into the historical facts by a painful straining of evidence. The conferences out of which the British North America Act originated were conferences among delegates from the colonies of Canada, Nova Scotia, New Brunswick, Prince Edward Island, and Newfoundland. The Canadian delegates were the members of the Canadian coalition cabinet of 1864; they spoke for Canada as a whole; they did not divide on racial lines. There were no delegates there who had been chosen by a French-Canadian or an English-Canadian "race" or "nation." If the Canadian delegates at these conferences spoke in any role but that of Canadians, they spoke as Conservatives and Reformers.

Finally, what did the Fathers and their contemporaries think would be the effect of Confederation upon the relations of British America with the United Kingdom and with the United States? There is no doubt about the overwhelming loyalty of all groups to the British connection and the British monarchy. If you want striking evidence of this, read the very racy account of *The Prince of Wales in Canada and the United States* written by N. A. Woods, who accompanied the Prince in 1860 as correspondent of the London *Times* on his tour through British America.[4] Woods got a good deal of amusement from the enthusiastic energy with which rival groups competed for priority in their attentions to the Prince, but he was tremendously impressed by this mass outpouring of loyalty.

In the Confederation Debates of 1865, John A. Macdonald gave classic expression to a conception that was general in British

America: "Gradually a different colonial system is being developed — and it will become, year by year, less a case of dependence on our part, and of over-ruling protection on the part of the Mother Country, and more a case of a healthy and cordial alliance."

The ideas of the Toronto *Globe* were very similar:

> We deny that the introduction of the federal principle is in any sense a step toward independence . . . The day may come when we shall be in a position to offer to Great Britain the friendship of a powerful and independent ally . . . But it is not for this that we are providing . . . Our object is to find a system of government which shall be just and equitable to all who live under it . . . This result can best be secured while we maintain, for at all events a very long time to come, our connection with the grand old British Empire intact and unimpaired.[5]

On the complementary aspect of Confederation — its meaning as an expression of sentiment toward the United States — there is also no doubt; it was fundamentally anti-American, a grand design to protect British America from American encroachments. The threat from the south was threefold: 1, a possible armed invasion at the time of the Civil War; 2, the abrogation of the Reciprocity Treaty of 1854, compelling the British-Americans to expand their own domestic markets; 3, the movement of American immigration northwards down the Red River into the Hudson's Bay territory and along the Pacific coast into British Columbia.

British-American statesmen, furthermore, did not like the American way of life. In strengthening Canadian political independence against the States, they conceived themselves also to be shutting out undesirable American political and social institutions. Every one of the Fathers was opposed to American manhood suffrage. To them democracy and republicanism were interchangeable terms, which meant the American tendency toward the rule of the uneducated mob, corruption in politics, violence and crime in social life. British connection, and in particular the British monarchy, would help to preserve the British colonies from these dangerous infections.

Yet, also, we must note that, already by the 1860s, this Canadian attitude to the American way of life showed a certain ambivalence. English visitors remarked the prevalence of American newspapers and magazines in Upper Canada. Representation by Population, whether accompanied by manhood suffrage or not, was American. Federalism was American; there were no British precedents for it. The absence of an established church and of a hereditary titled aristocracy, the equalitarian society, the existence of a publicly administered educational system from elementary school to university, the political party conventions, the independent farm owner on his family farm, all these were Upper-Canadian phenomena that were North American in spirit and origin. So was tariff protection for infant industries. Lower Canada, no doubt, was more insulated from some of these North-American tendencies. But the British-American people as a whole, in the beliefs by which they directed their lives in 1867, were not nearly so single-minded as they thought they were.

II

THE FIRST FINE CARELESS RAPTURE

| *Canadian Nationalism in the 1870s and 1880s* |

Nationalism was one of the great dreams of the nineteenth century. It has become one of the chief nightmares of the twentieth. To the liberal reformers or revolutionaries of the early nineteenth century, the democratic nation-state was the natural unit into which men gathered themselves to live the good life. "Nations" said a famous German historian, beginning a series of lectures, "are God's thoughts." All through the nineteenth century, it was the habit of English and other liberals to pour out their sympathies for "little peoples rightly struggling to be free." And the century closed triumphantly with the peace settlements of 1919, which broke up the old autocratic, multi-racial empires of Russia, Germany, Austro-Hungary, and Turkey, and set up in their place a bloc of new, independent nation-states across East-Central Europe and Western Asia, each state professedly based on an integral solidarity of race and language. The upheavals of our own day following World War II have extended this process to East Asia and to Africa. Nationalism has been the real religion of the modern age, absorbing, transforming, utilizing for its own purposes, Christianity, Democracy, Capitalism, Socialism, Communism, and Fascism.

In this evolution of nationalism it has been of more significance to us Canadians than we have ever quite understood, that our nation was born just at the transition point when one era was coming to an end and a second era was beginning. The first era was the liberal-romantic era. The nationalist faith that derived from the upheavals of the American and French revolutions regarded the self-governing nation-state as the instrument through which a great spontaneous outburst of creative popular energies would be released, once the old fetters of monarchy, feudalism, established church, and foreign rule were broken; and it looked forward to a world of democratic national communities that would live together in a new harmony and peace. But by the late 1860s, this messianic faith in the natural goodness of mankind when assembled in self-governing nation-states was being succeeded by a tougher, more realistic, more egoistic, more brutal type of nationalism. The second era is the anti-liberal, Bismarckian era.

The emergence of Bismarckian Germany was the sign of a change in the atmosphere of the western world. Bismarck's system was constructed to preserve and strengthen the conservative, anti-democratic forces. Since 1870, nationalism and liberalism have co-existed very uneasily. Nationalism for the last hundred years has meant a Darwinian struggle for existence among rival states, a struggle that may be carried on by economic and/or by military policies. In the powerful states, nationalism expanded into an aggressive imperialism. In the midst of this struggle for existence, the national state came to demand more and more the total, integral loyalty of all its citizens. As we can

now see, nationalism had in it, in its essence, some sinister totalitarian potentialities, which finally reached their full fruition only
in our own tortured generation.

Here in Canada, we began our national life in 1867 as if still
living in the early instead of in the later nineteenth century.
Those who welcomed Confederation did so in romantic, idealistic enthusiasm. Witness D'Arcy McGee, the hero of all Canadian
romantics.

I intend to dwell chiefly in this lecture on the Canada First movement.[1] Amid all the discussion that was stimulated by the great
event of 1867, Canada First best expresses the romantic enthusiasm, the first fine careless rapture of the new nationality. And since
about all that Canada First has left in our present-day memories is
its name, I think the story of its foundation and adventures is
worth telling once again. It was the first youth movement in our
politics, the first attempt of a group of intellectuals as such to
influence the tone and the content of political discussion. Also, it
was a Toronto movement, displaying both the energies and the
limitations of what was then the Queen City of the West.

Let me tell the story of its beginnings as Colonel George T.
Denison told it years afterwards in his book, *The Struggle for Imperial Unity*, of 1909:

> Business took me to Ottawa from the 15th April until the 20th
> May, 1868. Wm. A. Foster of Toronto, a barrister, afterwards a
> leading Queen's Counsel, was there at the same time, and through
> our friend, Henry J. Morgan, we were introduced to Charles Mair
> of Lanark, Ontario, and Robert J. Haliburton, of Halifax, eldest
> son of the celebrated author of "Sam Slick." We were five young
> men of about twenty-eight years of age, except Haliburton, who

was four or five years older. We very soon became warm friends, and spent most of our evenings in Morgan's quarters . . . These meetings were the origin of the "Canada First" party. Nothing could show more clearly the hold that Confederation had taken of the imagination of young Canadians than the fact that, night after night, five young men should give up their time and their thoughts to discussing the higher interests of their country, and it ended in our making a solemn pledge to each other that we would do all we could to advance the interests of our native land; that we would put our country first, before all personal, or political, or party considerations; that we would change our party affiliations as often as the true interest of Canada required it . . . It was apparent that until there should grow, not only a feeling of unity, but also a national pride and devotion to Canada as a Dominion, no real progress could be made toward building up a strong and powerful community . . . History had taught us that every nation that had become great, and had exercised an important influence upon the world, had invariably been noted for a strong patriotic spirit, and we believed in the sentiment of putting the country above all other considerations, the same feeling that existed in Rome, "When none was for a party; when all were for the State." This idea we were to preach in season and out of season.

Denison goes on to tell how Charles Mair, being appointed paymaster to the party of surveyors sent by the Canadian government to the North-West in preparation for the taking over of the Hudson's Bay territories, met another young man out at the Red River, Dr. John Schultz; how they became friends; and how Schultz was taken in as the sixth member of the Canada First group. Then, in 1869–70, came the troubles at the Red River, of which Riel was the hero, or the villain, and the death of Thomas Scott. Mair and Schultz were both put under arrest at one time by

Riel. They both eventually made their way to Toronto, and with their friends helped to stir up a great Ontario agitation over what was happening in the North-West. This was the beginning of the public activities of Canada First.

You can read it all in Denison — how they proceeded to proclaim their interpretation that there was a great conspiracy between the Catholic Church and Sir George Cartier to protect Riel and to make the North-West a French-Catholic preserve. "I went on to say" writes Denison, reporting a speech of his own at a meeting in Toronto, "that they (Mair and Schultz) had escaped and were coming to their own province to tell of their wrongs, to ask assistance to relieve the intolerable condition of their comrades in the Red River Settlement, and I asked 'Is there any Ontario man who will not hold out a hand of welcome to these men? Any man who hesitates is no true Canadian. I repudiate him as a countryman of . . . mine.'" In the excitement over the execution of Scott by Riel, you see, Canada First starts its practical activities as Ontario First. And this anti-French bias remained with it throughout its life in politics.

Who were these six young men? None of them in later years attained first rank in Canadian affairs, and the Canada First movement remained only an incident in their own lives. Of the five who met in Ottawa, four had been at college. The exception was Henry J. Morgan who had entered the civil service of Canada at the age of eleven, but who was to make his name in later years through the very useful series of biographical dictionaries and the *Dominion Annual Register* of which he was the editor.

The leading spirit in the group was W. A. Foster, a young Toronto lawyer with a taste for writing. Everyone who knew him has paid tribute to Foster's fine qualities. Unfortunately he died early from overwork in his profession and never realized the promise of his first years. The late Mr. John S. Ewart of Ottawa once told me a story about Foster. The two of them were young lawyers together in Toronto, each one a junior in a big law firm. They used to commiserate with each other from time to time about how juniors were overworked by their seniors in the legal profession. "Sometimes" said Foster to Ewart "the pile of papers on my desk gets so high that I just throw up my hands and abandon them. I go off down to the waterfront and spend my time watching the harbour and the lake; and when I come back next day or later, the pile has mysteriously disappeared." "That is," said Mr. Ewart, "Foster was a dreamer, rather lacking in hard practical drive." Mr. Ewart was a bit of a dreamer himself, and, happily for all of us, was to live long enough to see his dreams about the Kingdom of Canada come true.

Haliburton was, like Foster, a lawyer with a taste for literary pursuits. Mair has left a name as one of our early minor poets, distinctly, one would say now, more of a nationalist than a poet. Had he lived in our day he would undoubtedly have been an active member of the Canadian Authors' Association. Schultz, while a doctor, was an active and restless politician all his life, and ended as Lieutenant-Governor of Manitoba. Denison was a military man, a cavalryman, who was to become internationally known as the author of a history of cavalry. He was a fiery spirit, born a Tory, breaking with Macdonald over the Riel question, returning to Tory ranks when Commercial Union became a leading issue, tireless in his later years in defence of the British connection against subversives and traitors, i.e. against all who differed in political views from himself, tiresome in his passion for making declamatory speeches. Once, in a group at the National Club, when Goldwin Smith was trying to encourage discussion of the topic of Canadian independence, he announced that there was treason in the air and that he would discuss such a subject only on horseback. He was given to participating on horseback in all his political controversies — as has been the way with most Toronto loyalists, whether they are cavalrymen or not.

The really significant part of Canada First activities came after these excitements over the Red River. The original little group added steadily to their numbers, chiefly from friends in Toronto. In 1872, there was started in Toronto a new monthly magazine, *The Canadian Monthly and National Review*, for the purpose of providing a vehicle through which the new national spirit could express itself in literature, art, and philosophy, as well as in politics. In its second number it acquired a contributor who began to write a series of comments on current affairs under a byline that was to become famous: A Bystander. This was Goldwin Smith,[2] late regius professor of history at Oxford, who had come out to America to teach at the newly founded university of Cornell, and who moved north to Toronto in 1871. In 1874, a weekly appeared, *The Nation*, which lasted for only two years but which still remains the best weekly that has yet been published in Canada. Goldwin Smith was soon writing for it also; and apparently he supported both magazines with money as well. Smith arrived in Canada just when the ferment of the new nationality was at its strongest. He at once became the guide, philosopher and friend of the Canada First men. *The Nation* became practically their organ.

In January 1874, they decided to launch themselves officially as a political movement, and announced the formation of the Canadian National Association with an Address to the Canadian People and a platform of eleven points. Later in this year, in the fall, they formed a club, the National Club, to encourage the discussion of national affairs; and they built themselves a clubhouse, in which Smith gave the inaugural address. The rising young Liberal, the chief intellectual in his party, Edward Blake,[3] had been invited to lay the cornerstone of the new club, but declined after some hesitation. Almost at the same time that Goldwin Smith was making the inaugural speech in the National Club, however, Blake, at a Reform party picnic at Aurora, delivered what became famous as his Aurora Speech. The policies that Blake expounded at Aurora were almost identical with those of the Canadian National Association, and the young Canada Firsters quickly adopted him as their leader — without his consent, though there is some reason to suppose that the Aurora Speech was originally drafted as the inauguration speech for the National Club.

What were the particular policies for which Canada First, Goldwin Smith, and Edward Blake, stood, apart from their general thesis of the need of a truly national spirit in Canada?

Perhaps it would be well here to give the eleven planks in the Canada First platform. "We form a new and distinct political organization for promoting by a joint endeavour the national interest upon a particular principle on which we are agreed" said the Address of the Canadian National Association in January, 1874, in Burkean language. Their platform ran as follows:

1. British connection, consolidation of the Empire — and in the meantime a voice in treaties affecting Canada.
2. Closer trade relations with the British West India islands, with a view to ultimate political connection.
3. Income franchise.
4. The ballot, with the addition of compulsory voting.
5. A scheme for the representation of minorities.
6. Encouragement of immigration, and free homesteads in the public domain.
7. The imposition of duties for revenue, so adjusted as to afford every possible encouragement to native industry.
8. An improved militia system, under command of trained Dominion officers.

9. No property qualifications in members of the House of Commons.
10. The reorganization of the Senate.
11. Pure and economic administration of public affairs.

It is to be noted that plank 1 does not mention Canadian independence. The young men were divided on this question, as were their two chosen heroes. At Aurora, Blake came out for imperial federation. Goldwin Smith was an independence man, and the editors of *The Nation* agreed with him. But, of course, a party that was not agreed on this vital point bore a suspicious resemblance to older parties.

The same was true about plank 7 on the tariff duties for revenue, but so adjusted as to afford every encouragement to native industry. The most ingenious platform-maker of the Grit or Tory parties, in these days of the middle seventies when both parties were hesitating whether to go in for protection or not, could not have straddled the fence more skilfully.

The various clauses on constitutional changes were obviously not very radical or frightening. Some of them came straight out of John Stuart Mill. And when one came to the last plank, on pure and economic administration, *The Globe* had some justification for exclaiming sarcastically "There's a novelty for you now!"[4]

What got Canada First into controversy were three main points. One was their denunciation of the two old parties. Again and again *The Canadian Monthly* and *The Nation* came back to the theme that the old parties were merely factions fighting over again the old issues of the pre-Confederation era, the old issues of Brown versus Macdonald. "Party" said Goldwin Smith in *The Canadian Monthly*[5] "party without dividing principle becomes faction. The aim of faction is place, its bond is selfishness, the means which it universally and inevitably employs to hold together its forces and attain its ends are intrigue, jobbery, and corruption; its deliberations are conspiracies, its patriotism is the sacrifice of country to cabal; its eloquence is slander of opponents. The tendency of government by faction is always downward." And Canadian parties were made worse by the tone of *The Globe* and *The Mail*, the two chief party organs. "People are bewildered by the ceaseless storm of accusation and counter-accusation, deafened by the din of indiscriminating invective, and tacitly convinced that the government of faction must be a government of dishonesty."[6] *The Mail*, founded in 1872, was edited by a man who was supposed to have remarked that in his view the duty of a conservative newspaper was to stab the Grits under the fifth rib every morning. "*The Mail*" said Goldwin Smith "has saved us from a dictatorship (of *The Globe*), though much as we might be saved from typhus by having the small-pox."[7] And when party papers along with practical politicians urged Canadians to concentrate on immediate issues and to shun theoretical questions such as the implications of Canadian nationality, *The Nation* exclaimed "The authors of Confederation once appealed to the spirit of nationality . . . Now some of them tell us that their object was limited and that they set the forest on fire only to boil their own pot."[8]

Was Canada First, however, a party in the sense that it was seeking office and power against the old parties? Blake, whom they had welcomed as their prospective leader, who had been an independent Liberal at the time that he delivered the Aurora Speech, who had contributed money to keep *The Nation* going, and had helped to launch an independent morning paper in Toronto, *The Liberal*, to compete with *The Globe*, went back into party harness in the spring of 1875 when he became Minister of Justice in the Grit Mackenzie government. And *The Nation* gradually shifted its ground. "What is meant by party?" it asked on April 23, 1875:

A body of politicians organized under wire-pullers for the purpose of getting into office? Or merely a number of people animated by the same sentiment and moving spontaneously toward the same object? If the former, there is no such thing, so far as we are aware, as a national party. If the latter, there is a National party . . . The question of success or failure, in the case of such a party, is not to be decided on the same grounds as in the case of one of those parties which, when they have returned to dust, the uncourtly voice of history calls factions. Will the state of opinion, of feeling, of public life in Canada, ten or fifteen years hence be what it is now, or will a higher allegiance have begun to take root in the hearts and to mould the political character of our people? . . . Will our statesmanship still consist of a perpetual effort to hold together by "better terms" and bribery under various forms and names, a motley army of political contingents, drawn from districts which care little for each other, from self-seeking interests, from warring religions; or will this wretched and degrading necessity have been in some measure superseded by the ascendancy of a higher bond of union?

Alas, *The Nation* did not live to see the answer to its questions. Within about a year it had expired. And if it had lived, I am afraid the answer would not have been very satisfactory to it.

The second point that caused trouble to the Canada Firsters centred around the question of independence. Thoughtful men were agreed that to build up a national spirit what was needed was to give the new nation some wider responsibilities, some duties to perform that would concentrate public attention upon the nation as such, as distinct from the old provincial and sectional concerns, the old party controversies, the old religious divisions. Independence would surely confront the country with these wider responsibilities, but this meant separation from Britain, a subject that

English-Canadians could not discuss dispassionately. *The Globe* and *The Mail* combined to assault Goldwin Smith, *The Nation*, and Canada First, with sarcasm and invective.

Blake, for his part, advocated an advance in status and responsibility by which the colony would share with Britain in the control of defence and foreign policy. "We are four millions of Britons who are not free" he told his Aurora audience, pointing out how Canada was liable to be involved in imperial policies over which it had no control. But, while his policy of imperial federation would help to inspire wider views in Canadian minds, many critics pointed out that surely the end result would be an imperial sentiment rather than a national sentiment in Canada. Over this question of the ultimate destiny of the country, argument went round and round. But the prolonged depression which began in 1873 turned men's minds to more immediate and personal problems.

The third point was the question of the tariff. In 1874, *The Nation* at first welcomed George Brown's draft Reciprocity Treaty with the United States. But as the Canadian economy languished and as Toronto opinion hardened against the treaty, *The Nation* gradually became more critical of Brown's proposals also. It began to write about a national tariff in which duties would be adjusted to Canadian needs. Agriculture, it argued, might be the greatest Canadian interest at present, but statesmanship must provide for growing interests as well as for existing ones. In a word, on economic questions, as earlier on racial and religious questions, Canada First was becoming Toronto First. If *The Nation* had survived until the election of 1878, it would have been voting for Macdonald's National Policy.

Here we come to the end of Canada First as an active organized movement. I suppose that, since historians always conclude that what actually happened was inevitable, we must say that it had served its purpose and was no longer needed. By the end of the seventies, it had disappeared, though *The Canadian Monthly*, and later *The Week* and Goldwin Smith's own personal journal, *The Bystander*, continued to expound a good many of its ideas. The nationalism that captured the Canadian mind was not that of Goldwin Smith or Edward Blake or the young men of Canada First. It was that of John A. Macdonald.

There *was* developing a national sentiment in the new Dominion, but it was canalized along economic lines rather than political lines. It found expression in the National Policy tariff to protect native industries and in the building of the C.P.R. to tie the sections of the new Dominion together. The National Policy was, of course, a Declaration of Economic Independence. The first romantic phase of nationalism had passed quickly. Canada was living in the Bismarckian era. The realistic, practical politician, rebuilding one of the old parties after its downfall in the Pacific Scandal, had triumphed over the idealistic intellectuals.

III

History Against Geography

I shall begin this, my third lecture, with some considerations about the hard, practical national structure that was built up by Macdonald and his generation. Then I shall go on to the long debate, which still continues, as to whether the direction in which we should move as a people should be toward closer relations with Great Britain or with the United States — imperial federation or North American continentalism.

The nationalism that captured the support of the Canadian people was not that of Canada First or of Goldwin Smith or of Edward Blake, but that of John A. Macdonald — the nationalism of the protective tariff and the Pacific railway. To build up a national loyalty you must succeed in attaching some of the major groups in the country to the national government as the centre of their primary interest. The young men of Canada First lacked the basis of an effective political movement because they spoke for no particular social groups whose economic ambitions were to be furthered through the activity of the national government, and for no discontented groups who might form the basis of another Grit party. And, of course, they did not speak for the most solid group of all, the French-Canadians.

What Macdonald did was to attach to the national government the interests of the ambitious, dynamic, speculative or entrepreneurial business groups, who aimed to make money out of the new national community or to install themselves in the strategic positions of power within it — the railway promoters, banks, manufacturers, land companies, contractors, and such people. They supplied the drive behind his so-called National Policy, and they stood to reap the greatest benefits from it. They also required the fostering care of a Hamiltonian government and the lavish expenditure of taxpayers' money in public capital investment if their ambitions were to be realized. In return, their support was necessary to keep the Conservative government in office. "The day that the C.P.R. busts, the Conservative party busts the day after" said a slightly inelegant cabinet minister in the Macdonald government of the 1880s.[1] The actual, functioning nationalism, therefore, that emerged out of Confederation was based on a triple alliance of federal government, Conservative party, and big-business interests: government of the people, by lawyers, for big business.

The benefits of this nationalism were very unevenly distributed. As Norman Rogers pointed out in his Report on the Fiscal Disabilities of Nova Scotia, in 1934, the National Policy was the first step in making a national plan for Canada, and there should have been further steps to ensure that its benefits and costs were distributed equitably among the various classes and sections of the nation. But the chief beneficiaries of the tariff and the railway-building have seen to it that the word "plan" has remained a four-letter word in our Canadian political vocabulary down to the present.

The Macdonald system also involved a tremendous amount of corruption, which lowered the standards of our public life and has remained one of the heavy costs of this kind of nationalism ever since. For Macdonald's working principle was that every man has his price. "Generally I would charge against your party, as represented by the government in which you sat" wrote Sir John Willison to Sir Charles Tupper, as he looked back on this first generation of Confederation, "that it carried out a great constructive Canadian policy by bad political methods and gross corruption in the constituencies, and that the net result was to build up Canada and greatly to lower public morals."[2] This seems to me to be a pretty good summing up of that first generation of Canadian nationalism. But Willison lived to see his own party, the Liberals, in power for fifteen years after 1896. And his final conclusion was that all that distinguished Liberals from Conservatives in nation-building was their "voluble virtue."

Had the Liberals in opposition before 1896, apart from this voluble virtue, any distinctive national policies to offer that were based on a vision of a different kind of nation than that which expressed itself in a vulgar plutocratic capitalism? They had a different outlook on British and American relations. They attacked the tariff for the way in which it operated to build up a privileged class of industrialists at the expense of the mass of consumers. And they held up the ideal of a low-cost economy based on free trade. They also fought the railway alliance of the Conservative government, and the undue influence of the C.P.R. on Parliament Hill. But Blake, their wisest leader, gradually reached the conclusion that, the costs of national expansion being what they were, no government in office could afford to make any but minor changes in the customs duties that were the main source of public revenue. And, when it came to the point, public ownership was the only alternative to building a transcontinental railway by private enterprise with government financial help. No party was willing to contemplate the political pressures and corrupting influences that would flood in upon an administration that tried to build such a railway itself in the 1880s and to run it after it was built. In effect, then, the Liberals had no alternative vision of the new nationality that differed essentially from the Conservative vision.

Yet, twenty years after 1867, in spite of his political success, this Macdonald system was showing signs of breaking up. The long, world-wide depression, which had begun in 1873, pressed heavily upon Canada. Thousands of Canadians left the country and annexed themselves to the United States. By the time of the 1891 election, according to the American and Canadian censuses, there were about a fifth as many Canadian-born persons living in the States as in Canada. Inside Canada, the execution of Riel had produced an explosion of bitterness such as the country had never before seen. Ontario and Quebec were at one another's throats. In Quebec, Mercier was premier at the head of a new nationalist party, neither Rouge nor Bleu, which claimed to unite all members of the French-Canadian nation. By way of reaction to Mercier, there arose an extreme Protestant movement in Ontario, which started agitation against the French language and Catholic schools in the West. Their thesis was essentially that Canada was an English-Canadian country in one corner of which some French-Catholics happened to reside.

This combination of passionate antagonisms tearing the country apart with the long pressure of economic difficulties produced a deeper depression of spirit than has ever again captured the Canadian mind. The late eighties and early nineties mark the point when our national self-confidence reached its lowest level. "We have come to a period in the history of this young country" wrote Wilfrid Laurier to Edward Blake "when premature dissolution seems to be at hand. What will be the outcome? How long can the present fabric last? Can it last at all? All these are questions which surge in my mind and to which dismal answers suggest themselves."[3] There must have been a good many conversations along these lines in those days.

Out of this situation emerged a movement in 1887 for Commercial Union with the United States. The controversy that went on for the next five or six years raised deeper questions about the nature of the Canadian identity than Canadians had yet faced. I wish to pause over some of these questions as they were argued, not by the politicians of the day, but by some of the intellectuals.

Let me go back to Goldwin Smith. His book on *Canada and the Canadian Question* of 1891 is the most pessimistic book that has ever been written about Canada, and he advanced the most radical solution for the frustrations of the day — union with the United States. Modern Canadians no longer read Smith, and seem to have agreed that they dislike him. But he is the only intellectual in our history who was widely read in his own day, as can be seen from the controversies that his opinions stirred up in newspapers of his day and from the number of his books that have floated around second-hand-book shops in our day. So he is worth some attention.

After the collapse of the Canada First movement, Smith lost faith in the capacity of Canadians to rise to the responsibilities of nationhood. He became more and more impressed by the unwieldy size and the lack of geographical unity of the country. Also, having been an anti-clerical at Oxford, he was more easily worked up than native Canadians by the dangers to national unity of the ultramontane movement in Quebec. He knew more than they did about its challenge to the modern spirit in Europe.

Before he came out to America Smith had taken a lively part in English political discussion. In the crisis of the American Civil War he had been one of the small group of intellectuals who had refused to conform to the pro-Southern attitude of the English Establishment. During the war, in 1864, he paid a visit to the United States, coming as a sort of fraternal delegate to the Northern people from their sympathizers in England. Let me quote from a speech he gave in Boston, to illustrate how he interpreted the relations of the two great branches of the English-speaking peoples:

> To America, though an alien by birth, I am, as an English Liberal, no alien in heart . . . The real hour of your birth was the English Revolution of the seventeenth century, at once the saddest and the noblest period of English history . . . In England the Revolution failed . . . The feudal past sat too heavy on us to be cast off . . . But the yoke which in the mother country we had not the strength to throw off, in the colony we escaped; and here beyond the reach of the Restoration, Milton's vision proved true, and a free commonwealth was founded . . . Yet in England the party of Milton and Cromwell still lives. It still lives; and in this great crisis of your fortunes, its heart turns to you. On your success ours depends. Now as in the seventeenth century the thread of our fate is twined with the thread of yours. An English Liberal comes here, not only to watch the unfolding of your destiny, but to read his own . . . The present Civil War is a vast episode in the . . . irrepressible conflict between Aristocracy and Democracy . . . The England of Charles and Laud has been against you; the England of Hampden, Milton and Cromwell is on your side.[4]

To Smith, that is, the United States represented the quintessence of everything he admired in English society and civilization, purified of all the elements he detested. The hope of democracy in the English-speaking world rested upon the United States. This was why he dreamed of a reunion of the two separated branches of the race, and why he saw the union of Canada and the States as a possible first step toward this broader reunion. No doubt, he had some dreams that his own function in history would be to take a leading part in the achievement of this "moral federation of the English-speaking peoples," as he called it.

Note that French-speaking Quebec had no part to play in these dreams. The Catholic, ultramontane theocracy of Quebec was simply an obstacle in Canada to the progress of modern, liberal, democratic civilization. Smith never seemed to realize in the 1880s that Leo XIII had succeeded Pius IX in the Vatican. "Science and democracy" as he put it "do not go to Canossa." He failed to foresee the growth of Catholicism in America as a whole. It was Puritan America, as it had been Puritan England, that was his ideal.

Smith had also, while still an English citizen, made a name for himself by his outspoken views on the British Empire. We need to understand this Manchester philosophy of his if we are to appreciate why he was so certain that Canada could not remain indefinitely a British dependency. Here I quote from a book of his, *The Empire*, which he published before he left England:

We are keeping the colonies in a perpetual state of political infancy, and preventing the gristle of their frame from being matured and hardened into bone . . . We have given them all that we really have to give — our national character, our commercial energy, our aptitude for law and government, our language. We have given them the essence of our constitution . . . The accidents of that constitution — the relics of the feudal world in which it was wrought — we can no more give them than we can give them our history or our skies. England is a European aristocracy, Canada is an American democracy . . . I am no more against colonies than I am against the solar system, I am against dependencies when nations are fit to be independent . . . But grant that Canada cannot stand as a nation by herself, it is with a nation in America, not with a nation in Europe, that she must ultimately blend . . . And while she remains a province, Canada is, in fact, blending insensibly with the United States . . . There is but one way to make Canada impregnable, and that is to fence her round with the majesty of an independent nation.[5]

Smith had the early nineteenth-century, romantic, mystic faith in the miracle-working powers of nationhood. When, after experience in Canada, he decided that we had not the capacity for nationhood on our own, there was no other destiny for us than absorption into the great American nation that was the hope of democracy.

The book *Canada and the Canadian Question* of 1891 is the culmination of this thinking of Smith's. After a series of destructive, disillusioning chapters on Canadian history, he comes to "The Canadian Question" — the five possible choices that confront Canada, dependence, independence, imperial federation, political union with the States, or commercial union. Imperial federation among widely separated units he regarded as impossible, and he asked for details of the proposed federal constitution instead of vague uplifting generalities. Commercial union with the States would bring us prosperity by admitting us to the markets of our own continent. If we refused this opportunity, we were, as he put it, to remain "rich by nature, poor by policy."[6] Political union would mean that our influence in the republic would be thrown on the side of a better understanding with Britain, and so we would help to advance the greater union of all the English-speaking peoples.

"Annexation is an ugly word; it seems to convey the idea of force or pressure applied to the smaller state, not of free, equal and honourable union, like that between England and Scotland. Yet there is no reason why the union of the two sections of the English-speaking peoples on this Continent should not be as free, as equal, and as honourable, as the union of England and Scotland."[7] Let us admit, at least, that when Smith thought that we Canadians had enough vitality to play in an American republic the same part as that played by the Scots in the United Kingdom, he was paying us the highest compliment that we have ever received.

The best answers to the Goldwin Smith thesis about the destiny of Canada came from two Maritimers: George M. Grant, Nova Scotian by birth, then Principal of Queen's University; and George R. Parkin, a New Brunswicker, and a missionary for the cause of imperial federation, for which Grant was also an enthusiastic preacher.[8] It has struck me how often the best exponents of the imperial idea in Canada have come from the Maritime provinces: men such as Grant and Parkin among intellectuals; such as Howe, Tupper, Foster, Beaverbrook, among the men of affairs. Whatever careers some of them may have had in the larger Canada, Canada as such seems to have failed to answer to some deep emotional demand of their natures. Here in Ontario, our imperialists may have felt equally impassioned — they certainly expressed themselves vehemently enough — but one gets the impression about so many of them that a good deal of the attraction of the British connection to them has been its function as a status-symbol. It marks them off from mere French-Canadians who suffer from the misfortune of lacking a British mother-country, and from mere working-class or agrarian radicals whose zeal for narrow domestic causes shows that they have never mixed with the English governing classes.

Grant was an enthusiastic Canadian as well as an imperialist. He had accompanied his friend, the engineer Sandford Fleming, across Canada on the expedition that explored the Yellowhead route through the sea of mountains to the Pacific, and he was thrilled by the potentialities of his country. The challenge of difficulties only roused him to greater energy; these difficulties were only the growing pains in our history. His objections to Smith's ideas were temperamental almost as much as intellectual. His real objection was that Smith in his cold rational analysis paid no attention to all the traditions and sentiments that had grown up in our Canadian past:

> They (Canadians) feel that he is ignorant of the deepest feelings of Canadians . . . As an Englishman and an Oxford man, Goldwin Smith is incapable of understanding Canadian sentiment . . . Before knowing Canada he made up his mind what Canadian sentiment ought to be . . . He could do such a grand work for Canada if he would only lead us in reforming what should be reformed, one step at a time, instead of insisting that the whole house be pulled down about our ears . . . I look forward to the happy reunion of our race with as much longing as Dr. Goldwin Smith, but to begin it with a second disruption is out of the question.[9]

The best answer of all to Smith came from Parkin. Before he made his name as a propagandist for imperial federation, Parkin had been headmaster of the collegiate school in Fredericton, which he had vainly tried to persuade his community to turn into a residential school modelled on the English public schools. His object had been to train the minds and characters of young men, some of whom would in due course show themselves capable of a higher form of politics than was current in New Brunswick. Parkin and Grant and all our later imperialists have been moved by one great vision, that of raising the standards, moral and intellectual, of Canadian public life. One of the great attractions of imperial federation to them was that Canadian statesmen, by becoming partners in a wider enterprise, would acquire wider viewpoints and a more mature sense of responsibility.

Parkin's reply came in a book that he published in 1892: *Imperial Federation, The Problem of National Unity*. One word in that title reveals more than Parkin quite realized, the word "national." The nation of which he was thinking was the British Empire as a whole. Canadian nationality seemed to him relatively insignificant. He continuously uses the words "nation" and "national" to apply to the wider entity. This was implicitly a denial of the thesis on which Canadian Liberals by the 1890s were beginning to unite, that the relations between Canada and Great Britain must be diplomatic relations between two national states and not constitutional relations within one federal state. And the Liberals, of course, had the future with them.

Parkin, however, had more than this to his argument. His main preoccupation was with defence. In his thinking here, he was a generation younger and more up to date than Goldwin Smith. He understood that the balance of power in Europe and the world was changing to the disadvantage of Britain and the empire that she guarded, and that Canada could no longer regard herself as insulated from the outer world by British protection. He might be said to have been our first geopolitician. The function of Canada, in his vision of defence, was that of a country that, possessing harbours and coal on both the Atlantic and Pacific coasts, occupied a vital strategic position in global imperial defence. Added to this, he argued, correctly, her wheat surplus would find its markets across the ocean, not in the United States. Every interest, economic as well as military, made the connection between Canada and Britain a vital one.

Parkin's vision rose to grander heights still:

> If we really have faith in our own social and Christian progress as a nation; if we believe that our race . . . can be trusted better than others to use power with moderation . . . and a deep sense of moral responsibility . . . then it cannot be inconsistent with devotion to all the highest interests of humanity to wish and strive for a consolidation of British power. It is because I believe that . . . there is this strong faith in our national integrity and in the greatness of the moral work our race has yet to do, that I anticipate that the whole weight of Christian and philanthropic sentiment will ultimately be thrown on the side of national unity . . . inasmuch as it will give us the security which is necessary for working out our great national purposes.[10]

This on the eve of the Jamieson Raid and the Boer War! When political argument reaches religious heights in this way, one needs to beware of it.

In discussing these intellectuals I have got a little ahead of events. Let me return to that Unrestricted Reciprocity election of 1891. In that first trial of strength over relations with the outer world, the division of opinion about the direction that Canadian evolution should take was really very close. Of the voters of Ontario, 49.1 percent voted for Unrestricted Reciprocity, and 49.4 percent against it. In Quebec, 45.4 percent were for, and 52 percent against. Ontario and Quebec, taken together, were divided fairly evenly both in votes and in seats won. What saved the Macdonald government was its majority in the outlying provinces, east and west — the rags and tatters of Confederation, as Sir Richard Cartwright very untactfully called them. Along the main line of the C.P.R. from Montreal to Vancouver it was observed that only one constituency (in Manitoba) voted for Unrestricted Reciprocity. When Van Horne, the head of the C.P.R., was asked about this, he replied that that particular constituency must have been a case of pure oversight on the part of the railway company.

One of the striking features of our history since 1867 has been this tendency of Canadian public opinion, which first showed itself at the end of the 1880s, to return periodically to what might be called a continental attitude, to see our destiny in closer relations — economic, political, and cultural — with our American neighbour. We had another public debate about this in the Reciprocity election of 1911. And today again there is widespread talk about continental free trade. Should we conclude that this persistent phenomenon in our communal life, which keeps showing up periodically in spite of the best efforts of our Establishment to suppress it, is a sign of the direction in which our ultimate goal lies? Or should we be more impressed by the fact that, every time the Canadian people are confronted with a conscious choice in a general election, they have nobly put the Satanic American temptation behind them?

Furthermore, did Unrestricted Reciprocity in 1891 inevitably involve the absorption of Canada by the United States? We know now that a good many Liberals, who were not prepared to go the length of breaking with their party as Edward Blake did, privately agreed with him and Macdonald. But here again we run into one of those myths of our Canadian life to which I have referred previously. I know of no method of scientific analysis by which it can be proved or disproved that free trade between the two peoples, in 1891 or in 1963, would be destructive of our Canadian identity. Perhaps a social psychologist would tell us that it is necessary for

Canadians to believe in an American hell in order to preserve the vital force of the Canadian national religion. To be a Liberal rather than a fundamentalist in one's political religion requires a very high type of mind and character.

At any rate, after all the excitement of the Reciprocity election was over, Sir John Macdonald, having saved his country from the American danger, as his admirers believed, died a British subject as he had been born a British subject. According to what I have just been reading in *Ontario History*, the journal of the Ontario Historical Society, he was buried in a casket which was imported from West Meriden, Connecticut, and which was an exact facsimile of the casket in which President Garfield of the United States had been buried a short time previously.[11] Well, it is always other Canadians and not ourselves who are liable to be demoralized and de-Canadianized by truck or trade with the Yankees.

IV

CANADA'S RELATIONS WITH BRITAIN

The Boer War was a great watershed in our history. While the amount of energy that we expended on it and our sacrifices of men and money were insignificant as compared with what we went through in the two great wars of 1914 and 1939, it marked a new stage in our national experience. We ceased to be a secluded, protected colony, insulated from the direct impact of world affairs by British power and diplomacy. We began to play a part in the great twentieth-century struggles of world power-politics. All the issues about our relationship to the overseas world first became acute in these years of the Boer War. And so I propose to pause over it for a while, since the issues as they were discussed in the two world wars are still relatively familiar to most Canadians, whereas we have largely forgotten about the earlier war. It was when we entered upon this new experience in 1899 that we discovered that the image that English-Canadians had of our place and function in the world was widely different from the image in the minds of French-Canadians. A new cause of bitter conflict arose in the long, unending, domestic cold war between Ontario and Quebec.

This participation by Canada in an imperialist war for power on the African continent happened to coincide fairly closely in time with the Spanish-American War in which our American neighbours took their first step toward an American overseas empire. In the United States, there was a great debate about this abandonment of North American isolation, about the morality as well as the expediency of this plunging into imperialist, overseas conquests. American liberals who were distressed at the spirit of aggrandizement displayed by their country, were defeated in this debate; but it was a great debate over the moral implications of foreign policy. How immature we still were as compared with our American neighbours was shown by the near unanimity with which English-Canadians accepted the British advance in South Africa simply because it was British.

There were critics, of whom Henri Bourassa was the most prominent. And it was soon clear that he expressed a general French-Canadian distaste for this adventure. Goldwin Smith, as an English Manchester liberal, was also opposed. Principal Grant of Queen's, who had visited South Africa and seen the activities of the gold-mining crowd on the spot, was a Pro-Boer before the war, but had to agree that there was no alternative to fighting it out when once the Boers themselves precipitated armed action.[1] Over in London, Edward Blake, late Liberal leader, who was now an Irish Nationalist M.P. in the Imperial Parliament, stood with his fellow Irishmen in opposing the war; he had been a member of the parliamentary committee that investigated the Jamieson Raid, and he knew more than did his fellow Canadians about the sordid realities of the Rhodes high-flying dreams of empire. But these were voices in the wilderness, which went largely unheeded

in the great outburst of imperial enthusiasm that swept over
English-Canada.

By 1899, when the Boer War came, some important changes in
the Canadian outlook were taking place. The clouds caused by the
long decline in world prices were lifting, and the sun of the great
wheat boom was coming out. As our exports of wheat and foodstuffs to the British market came to be the dominant element in
our foreign trade, it was, for the time at least, no longer necessary
to dispute whether the American market represented the chief
promise or the chief threat to the Canadian future. And as the
clouds lifted, Canadian self-confidence revived. Sir Wilfrid
Laurier was shortly to declare that the twentieth century belonged
to Canada. This renewed national vitality, seeking outlets in which
to express itself, tended among English-Canadians to take the
form of an urge toward imperial adventures.

The appeal of the British connection was, moreover, strong
among all English-speaking Canadians, no matter to which political party they belonged. J. W. Dafoe, in his little book on Laurier,
had some interesting remarks on this subject. They are interesting
because, while they are critical of his fellow English-speaking
Canadians, they come from a man who was to become, by 1917,
one of the most determined anti-French leaders in the country:

> English-speaking Canadians were more British than the British,
> they were more loyal than the Queen ... Imperialism, on the senti-
> mental side, was a glorification of the British race; it was a fore-
> shadowing of the happy time when this governing and triumphant
> people would give the world the blessing of the Pax Britannica ...
> It kindled their imagination; from being colonists of no account in
> the backwash of the world's affairs, they became integrally a part of
> a great imperial world-wide movement of expansion and domina-
> tion; were they not of what Chamberlain called "that proud,

persistent, self-asserting and resolute stock . . . which is infallibly bound to be the predominating force in the future history and civilization of the world"? Moreover it gave them a sense of their special importance here in Canada, where the population was not "homogeneous in blood, language, and religion"; it was for them, they felt, to direct policy and control events.[2]

This racist tone, which ran all through the imperialism of Chamberlain and Kipling in Britain, naturally repelled the French-Canadians. The more this type of Anglo-Saxon nationalism became prominent in Canada, the more the two main communal groups were alienated from each other. And the more that the fervour of Anglo-Saxondom came to centre in the Conservative party, the more inevitable it was that the French-Canadians should attach themselves to the Liberals. For this reason, if for no other, the Liberal form of nationalism had the future with it.

English-speaking Canada had been growing more and more emotionally imperialist in the decade before 1899. One little incident that illustrated this occurred in Toronto in 1896 over a proposal in the university to give an honorary doctorate to Goldwin Smith, the city's most distinguished citizen. Colonel George Denison, he of the Canada First movement in the 1870s, asked that his name be struck from the list of graduates. It was reported that the Vice-Chancellor of the university would refuse to preside at the degree-conferring ceremony. So great was the rumpus, because of the charge against Smith of disloyalty to Britain, that he wrote declining the honour. "I will therefore beg to withdraw my acceptance of the honorary degree of Toronto University" he wrote "and rest content with that which has already been conferred upon me by my own University of Oxford."[3] The old gentleman distinctly got the better of Toronto on this exchange.

The diamond jubilee of Queen Victoria in 1897 also helped powerfully in the growth of imperial sentiment. Special jubilee stamps were issued, containing a map of the world that was splashed with red wherever there were British possessions, with a proud declaration at the bottom of the stamp: "We hold a greater empire than has been." Who were the "we" who held this great empire? We Canadians? Of course not. But our Postmaster-General was identifying us with the British people who did hold it. I can remember, as a small boy of some eight years, collecting these stamps eagerly.

Perhaps equally significant, though I was too young to be aware of this, was the fact that, when the South African crisis came two years later, there were two books by Canadian intellectuals published in Canada and expounding the British case with much learning — one by David Mills, the Liberal lieutenant of Blake and Laurier, who was professor of law in the University of Toronto, and one by James Cappon, who was professor of English in Queen's University.[4]

In the summer of 1898, the year between the jubilee and the war, my childhood companions and I were playing war games introduced by an American boy, a visitor in one of the homes on our street; we were capturing Havana and Manilla for the Anglo-Saxon, Protestant American forces, who were also, as I vaguely sensed, part of "that proud, persistent, self-asserting and resolute stock which is infallibly bound to be the predominating force in the future history and civilization of the world." A small boy in a little Ontario village was well prepared by 1899 to sing "Soldiers of the Queen," that most vulgarly boastful of all imperialist war-anthems.

In 1885, Sir John Macdonald had coldly turned down the proposal to send an official Canadian force to take part in the Soudan expedition for the relief of General Gordon, though he allowed a body of boatmen to be recruited by the British authorities for service on the Nile. He pointed out to Sir Charles Tupper, who was Canadian High Commissioner in London and who was eager to seize the opportunity to advertise Canada in Britain, that Canada had no direct interest in the Nile or the Suez Canal, and that "our men and money would therefore be sacrificed to get Gladstone & Co. out of the hole they have plunged themselves into by their own imbecility."5 In 1899, Sir Wilfrid Laurier, if left to follow his own view of the situation, would no doubt have shown a similar detachment from South African affairs, and would have declined to make Canadian sacrifices to get Chamberlain & Co. out of the hole they had plunged themselves into by their own imbecility. But his hand was forced by the enthusiasm in English-speaking Canada for taking part in the war. He felt that his government must act on Canadian majority opinion. So the first contingent was sent off without waiting for parliamentary sanction — a momentous step in our history, which was defended by the provision in the Order-in-Council authorizing the action that declared that this step should not constitute a precedent.

Young Henri Bourassa, the rising lieutenant of Laurier, at once raised a protest. The debate between him and Laurier on what was involved in this sending of Canadian troops overseas was one of the finest that has ever taken place in our Canadian Parliament. I quote at some length from it because the issues were so important (Bourassa's protest was twofold. In the first place he associated himself with the British Liberals who opposed Chamberlain's policy. His other main point was that this was a change in the constitutional relations of mother-country and colony. Hitherto both of them had recognized that the colony's military obligations were confined to the local defence of Canada, and that the metropolitan power had the responsibility of general imperial defence):

> This great display of Imperial militarism is not intended for the purpose of this war, but is being organized to give an example and warning to the world . . . If we send 2,000 men and spend $2,000,000 to fight two nations aggregating a population of 250,000 souls, how many men shall we send, and how many millions shall we expend to fight a first-class power or a coalition of powers? And it is, no doubt, to first-class powers and to possible coalitions that the lesson and the warning were intended to be given. If we judged proper to share in the teaching, it must mean that we are ready to share in the action when the time comes of applying the lesson . . . It is the starting-point of a new policy which opens a serious point of view on the future of the country. The point of view may be glorious for those who aspire after military honours . . . But it prepares a gloomy future for the farming and labouring classes of this country.

As to the no-precedent clause, he repeated what he had said in an open letter to the prime minister: "The precedent, sir, is the accomplished fact." And he quoted from utterances of Chamberlain and the Governor General to show how they had deliberately greeted the sending of the troops as a precedent for the future co-operation of Canada and Britain in war. Canada's future involvement in European militarism was being determined now.

> I do not ask for independence now, nor at any period within ordinary foresight. Not that independence is not, to my mind, the most legitimate and natural aim to which any colony should tend . . . But clear propositions as to military co-operation must be laid before parliament and thoroughly discussed, and when the terms are agreed

upon, a plebiscite must be taken on the question, free from all other political issues . . . I am a Liberal of the British school. I am a disciple of Burke, Fox, Bright, Gladstone, and of the other little Englanders, who made Great Britain and her possessions what they are.

He ended by moving "that . . . this House declares that it opposes any change in the political and military relations which exist at present between Canada and Great Britain, unless such change is initiated by the sovereign will of Parliament and sanctioned by the people of Canada."[6] Note two things about this Bourassa stand. He is speaking as a Liberal who agrees with what English Liberals were saying about the moral issues of the war. How strange that English-speaking Canadian Liberals seemed so blind to this aspect of the question! He also remains still a colonist, insisting on colonial detachment from these wider imperial responsibilities. He is not yet a full Canadian nationalist demanding that Canada assume responsibility for her own defence and foreign policy.

Laurier replied that his young friend was making too much of the situation. "He is at that age, that happy age, where the pride of cherished theories far outweighs, and indeed usually makes light of all considerations of practical reality." He went on:

If we had refused at that time to do what was in my judgement our imperative duty, a most dangerous agitation would have arisen . . . which would have ended in a cleavage in the population of this country upon racial lines . . . If there is anything to which I have given my political life, it is to try to promote unity, harmony, and amity, between the diverse elements of this country . . . I am fully convinced in my heart and conscience that there never was a juster war on the part of England . . . I altogether repudiate that doctrine, that we have changed the relations, civil and military, which now exist between Great Britain and Canada . . . If we were to be compelled to take part in all the wars of Great Britain, I agree with my honourable friend that, sharing the burden, we should also share the responsibility . . . But there is no occasion to examine this contingency today.

Laurier concluded with an eloquent appeal on his standard theme of unity within Canada:

Today there are men in South Africa representing the two branches of the Canadian family . . . Already some of them have fallen . . . Their remains have been laid in the same grave, there to rest to the end of time in that last fraternal embrace. Can we not hope . . . that in that grave shall be buried the last vestiges of our former antagonism? If such shall be the result, if we can indulge that hope . . . the sending of the contingents would be the greatest service ever rendered to Canada since Confederation.[7]

Alas, what English-Canadians observed was that there were many more of them offering their lives in South Africa than of French-Canadians. The former antagonism was not buried. And what French-Canadians were to observe in the next few years was that Bourassa had been right: "The precedent, sir, is the accomplished fact." He was prophetic. By 1914, we were plunged into that greater struggle among European powers that he had foreseen.

The immediate results of the war were seen in the elections of 1900, which came a year after this Bourassa-Laurier debate. Laurier won seats in Quebec over his 1896 figure, although he had just done something that his province did not like . . . His fellow French-Canadians preferred to have him in office rather than someone else who might do more. In Ontario, he lost seats, though he had now twice done things of which Ontario approved, in the Manitoba schools question and in the sending of troops to South Africa. Quebec and Ontario were squaring up for another fight.[8] The fight came to a climax in 1917, when English-Canada imposed its will upon French-Canada — the worst of all possible situations that could arise in our Canadian politics.

How we gradually worked out the problems of our relations with Britain, which showed up first in an acute form in the Boer War period, would take too long to tell here. The war itself, since the Canadian part of it was exciting but not very costly, undoubtedly increased the eagerness of many English-Canadians for the active partnership of Canada in imperial affairs. But, on the other hand, it revealed that there was a strong anti-imperial feeling in Canada also. And because it sharpened in this way the two opposed points of view, the Boer War is a great watershed in our history.

Let me quote, as one example of the imperial spirit among English-Canadians, some paragraphs from an article by Stephen Leacock in *The University Magazine* of April, 1907. *The University Magazine* was a joint publication of McGill, Toronto, and Dalhousie universities; and it is full of pronouncements like this of Leacock's, though usually not such brightly written ones, calling for closer imperial integration; confidently announcing, after 1914, that the integration is taking place; expressing an ecstatic exaltation at the purifying effects that war will have upon Canadian life and politics; expressing on the other hand deep anxieties lest the mass influx of immigrants will have lowered our standards; and, in general, from one number to another, displaying an almost blissful unconsciousness of the existence of the French-Canadians. Most of these articles seem to be by McGill men. When one reads them today, with our knowledge after the event of what actually was happening, one can hardly avoid exclaiming "O God, O McGill!"

Well, here is Leacock in the spring of 1907:

Now, in this month of April, the ministers of Canada take ship for the fourth Colonial Conference in London. What do they go to do? Nay, rather, what shall we bid them do? We — the six million people of Canada, unvoiced, untaxed in the Empire, unheeded in the councils of the world — we the six million colonials sprawling our over-suckled infancy across a continent — what shall be our message to the motherland? Shall we still whine of our poverty, still draw imaginary pictures of our thin herds shivering in the cold blasts of the North, their shepherds huddled for shelter in the log cabins of Montreal and Toronto? Shall we still beg the good people of England to bear yet a little longer, for the poor peasants of their colony, the burden and heat of the day? . . . Or shall we say to the people of England, "The time has come; we know and realize our country. We will be your colony no longer. Make us one with you in an Empire, Permanent and Indivisible." I that write these lines am an Imperialist because I will not be a Colonial. This Colonial status is a worn-out, by-gone thing. The sense and feeling of it has become harmful to us. It limits the ideas and circumscribes the patriotism of our people . . .

Our politics, our public life and thought, rise not to the level of our opportunity. The mud-bespattered politicians of the trade, the party men and party managers, give us in place of patriotic state-scraft the sordid traffic of a tolerated jobbery. For bread, a stone. Harsh is the cackle of the little turkey-cocks of Ottawa, fighting the while as they feather their mean nests of sticks and mud, high on their river bluff . . .

Nay, on the question of the cost, good gentlemen of the council, spare it not. Measure not the price. We are buying back our honour as Imperial Citizens . . . Thus stands the case. Thus stands the question of the future of Canada. Find for us something other than mere colonial stagnation, something sounder than independence, nobler than annexation, greater in purpose than a Little Canada. Find us a way, build us a plan, that shall make us, in hope at least, an Empire Permanent and Indivisible.[9]

It was significant, perhaps that in the number of *The University Magazine* that immediately preceded this one, Leacock had an article on American humour in which he took pains to point out that by American he meant North American, and that he included Canadian humour in all his remarks.[10] He was culturally a North American but emotionally a Britisher.

Of course this ardent aspiration for a closely organized British Empire, with Canada a full partner in it, was never to be realized. And today we seem to have reached a general acceptance by the Canadian people as a whole of a position in which the aloofness of the French-Canadians is more effectively expressed than the organic imperial unity longed for by the federationists. English-Canadians no longer insist that French-Canadians must adjust themselves to a great world-wide English-speaking empire. Out of all the controversies that filled the air from 1899 to 1945, what emerged was a Canadian nationalism that insisted on the complete national sovereignty of Canada, and that refused any economic or military schemes such as would bind us in one community with Britain. Canada has, however, accepted responsibilities in Europe that spring from our partnership in an Atlantic alliance rather than a Britannic alliance, and responsibilities in the world at large that are undertaken as a member of the United Nations rather than of the British Commonwealth.

This development was not foreseen by any Canadian before 1919, and the logic that was driving us toward it was denied by many Canadians during the long armistice from 1919 to 1939. We have arrived at a conclusion that was beyond the categories of our thinking during most of the time we were moving toward it.

As one looks back now, it seems evident that the North American isolationists, English-Canadian and French-Canadian, were blind in their failure to see the realities of the international balance of power in this twentieth century. In 1914 and 1939, we were bound to come into the war because we could not afford to see Britain and France eliminated as great European powers. The United States came in for the same reason, and it did not matter how much we may have disapproved certain aspects of British and French policy. Today we keep armed forces in Europe because we cannot afford to see the West European powers overrun by totalitarian invasion. This continuous policy of intervention in Europe was really all the time based on inescapable calculations of power politics and not on a sentimental attachment to Britain.

Today our ties with Britain have weakened, in spite of the common Crown, because Britain is no longer a great world power. It was British power that guaranteed our security in the world, acted as a counterweight against American pressures, and made it worth while for us to follow the British lead in two world wars. But now that British power has been so drastically reduced, the British connection has lost that magnetic attraction that it used to exercise over us. The power that guarantees our security now is that of the United States as the leader of the Atlantic alliance. We have to contribute what we can to make that alliance effective.

But as British power declined, something else happened to us. Canada's move toward complete constitutional independence (of which the story is told in all our history books) did not for some time alter the fact that most English-Canadians continued to look to Britain for intellectual and moral leadership, even if she could no longer give political or military leadership. We accepted British standards as those at which we should aim. We assumed the superiority of British political and diplomatic methods. And then gradually it began to dawn upon us that all these ways of thinking were irrelevant to our real problems in this dangerous world in which we now live.

The historian has great difficulty in fixing the dates of changes in the ideas that govern people's lives. These subtle intangible movements are more difficult to trace than events on the surface of politics. But it is possible to pin-point the date at which the long-settled habit of looking to Britain for standards of conduct came to an end. It was the date of the issue of *Maclean's Magazine* in which Beverley Baxter was dropped from its pages. That fellow had a genius for creating in the minds of thousands of ordinary Canadians the feeling, through his fascinating pictures of life and politics among the top people in England, that they were participating in these great events, sharing in great decisions, living at the centre of things. He himself, according to his own account, had the uncanny faculty of a Lanny Budd in being always on the scene when great events happened and knowing all the actors by their first names. Then suddenly he was cut off; and the lives of thousands of ordinary Canadians went on placidly as if nothing had happened. No doubt *Maclean's* had discovered that he no longer interested its readers. This was the moment at which the umbilical cord binding our minds and imaginations to Britain was finally cut.

So we are now out in the world on our own. We English-Canadians can no longer, when we try to distinguish ourselves from the Americans, announce that we are British. Somehow or other we have to put a distinctive meaning into the declaration that we are Canadian. This is a hard world in which we live. We can no longer creep back into our British mother's womb. And it is a rather sad world too, considering all the aspirations, passions, exaltations, that have characterized the British connection for us in that past which is now dead beyond recall.

V

FRENCH-ENGLISH RELATIONS IN CANADA

Wilfrid Laurier was the greatest of all Canadians. Let us remember this today in the midst of all our troubled discussions between English-Canadians and French-Canadians. The name of Laurier and the Laurier tradition are not popular, so I gather, in present-day Quebec. Yet, if we are to solve our difficulties between the two main communal groups today, we need men with Laurier's qualities both in Quebec and in English-speaking Canada.

He was the greatest of all Canadian public men because he devoted his life to this most intractable of all problems, the finding of the terms on which English-speaking and French-speaking Canadians can learn to live together here in Canada more or less amicably. I stress the phrase "more or less" because it is foolish to pretend to believe that we are likely to turn good neighbourhood, if we achieve it, into good brotherhood within the lifetime of any individuals now living. There has been too much bitterness in our generation for that. At the end of the 1940s the Frenchman,

André Siegfried, who had been studying Canada for fifty years, concluded that all that we had achieved was a "*modus vivendi* without cordiality."[1] We need to aim at something a little better than this. At present, we seem to be moving toward something a good deal worse.

But if we are to achieve this something a little better, it can only be done through leaders from both sides who achieve something a good deal better in their personal relations with each other, who reach a degree of understanding and cordiality that approaches brotherhood. There will always be leaders springing up who make profit for themselves by extremist exploitation of mean tribal suspicions and selfish particularist ambitions. We cannot eliminate these adventurers. We can only hope to counteract their bad influence through the leadership given by another type of statesman who appeals to our better selves, who tries to induce us to stretch our imaginations and sympathies, to display a generosity of spirit toward people who are different from ourselves.

Incidentally this problem of the relations between different groups inside Canada is at bottom the same as the problem of international relations in the world at large. Neither problem will be solved by paper documents, by constitution-making, but only by the emergence in all groups of a general feeling that it is our duty to act as if we were a little better than our normal parochial selves.

Laurier should be our great example because he tried to practise what he preached. Of course, the mouthing of noble *bonne entente* sentiments has become a ritual in our public life. O Canada, O Canada, O can a day go by without some orator orating on this theme of harmony between the two communal groups! Here I am doing it myself at this moment. What distinguished Laurier as a Canadian statesman was, firstly, that he never gave up warning his own French community against the particular form of sin that doth so easily beset it; and, secondly, that he steadily tried to keep in personal touch with the other community. He is unique among Canadian leaders in both respects. Today, more than ever, we need leaders who are capable of both forms of action.

The tendency against which French-Canadians need to be on guard is that toward the particularist, isolationist, Sinn Fein type of tribal nationalism to which they have always been tempted when things have been going wrong — under Mercier, under Bourassa, under Duplessis. This is a tendency natural to all uncomfortable minorities. The tendency against which we English-Canadians need to be on guard is that toward the unconscious or subconscious assumption that, because British sovereignty displaced French sovereignty over Canada in 1763, and because since then the English-speaking population has become an overwhelming majority, therefore Canada is fundamentally an English-speaking community, and our English-Canadian habits, methods, forms of social organization, and way of life generally, must in the end be accepted by the French-Canadians as their way of life also. This is a tendency natural to all comfortable majorities. And we have always lacked English-Canadian Lauriers to warn us against our besetting English-Canadian sins.

Laurier spent a considerable part of his career warning his community against the temptation to form a racial national party for political purposes. He pointed out to them that this would only lead to a combination of the English majority against them, as it did in 1917. He told them the unpleasant truth that as a minority they must from time to time make adjustments to what the majority wanted. He did his best to get minority and majority to divide on political issues as Liberals and Conservatives rather than to confront each other as French-Catholics and English-Protestants.

He did not preach moderation and concession only to his own group. He was always going on political tours into English-speaking

Canada, especially into Ontario, speaking to English-Canadians in their own language, which he used with a special gracefulness and polish. More than any other Canadian leader whose speeches I have read, he followed the honest but unpopular practice of saying the same thing on controversial issues to both English and French audiences. He was always preaching the principles of British constitutional liberalism to both. He mixed readily and naturally with members of the other racial group; he had many personal friends among that group. By his generous bearing, his good manners, and his moderation, he built up a personal following in English- as well as in French-Canada. Men who had once worked with him nearly always found it painful to part company with him on political issues. Even Bourassa, who attacked him most bitterly over a long period of years, declared that he loved the man.

This was the happy warrior. This was he that every man in arms should wish to be. Yet Laurier ended his career in defeat.

Laurier's dealings with the intellectuals of the two racial groups are specially noteworthy today. In Quebec he had to fight first the group of fanatical, doctrinaire, ultramontane Catholics;[2] he had to fight them for the right of Catholic voters to vote Liberal freely. And then he had to fight his own Liberal lieutenant Bourassa. Both of these opponents accused him of disloyalty to the French-Catholic group, and of giving in to pressures from the English majority who represented a threat to the French-Catholic way of life. In English-Canada he had Willison of Toronto against him for the opposite reason, for giving in to the sinister ambitions of the French-Catholic hierarchy over Saskatchewan schools and for betraying the principle of provincial rights. And then later he had Dafoe of Winnipeg against him for being so afraid of losing Quebec to Bourassa that he failed to rise to the necessities of the world struggle against German aggression.

Laurier had to steer a difficult middle course between these two

opposed sets of intellectual doctrinaires, and to try to make them
see that liberal principles as he interpreted them furnished the
only guide for peace and freedom within Canada. It is in his
discussion of principles, in his frank, face-to-face argument with
men of both racial groups who professed to be mainly interested
in principle, that Laurier is so superior to both Macdonald and
King, who shared his belief that the supreme necessity of statesmanship in Canada is to find a way of conciliation between French
and English. One of these two prime ministers disliked talking
about principles; and the other, in spite of his Harvard Ph.D., was
incapable of handling abstract ideas.

The root of our current difficulties is that French-Canadians and
English-Canadians have different pictures in their minds of what
the meaning of Confederation was in 1867, of what our national
purpose was or should have been in the years since then, and of
what Confederation has accomplished so far.

To the French, as they look back on their two centuries of
history since 1763, the two centuries have been clearly and unhappily divided. In the first, from being a conquered people they won
their way, after long struggles, which included an armed revolt
under Papineau, to political liberty, to Responsible Government
with full French participation under Lafontaine, Morin, and
Cartier. Then came the second century, in which they have had to
suffer a series of defeats — over the settlement of the West, over
Riel, over schools and language outside Quebec, over our Canadian relations with Britain, over conscription; a century in which
they have seen their Quebec economy, as their province entered
fully into the second industrial revolution, fall more and more
under the control of English-Canadian and American capitalism.

To the English-Canadian, it seems that Quebec is suffering

today because she deliberately isolated herself in the nineteenth century under the guidance of a church that was determined to keep its people separated as far as possible from dangerous contacts with Anglo-Saxondom. She accepted the clerical doctrine that in order to preserve her language and religion she should adhere to a static, agrarian, habitant economy. Curiously enough, this agrarian gospel was preached by clerics, journalists, and writers, who themselves lived in cities. Clerically directed education in classical colleges meant that a small élite was turned out who lacked training in science, technology, and business enterprise, and thereby the province cut itself off from the possibilities of economic advance that were so eagerly being seized by the English-Canadians west of the Ottawa River. Quebec lost the competition with Ontario for the West because her teeming surplus population drifted southward to find employment in the American factories, and because she showed no willingness to try to assimilate some of the non-French and non-English population that poured into Canada after the turn of the century. If she fell behind, it was her own doing.

English-speaking Canada has another point to make also. The demands for separate French-Catholic schools outside of Quebec have always been demands for clerically controlled teaching. It is this to which English-Canada generally objects, it seems to me, rather than to the teaching in another language. If Quebec in her present revolution should put her own education under lay control, would English-Canadian distaste for French schools be so marked, so obstinate, so fundamentalist?

I think it might be enlightening at this point to quote some of the criticisms made by André Siegfried of both the French and the English groups as he saw them in Canada in the period just after the Boer War. It was at this time that he published his first book on our country, *The Race Question in Canada*, 1907. Siegfried came from Alsatian-Protestant stock; and he is an interesting commentator because, as a Frenchman, he felt a natural sympathy with the fortunes of the French people in America, while as a Protestant anti-clerical, he had no sympathy with the far-reaching ambitions of the French-Canadian church.

He gives a striking picture of the control that the church exercised over the mind of Quebec through its domination of education and its interference in politics. And he concludes:

> The protection of the church is precious, but the price paid for it is exorbitant. Are not the intellectual bondage in which the church would keep them, the narrow authority she exercises, the antiquated doctrines she persists in inculcating, all calculated to hinder the evolution of the race and to handicap it in its rivalry with the Anglo-Saxons, long since freed from the outworn shackles of the past.[3]

This analysis and conclusion will not surprise us Anglo-Saxons.

What may surprise us, however, is what he has to say about the relation of English-Canadian education to politics.

> If Catholicism is one of the essential factors in the development of the French-Canadians, Protestantism does not count for less in that of the English race in the Dominion . . . To all appearances the independence of these [Protestant] churches in regard to the State has been absolutely established. Perhaps it would not be safe to say quite so positively that the State's independence of them is established in the same degree . . . They have never been able to imagine a State entirely devoid of religious prepossessions. The Protestant clergy do not aim at controlling the government in the

ultramontane Catholic fashion, but they do aim at informing it with their spirit . . . Canada, never having had its 1789, has no real comprehension of the theory of the neutrality of the State.[4]

As English-speaking Canada intends the State to be Protestant, so also, says Siegfried, it intends it to be Anglo-Saxon:

Another characteristic of the English school is the very keen national spirit that flourishes in it. Public opinion decides that the boys shall have instilled into them a thoroughgoing Anglo-Saxon patriotism . . . This is precisely why the French, who don't wish at any price to be absorbed, have a deep distrust of the distinctively English public school . . . Both French and English school systems are national in spirit. That is to say, that the one seeks to produce French-Canadians, the other English-Canadians . . . Both schools are permeated by religion.[5]

Siegfried went on to deal with Canadian political parties. He is interesting on this subject, too, because he came from a country in which parties were so much more ideological than with us, and political controversy, especially at this moment of the separation of Church and State, was concerned with the principles on which the good society should be based to a degree that we English-Canadians would find nearly incomprehensible:

Originally formed to subserve a political idea, these parties are often to be found quite detached from the principles which gave them birth, and with their own self-preservation as their chief care and aim. Even without a programme, they continue to live and thrive, tending to become mere associations for the securing of power . . . This fact deprives the periodical appeals to the voting public of the importance they should have . . . Whichever side succeeds, the country, it is well known, will be governed in just the same way; the only difference will be in the personnel of the Government . . . Canadian statesmen . . . seem to stand in fear of great movements of public opinion, and to seek to lull them rather than to encourage them and bring them to fruition . . . The reason for this attitude is easy to comprehend. Canada, as we have seen, with its rival creeds and races, is a land of fears and jealousies and conflicts. The absence of ideas and programmes and convictions is only apparent. Let a question involving religion or nationality be boldly raised and . . . the elections will be turned into real political fights, passionate and sincere. This is exactly what is dreaded by farsighted and prudent politicians, whose duty it is to preserve the national equilibrium . . . They exert themselves, therefore, to prevent the formation of homogeneous parties, divided according to creed or race or class. The purity of political life suffers from this, but perhaps the very existence of the Federation is the price.[6]

Siegfried was so French in his understanding of how politics should be carried on that he was not quite fair, in this rather cynical account, to our Canadian parties. For the composite bi-racial, bi-cultural party, uniting both French and English voters, had been one of our great political inventions. It has been the only effective instrumentality that we have been able to devise for overcoming the deep cleavages between the two communal groups and for keeping them going along together in some kind of rough jolting co-operation.

The experiment began with the Reform party of Lafontaine and Baldwin in the 1840s, which won Responsible Government. When it broke up after ten years, it was succeeded in 1854 by the Liberal-Conservative party of Macdonald and Cartier, which dominated Canadian politics for forty years, taking over the

French majority group that had called itself Reform under Lafontaine and Baldwin. Then came the Liberal party of Laurier, which took over most of the Quebec Bleus who had supported Macdonald. With some short breaks, it provided the government from 1896 to 1957. Apparently we are capable of producing only one of these bi-racial parties at a time. The opposition party is never able to function so efficiently as the government party because the French have instinctively given the bulk of their support to the party that sits on the right of Mr. Speaker.

These successful bi-racial governing parties are marked by certain characteristics. Whatever their name, they are really coalitions of the moderate men in each of the French and English communities. Above all, their leaders are moderates. The extremists after 1854, the Grits and Rouges, never quite succeeded for a long time in forming a nation-wide party that was a going concern. The Diefenbaker and the Duplessis groups have been equally unsuccessful in our day. The successful party is based on the men of the centre.

This composite party, with membership from the two races, is always in a state of internal tension, and is frequently torn by dissension. Its unity is always somewhat doubtful, for French and English find it difficult to understand each other even when they can speak one another's language. What holds the party together in the end is the quality of its leaders, their determination to stick together personally through thick and thin, their loyalty to one another and fondness for one another — usually, also, their similarity in temperament as well as in political philosophy. The party, in effect, has had a joint leadership when it was most successful — Lafontaine and Baldwin, Macdonald and Cartier, King and Lapointe.

To judge from the fact that this experiment has been going on with more or less success continuously since the 1840s, this kind of a bi-racial party would seem to be essential if political co-operation between French- and English-Canadians is to work in practice. This is our *articulus stantis aut cadentis imperii*. It does not matter what else we may do or try to do in the next few years; if we can not keep in operation a governing party at Ottawa composed in this way, Confederation will fail. If leaders of the requisite quality, who will devote themselves to holding together a party of this kind, do not arise from both communal groups, Confederation will fail.

The most alarming feature of our present situation is that so many of the French leaders no longer seem to be led by ambition or by a wider patriotism to play their part in federal politics. If they are not attracted to our national capital, what hope is there of the ultimate loyalty of the masses of French-Canadians being attached to the larger Canadian experiment? The future of Confederation depends upon the future of this bi-racial, bi-cultural political party.

There is a great tradition in Quebec of service in this larger party; and it is one of Quebec's essential traditions, just as much as is the tradition of the narrow provincial nationalism — though there seems to be a strange reluctance among leading figures in Quebec just now to come out bluntly and say so. Consider the names that are attached to this wider national tradition: Lafontaine, Morin, Cartier, Dorion, Chapleau, Laurier, Lapointe, St. Laurent.

At present the more vocal nationalist thinkers in Quebec tend to sneer at efforts to make the Ottawa government work successfully, on the ground that Ottawa is in reality only the seat of an English-Canadian government, and that the only government that matters to French-Canadians is their own government in Quebec. They are forgetting a large part of their Quebec political history.

It is true that we English-Canadians, the overwhelming majority of us anyway, take for granted that our first loyalty is to the federal government in Ottawa rather than to our particular provincial government. Good heavens, how could a citizen of Ontario, since the days of the rise of Mitch Hepburn, possibly feel that he was first an Ontarioite and only secondly a Canadian? French-Canadians have found it more difficult to feel in this way, especially in this last generation when their younger men have been subjected to passionate teaching in the classical colleges, which inculcated narrow, provincialist nationalist doctrines. But Quebec's destiny as part of a larger whole has never quite disappeared from their minds as an ideal.

It was Bourassa who first enlarged the conception that French-Canadians had of themselves as full citizens of the Dominion, and who also unfortunately encouraged them toward a narrow, tribal nationalism. When he started his campaign against Laurier at the time of the Boer War, he was functioning, as he himself emphasized, as a Liberal. He was demanding that Canada's constitutional autonomy should not be infringed by a gradual process of getting entangled in British military imperialism overseas. This was a good Liberal cause; Laurier shared Bourassa's abhorrence of militarism and his constitutional objection to any infringement of Canadian autonomy. This was also a cause on which both French-Canadians and English-Canadians might be hoped to unite. They did rally around it in the next generation, in the King era. It might have been a great unifying cause in these early years of the twentieth century, as Bourassa hoped it would be.

But at the same time he was caught up in a great struggle for French rights within Canada. He put himself at the head of a campaign to protect these rights as he understood them, in the controversies, first, over schools in Saskatchewan and Alberta, and then, over schools in Ontario and Manitoba. He insisted that French-Canadians had the right to be equal citizens with English-Canadians all across Canada, and that they must not allow themselves to be herded into something like an Indian reserve in Quebec. This also was surely a good Liberal cause for which he was fighting. But he became so emotionally wrought up over it, so violent in his attacks on English-Canadians, that he defeated any hopes he might have had earlier of uniting the two races in a common Canadianism. His liberalism gradually transformed itself into a militant, ultramontane Catholicism. The Castor side of his nature overwhelmed the Rouge side. The issue of Regulation xvii overshadowed for him the issue of the war. The real enemy, he told his fellow French-Canadians, was not German militarism in Europe but Anglo-Saxon materialism in North America. Let the French-Canadians collect money, not for the wounded in France and Flanders, but for the French-Catholic sufferers in Ontario, *"les Blessés d'Ontario."*

And Laurier became to him more and more a pure villain. Laurier's doctrine of mutual concession became purely evil. "When Sir Wilfrid Laurier arrives at the gates of Paradise, the first thing he will do is to propose a compromise between God and Satan," he declared. This was a brilliant sarcastic sentence, not without considerable point. But it revealed more about Bourassa than about Laurier. Canadian domestic politics had become for him a struggle between God and the Devil. Peaceful constitutional politics is impossible on that basis.

Bourassa's pilgrimage of passion up and down Quebec inevitably stirred up an extremist form of Quebec provincial nationalism, especially among his excitable younger followers. Yet he himself never gave up his belief in the wider Canadian nation. The charge against him is that you cannot advance this wider nationality by preaching that the differences between the two branches of the nation are part of a great struggle between God and the Devil.

Later, after the war was over, Bourassa became critical of the excesses of this provincial nationalist spirit that he had helped to foster by his impassioned oratorical campaigns. In an audience with the Pope in 1926, he apparently received a long lecture on the evils that excessive nationalism of this kind was producing in the contemporary world and on the incompatibility of this kind of nationalism with the Catholic religion. When he came home, he proclaimed that his Catholicism was more important to him than his politics, and he tried to dampen down some of the racial feeling he had helped to stir up.

It would be difficult to over-emphasize the importance of Bourassa's career. He was one of our greatest Canadians. As an intellectual he insisted on issues always being clearly defined, and was thus a useful trouble-maker, though a confounded nuisance to the practical politicians of both parties who do not like to have party unity upset by too much clarity. He always saw the relation of Canadian issues to wider world affairs, and helped in this way to make his people, English-Canadian as well as French-Canadian, more mature. The process of becoming mature, however, is apt to be a painful one for peoples as well as for individuals. And you cannot unite a people in a common Canadianism by continuously declaiming at the top of your voice on the grievances that separate one group of Canadians from another.

The epigoni who followed Bourassa in Quebec narrowed his appeal, and the sad result is our present situation. We need a return to the spirit of Laurier.

Today, it seems to me, many of the claims put forward by the spokesmen of Quebec nationalism must be accepted as valid by reasonable English-Canadians. Equality is always a difficult concept to define in practice; but some of their claims to equality in our common country need wider recognition. However, the exaggerated language in which these claims are phrased, the presentation of claims in the form of ultimata, do not bode well for our future. What we should ask now of the spokesmen of Quebec is not so much a definition of what they claim for their province and for their racial group as of what they consider all of us still to have in common if their claims are granted. Nothing is so alarming in these French-Canadian speeches as the almost complete absence of any consideration of what French and English can still look forward to doing together through their common government in Ottawa, if Confederation is to continue for a second century. A nation is a body of men who have done great things together in the past and who hope to do great things together in the future. Confederation will not be saved by any new constitution-making between now and 1967 if the minds and hearts of men of both groups are not moved by dreams of the great things that we may yet do together in the future.

VI

Conclusions

My original intention, when I first made plans for these lectures, was to give them the general title of *The Canadian Rainbow*. I was borrowing from a French-Canadian of 1865, who was a member of the Canadian legislature in which the Confederation Debates took place — Henri Joly de Lotbinière. Joly was a Rouge, at that time a critic and opponent of the Confederation scheme, though he was later to have a distinguished career in the Dominion of Canada. He was a polished, urbane gentleman, a sceptic all his life about many of the passions and fanaticisms that swept over his fellow Canadians. On this occasion he allowed himself to wax ironical about the possibilities of the new Canadian nationality:

> I propose the adoption of the rainbow as our emblem. By the endless variety of its tints the rainbow will give an excellent idea of the diversity of races, religions, sentiments and interests of the different parts of the Confederation. By its slender and elongated

form the rainbow would afford a perfect representation of the geographical configuration of Confederation. By its lack of consistence — an image without substance — the rainbow would represent aptly the solidity of our Confederation. An emblem we must have, for every great empire has one; let us adopt the rainbow.

I think that we can all see the point of Joly's suggestion today.

But I came to feel, considering the seriousness of the crisis that we are now facing as we prepare to enter the second century of Confederation, that I might justly be accused of frivolity if I proposed today, a century after Joly, that we adopt the rainbow as our Canadian emblem. So I decided on a non-committal title, more fitting for a man of my years, and more fitting for this cautious, non-committal country of which I am a citizen; and I have called my series *The Image of Confederation*.

Joly, I hope you will have noticed, was using this concept of "image" as long ago as 1865, though we are apt to think of it as a very modern one, invented on Madison Avenue. I have been trying to suggest in these lectures that we have not yet arrived at any clear, distinctive image of Canada in our minds, that we have not achieved a sufficient degree of consensus about our national purposes and goals to satisfy either ourselves or outsiders as to what the word Canada means. We shall enter our second century without feeling very confident about the nature of our identity.

I have not tried to cover my subject in any comprehensive or complete manner. I have picked out for comment certain periods, such as that of the Unrestricted Reciprocity election of 1891 or of the Boer War, and certain themes, such as that of the Canada First movement or of English-French relations, in order to illustrate some of the major continuing controversies about our national purposes and goals in which we have been engaged. When I have talked about individuals, I have picked out mainly certain detached intellectuals, or some of the more intellectual of our statesmen, such as Laurier and Bourassa, rather than the practical men of action in politics and business on whom the stage-lights are focussed in most of the standard histories of Canada. It strikes me that, if we are to understand ourselves better, we need to devote a great deal more study to our intellectual history, to the values, to the guiding ideas and ideals, that have influenced the minds of different groups of Canadians at different times. This is what I have been trying to do in a sketchy way in these lectures.

"Our national purposes and goals." Some words of warning are needed here. We Canadians are not a people who have ever shown much aptitude or genius for whole-hearted, deeply felt dedication to purposes and goals beyond those of our particular individual lives. We differ from our American neighbours in this; for, from the moment that the Puritans landed in New England, they have conceived themselves as a people uniquely chosen by destiny to give the world a model of a new, finer civilization than Europe had been capable of producing, and to spread that civilization among more backward peoples. We ordinary Canadians lack the capacity to be caught up in a great crusade for an idea. And this statement is true both of French- and of English-Canadians.

The French were taught by their intellectual and spiritual leaders that their true function was to build up an agrarian peasant society, which would be an oasis of Catholic piety and virtue in the great North American desert of Anglo-Saxon industrialized commercialism. And, all the time, while they dutifully said yes to this proposition, they kept flocking into Montreal and smaller urban centres to work in factories. We English-Canadians dedicated ourselves to maintaining an identity separate from the American one; but, all the time, thousands of our best spirits kept emigrating to the United States, while those of us who remained behind steadily Americanized ourselves in our mass culture so that in our everyday life we became more and more indistinguishable from the Americans. And the most indistinguishable Canadians of all are our politicians who daily save us from the United States. Our capacity for a genuine dedication to national purposes and goals is definitely limited.

For, behind all this talk about loftier national purposes and goals, it is obvious that the individuals who make up our community have individual purposes. In a way, the cumulation of these individual purposes makes up a nation-wide purpose. But these individual purposes are what? — more money, more comfort, more apparatus of all kinds for affluent living, more status, more sex, more leisure, more self- and family-indulgence. The cumulation of such purposes stands in the way of a genuine emergence of any national purpose that might involve the disciplining or sacrificing of individual purposes, the putting of the general good ahead of the individual good and pleasure. This universal reaching out for "more" makes the mean sensual Canadian very much like the mean sensual American or Englishman or Frenchman or German. And we need to remember that in the Western world the men who have talked most loudly about national purpose in our generation were those who went on to impose a national purpose arbitrarily upon their people by means of an authoritarian totalitarian government. Perhaps this whole idea of a national purpose should meet with a certain amount of scepticism and suspicion when we contemplate it today.

With these qualifications in mind, let me turn to consider a little further some of the controversial issues with which I have been dealing in earlier lectures. Firstly, a little more about the form taken by our economic nationalism; and then about the issues of

English-French relations within Canada and about Canada's relations with Britain and with the United States.

Firstly, then, as to our Canadian economic nationalism. I pointed out in my third lecture that, during the generation after Confederation, we adopted a national policy based on economic expansion through railway building and tariff protection, a policy carried out under the leadership of, and for the primary benefit of, a group of great capitalist entrepreneurs working in close alliance with the national government. We have since then made no fundamental modification in this form of society. Other interests have learned how to organize themselves into effective pressure-groups; and the government, in the benefits that it has to distribute, tends to become a sort of arbitrator among competing groups. But in the economic jungle that results from this régime of Darwinian competition, the lion's share continues to be distributed to the lions.

At the end of World War I, there was a great protest movement against the domination of our society by these big-business tycoons in their offices in Montreal and Toronto. But the protest failed. The farm leaders of the prairie had a vision of what they called a New National Policy, a vision of an economy and policy based on freer trade with the outer world, on an international policy centring in the League of Nations, on public ownership and operation of the basic economic activities, on a system of politics emancipated from the control of the old parties, which, in their view, had become the instruments of big-business corporations in Montreal and Toronto. When I was a young man living on the prairies in the 1920s, this seemed to me the vision of a new dynamic democracy in which the common man might become an actively participating citizen instead of a passively manipulated consumer.

But the farmers' revolt, from the Progressive movement of the 1920s into the C.C.F. and Social Credit movements of the 1930s, did not turn out to be the springtime of a new era. It was really the last stand of agrarianism against the urbanization and industrialization of our society, against leadership by the big metropolitan centres. The farmers were unable to enlist the co-operation of the industrial workers in their trade unions. And the prairie fire sweeping eastward was stopped by the fire-break of the Ottawa River. For the French-Canadians remained aloof in the 1920s; and, when the depression of the 1930s at last produced upheavals in their society, these were canalized into narrow, racial, nationalistic channels, producing a variety of Sinn Fein nationalist movements. As for the Maritime provinces, nothing, of course, ever happens down there. For Canada as a whole, no new form of co-operation among racial and sectional groups in a programme of social reconstruction led by forces of the left came about. No new National Policy was worked out.

Since then, the western farmers, who once considered themselves the pioneers of a new national outlook, have sunk back into becoming a mere pressure-group, getting what they can out of the old society. They no longer aspire to the responsibility of thinking out the forms of a new society. If this task is to be undertaken today, it will have to be done by some groups in our urban centres — some middle-class groups, since the new trade unions of the 1930s have also sunk back into being just another pressure-group.

If we are to acquire a new image of ourselves and a new sense of purpose, what is needed is a great campaign of education and propaganda to raise us out of our narrow, inward-looking protectionism. What is really wrong with us, both French and English, is our belief that we can defend our identity by turning our backs upon the outer world, by retreating into ourselves. The French are going through an acute attack of this isolationist nationalism just now, which we English-Canadians profess to regard with the superior attitude of a broader-minded people. But the anti-Americanism that afflicts us in a virulent form just now is a disease of exactly the same nature. Canada needs an Adam Smith or a Cobden, backed by a movement something like that of the Anti-Corn-Law League of the 1840s, to tell us that the affluent life at which we aim cannot be attained if we shut ourselves into the limited intercourse, economic and intellectual, of our own local markets.

That radical farm movement, while it lasted, represented something else of significance in our Canadian experience. It was an outburst of local populist democracy, a rising up of the common people at the grass roots, who were refusing to accept the leadership that had hitherto provided both the ideology and the practical politics for our country. In our equalitarian North American society these outbursts of populist democracy, protesting against a central authority in the hands of the Top People of the Establishment, are endemic. They are healthy because they provide a popular balance against too much authority in the hands of an oligarchy at the centre. But in the complicated technology of modern society, populist democracy by itself is not enough. We need the guidance at the top of specialists, trained administrators, experts in economics, finance, and science, of men without whose advice the representatives of populist democracy are likely to go wildly astray.

Nevertheless, it was out of this populist democracy, in its more promising days after World War I, that there came the one creative idea in our contemporary generation of politics. The man whose name is most closely connected with it was J. S. Woodsworth. As Professor W. L. Morton has put it in his recent one-volume history, *The Kingdom of Canada*:

A social reformer of a prophetic more than a political bent, Woodsworth entered politics in a heroic endeavour to make society more humane . . . His principal work was a work of the spirit. More than any other Canadian public man, he helped transform Canadian politics from the politics of special sectional interests to the politics of collective concern for the welfare of the individual in a society collectively organized.[1]

Alas, our national life today is once again dominated by the politics of special sectional interests. The idea of a general national interest transcending these special and provincial interests seems unable to be born. It is time for a Canada First movement more sophisticated and more effective than the Canada First movement of the 1870s. We are in search of the next National Policy, on the basis of which a new national consensus can be built up. This will come when our imaginations are once more moved by a conception of the great things that are waiting for us to do together again in the future.

As things are, however, our national government in recent years has approached the ten lusty provincial governments, and especially that of Quebec, in an attitude of timorous politeness, as if apologizing for the fact of its own existence. And the Canadian people as a whole cannot apparently reach any agreement to entrust their fortunes to any one political party with a majority support. They watch apathetically while our unprotected federal quarterback, looking in vain for a pass receiver, is overrun by the big husky linemen of the provincial defensive team and thrown for another loss.

In an environment that changes every decade with the revolutionary advances of science and technology, our future depends on our flexibility, our adaptability to changing conditions. And this depends upon the quality of the education that we make available to our young people. This is a national interest that we all have in common; in the conditions of the second half of the twentieth century, our rigid division of powers in which we insist that education is a function belonging entirely to the provinces is self-defeating. In a world economy in which all groups are becoming daily more interdependent for their economic health and prosperity, we need a strong, well-equipped national government to direct and supervise the growth of our economy as a whole in its relations with the world as a whole. In a world divided as ours is into two great political blocs competing for power and for the minds of men, we need a strong national government to advance our conceptions of what constitutes the good society and to work in concert with like-minded governments. There is a great constructive role to be played in the Atlantic alliance by a power such as Canada, if we have a government equal to playing that role. And within our own domestic society, as we become a more and more industrialized and urbanized people, we need an active national government to deal with these new problems of urban civilization.

Yet it is at this time, confronted as we are by opportunities and dangers so momentous, that our ambitious provincial governments are doing their best to erode the basis of national authority and to add to their own importance and prestige. The assignment of greater responsibilities and greater financial resources to the provincial governments is, of course, in the interest of the provincial politicians and bureaucrats. I can see no evidence that it is necessarily in the interest of the people of the provinces who are also citizens and taxpayers of the Canadian national state.

In these circumstances, the case of Quebec presents us with a very difficult situation. That we should agree to the demands of the French-Canadians for equality of the French language in the sphere of the federal administration seems inevitable. That the English-speaking provinces should make concessions in the matter of language rights to the French minorities within their boundaries seems reasonable, though the extent of these concessions is debatable. But the Quebec conception of the future nature of our federal structure is another thing.

Quebec, through its premier, demands complete, exclusive control of all the new social services that have developed since Confederation and that — since they were not dreamt of by the Fathers in 1867 — have been assigned by the Privy Council to the provinces. But, while the B.N.A. Act is to be sacrosanct in the fullest interpretation that can be given to it of provincial rights, it is to be of little account in what it says of federal jurisdiction. For Quebec, so it appears, must also be consulted about federal monetary and fiscal policies, about tariffs, even apparently about some aspects of international policy. One wonders how the Quebec premier will find time both to run his own province and to keep the federal prime minister properly advised on how to run the Dominion. One wonders also what financial resources will be left to the Dominion after the claims of Quebec and the other provinces have been satisfied. To go to such lengths as this in the fragmentation of national unity seems a strange, fantastic way of celebrating the centenary of Confederation.

One can sympathize with the passion of French-Canadian leaders for recovering the control of their province from the English-Canadian and American big-business corporations who have come to dominate its economic life. But it must be pointed out also that no little local communities, whether they call themselves nations or not, can achieve full autonomy in this contemporary world of economic interdependence except at the price of seclusion and poverty. Though she is emancipating herself from clerical control, there still seem to be rather too many lay priests among the Quebec intellectuals who are giving the lead in the quiet revolution of their province — with an occasional lay bishop. And they still exhibit rather too much of the dogmatism, inflexibility, and fervour for isolation, that marked those former clerical prophets, Bishops Bourget and Laflèche.

One senses, also, as one reads them, that these intellectuals are suffering from that last infirmity of noble minds, the dream of a community in which intellectuals will function as Platonic philosopher-kings. Alas, intellectuals are always compelled, sooner or later, to wake up from this dream and to discover that the real kings are hard-boiled, practical administrators. It will not matter much whether these managers are at the head of socialist institutions in Quebec or not. They will be very much like the managers who run our English-Canadian, private-enterprise corporations. "There is more in common between two managers, one of whom is a socialist, than there is between two socialists, one of whom is a manager."

Let me go on to the question of the relations between Canada, Britain, and the United States.

Have we English-Canadians emancipated ourselves sufficiently from our old worship of Britain? It is obvious that most of the sentimental appeal that the Commonwealth has had for us has now degenerated into the ritual of after-dinner oratory. An Englishman[2] a short time ago referred to the Commonwealth in these terms: "As a stimulant nothing could be flabbier than the Commonwealth, that sop to our self-esteem, that dim intermittent vision of universal niceness." The British have, of course, been under the temptation to exalt the significance of the Commonwealth in world affairs in order to hide from themselves their own loss of the position of a great world power. But when Commonwealth ministers now try in conference to do something more specific than to summon up this vision of universal niceness, they usually find that they disagree and cannot reach a common policy.

To Canadians, the Commonwealth has always meant primarily our connection with Great Britain. This has fulfilled a necessary function for us, because, in the North Atlantic Triangle, Britain acted as a counterweight at one corner against the weight of the United States at another. We still need such a counterweight if we are to escape the necessity of confronting the United States all alone by ourselves here in North America. But Britain has no longer the power nor the economic capacity to provide that counter-terweight. It can only be provided by a strong united Western Europe of which Britain is an active and influential part. The failure of the rather half-hearted British attempt to enter the West European union was a major defeat for Canadian interests. We should have been much more vigorous in pushing Britain into Europe rather than in holding her back, whatever immediate short-term losses our trade might have suffered.

Of course, for the moment, this Atlantic Community, which I am holding up as an object of Canadian policy, has sunk to be almost as much a theme for pious incantation as is the British Commonwealth. President Kennedy's Grand Design was meeting with frustration before his death, both in the European foreign offices and the Congress of his own country. But this does not alter the fact that the Atlantic Community should be the grand design of Canadian policy also.

In the long run, this is the only way in which we shall be able to free ourselves from all our present neurotic anxiety as to whether we are capable of achieving a distinctive Canadian identity here on the North American continent. We need some constructive activity to take us out of ourselves and to save us from degenerating into the gloomy, bad-tempered Ulster of North America, forever brooding hysterically on the dangers of absorption by the more numerous and more lively people to the south of us. If we were playing a part in a vigorous and progressive Atlantic community, we would not be so obsessed by doubts as to our ability to continue to play an independent, self-respecting part in North America.

For we are inescapably North Americans. In the long run our Canadian civilization will be a North American one. It is foolish to hope for anything else. If we are eventually to satisfy ourselves that we have at last achieved a Canadian identity, it will be only when we are satisfied that we have arrived at a better American way of life than the Americans have. A better *American* way of life, not just a better way of life. Whether we have the capacity to reach that goal, nobody knows. Of course, we cannot produce such big business corporations and corporation managers as the American ones. Probably we cannot produce such big racketeers. We cannot produce such big universities or research laboratories or advertising agencies or entertainment industries. But we simply do not know in what fields we may be able to reach better forms of North American excellence, because we have not yet really tried.

This brings me to my last point. In the present circumstances, with our minds intent upon the commemoration of the first century of our Confederation, we are liable to become too self-centred. An inward-looking, self-centred nationalism is a dangerous thing. There are too many such nationalisms rampant in the world at present. So far as one can see, the nation-state is going to continue to be the unit in which peoples naturally group themselves. It will be through his membership in his national group that the individual will achieve his own personal identity. But the sovereign, autonomous, separatist nation-state is now obsolescent, and the nationalist faith of the nineteenth century needs to be expanded and transformed into something wider.

In 1867, our Fathers created something new, "a new national-ity." The best way in which we can commemorate their work is not by breaking up what they did but by going forward ourselves to create something new, some wider, international, transnational community, which will unite us more closely with other peoples. At any rate, let us try to make our Confederation a community that is outward- rather than inward-looking, a community that is ambitious to play a worthy part in the world at large.

Our American neighbours, since the tragedy in Dallas, have been going through a crisis of conscience. They are being led to confess to themselves that the assassination of President Kennedy was, only too clearly, the ultimate manifestation of the violence that has never been far from the surface in their national life, and that has erupted too frequently of late in the displays of hatred and bitterness between segregationists and integrationists, between rightists and leftists, between isolationists and internationalists. The more thoughtful of them have been speculating whether this most recent outburst of violence may produce a catharsis in their national life.

We Canadians are largely free from the violence and extremism in action that have marked the American experience. But we have been indulging of late in far too much extreme language to express the differences of opinion among the various groups who make up our Canadian community. And this extreme language has led us into a defeatist attitude of doubt as to whether the bonds that hold us together have any longer the old strength. As we approach 1967, it is time for us to turn our minds once again to the things that unite us as a people. A nation is a body of people who have done great things together in the past and who hope to do great things together in the future.

TIME AS HISTORY

by

GEORGE GRANT

I

Chapter One

"History" is one of the key words in which English-speaking people now express what they think they are and what they think the world to be. There are similar words in the other modern western languages. English, however, is our destiny, and it is now also the destiny of others. In the events of the last two hundred years, English has become the predominant language through which the culture of the western world expresses itself throughout the globe — whether for good or ill. The polyglot language from that small island off the north-west of Europe is now more than any other the "lingua franca." It is well to remember that in speaking our own, we are speaking a world language. And in that language the word "history" comes forth from lips and pens near the centre of what is most often said. "History will judge my Vietnam policies," says a president. "This is a history-making flight," says an astronaut. "History" demands, commands, requires, obliges, teaches, etc., etc.

Whatever may be, it is clear that human beings take much of what they are and what their world is through the way that words bring forth that world and themselves to themselves. Other words such as "freedom" and "value," "science" and "nature," "personality" and "attitudes" are also at the core of what we conceive ourselves to be. But "history" has particular significance because it is one of those words which is present for us and was not present in any similar sense in the languages of other civilizations — including those from which ours sprang.[1] Therefore if we desire to understand our own understanding of ourselves, it is well to think about this word which has come to have such a unique connotation amongst us.

It is not in language in general, but in the words of one collective that the world and ourselves are opened to us. In all groups of languages, for example the European or the Indic, certain languages such as Sanskrit or Greek appear marvellously to transcend limitation, and so have been thought of as called forth for a universal destiny. However, the very liberation through language takes place by the moulding of particular forms. Like food, language not only makes human existence possible, but can also confine it. It is, therefore, useful to think about those parts of our language which particularly express our civilization, and to judge just how these key words have come to determine our apprehensions of what is.

Anybody aware of living in the spearhead of modernity as a North American hears much talk about a crisis in our life. Indeed one manifestation of that crisis is the division between us as to whether the crisis is fundamental. Many of our rulers seem to assume that our way of life may have faults in detail but that basically we are on the right track and that our civilization is the highest ever. On the other hand, significant minorities see what is happening as more than a crisis of detail. Western civilization becomes world-wide just as it becomes increasingly possible for some to doubt its assumptions.

The causes of that doubting cannot be fully described in language that concentrates simply on either outward or inward phenomena. To speak of outward problems, of cities, water and air, poverty, monstrous weapons and expanding populations, is not sufficient. On the other hand to speak of such inward difficulties as banality in education, alienation from meaning, and widespread nihilism is also not sufficient. Whatever the distinction between outward and inward may mean, our present uncertainties can only be held in our minds by transcending such a distinction. If there be a crisis, it is a crisis about what we are and what we are becoming, both inward and outward. Language itself transcends the distinction between inward and outward. We can hear it and measure it as sound waves; at the same time we know the difference between listening to a foreigner whose speech is meaningless sounds to us, and listening to someone speaking in a language we know and conveying to us intelligible meanings. Like sexuality or religion or music, language transcends the inward-outward distinction.

In this crisis of our present lives in North America, an effort is required to think what we have become. That is manifested to us in language, and central to our language is the word "history." To use then the very language that encloses us, it may be said that one of our present historical tasks is to think what we are summing up to ourselves when we use the word "history." To touch upon that task is the purpose of the following pages.

"History" is used for many different purposes in our language with shades of differing meaning. There is one division of its use, however, which is more important than any other and which is often a cause of ambiguity. On the one hand the word is used to denote an activity which some men pursue — the study of the past. It is also used to denote a certain kind of reality — human existing — the whole of which, whether in the past, present or future, we call "history," and which is distinguished from other kinds of existing. The ambiguity caused by this central division of usage can be seen when we compare the words "history" and "biology." In our educational institutions we study "life," not in departments of life, but in departments of biology or in departments of the life sciences. On the other hand, we study history in departments of history, thus using the same word both for the study and what is studied.

Some people like to describe this fact by speaking of the subjective and objective uses of the word "history"; the subjective being the activity of studying, the objective being what is studied. This subjective-objective language about the two uses is misleading, because history as a sphere of reality is something in which we take part, and which is therefore only an object for us in the most artificial sense of the word "objective." There is indeed an English word "historiology" meaning the study of history. In some ways our language would be clearer if we used that word for the study of history, and kept the word "history" and "historical" for a special dimension of existence. In fact, we are not going to use the word "historiology" (technical pedantry does not yet entirely determine the development of our language), and therefore the ambiguity of using the same word to describe a dimension of reality and the study of that dimension is going to stay with us. The Germans are coming to make this distinction more clearly in their language by the use of two separate words: "*Geschichte*" for that particular realm of being, historical existence, and "*Historie*" for the scientific study of the past. Perhaps in English the word "history" should be kept for the systematic study of the past, while we should find some other word to denote the course of human existence in time. Certainly the Greek original "*historie*" was used to denote some kinds of human inquiry. It is easy to see how the word for inquiry moved in the direction of the study of human affairs. If you wanted to inquire about an event far away in time or space, you went and asked an old person or somebody in another country. Thereby a general word for inquiry came to be used for what had happened in human affairs.

The two uses of the word "history" — as a study and as an aspect of reality — cannot finally be separated because they are interdependent. We see the enormous interest in the last two hundred years in the study of man's past from the way that resources have been poured into those studies. Men spend a lifetime understanding the administrative details of earlier empires; a day to day description of the literary life of eighteenth-century London is available to us. This would be unlikely outside the belief that knowledge about man will be brought forth by the assiduous study of his genesis and development. Thousands of grown men have believed that they could penetrate to the core of the Christian religion by historical studies about its origins. In other civilizations, men have been quite interested in their past, but never with the passion and hope for illumination therefrom which have characterized western historical studies. This is surely because we have believed that man is essentially an historical being and that therefore the riddle of what he is may be unfolded in those studies. The thinkers of other societies have not believed that man was finally understandable as an historical being. Our interest in history as a study is directly related to our belief that we are historical beings.

It may be argued that the word "history" to distinguish human existence from that of stones and animals is poor usage, because we now know that birds and stars have a history as much as men. Two of the great scientific achievements of the nineteenth century were the discovery of the history of the earth in geology and of the development of life in evolutionary biology. When pre-modern biology, with its doctrine of unchanging species, is compared with modern biology, which accounts for the origin of species, (how they came to be and their development through time), one must surely say that the earth and the beasts have history as much as man. Indeed in modern thought the idea of history is everywhere. Not only men and stones and animals have history, but philosophers such as Whitehead write as if God has a biography. Even reason, which was traditionally conceived as transcending all development, has been given its own history. The most beautiful modern book on the subject, Kant's *Critique of Pure Reason*, ends with a section on the history of pure reason.[2] The modern concentration on man as historical is but an aspect of a whole way of conceiving temporality, which, it is claimed, allows us to understand more adequately the story not only of our own species, but of everything. In such a usage, the account of man's collective development through the ages is held together with the development of other beings, for example, the beasts evolving and the earth coming to be through millennia. The word "history" does not mean a particular kind of reality, because it is used about all forms of reality. It is what we must know about something to understand that something. To know about anything is to know its genesis, its development up to the present and as much of its future as we can. Perhaps it may be said that the greatest difference between the ancient and modern accounts of knowledge is this modern concentration on the genesis of something in order to know it. History (call it, if you will "process") is that to which all is subject, including our knowing, including God, if we still find reasons for using that word.

Yet as soon as this is said we must see that within the modern project the human is at other times clearly distinguished from the non-human, and the word "history" appropriated for this distinction. "History" is distinguished from "nature." The modern physics of Galileo, Descartes, and Newton accounted for the "physical" world (including our own bodies) as understandable in terms of mechanics, and without final cause. But immediately, questions about men arose for those who so conceived nature; how men, who are part of such a nature, have still the freedom to know it, and even more, how their determination by this nature affects their freedom to do good or evil. Those thinkers who were unwilling to reduce what they considered the undoubted "given" of morality, and at the same time accepted the new account of nature, reconciled any difficulty in so doing by showing forth our lives as lived in two realms — that of nature and that of freedom. It was indeed in this intellectual crisis (the attempt to understand the modern scientific conception of nature, which excluded any idea of final purpose, and to relate that conception to human purposiveness) that the modern conception of history first made its appearance in the thought of men such as Rousseau, Kant, and Hegel. The realm of history was distinguished from the realm of nature. "History" was used to describe the particular human situation in which we are not only made but make. In this way of speaking, history was not a term to be applied to the development of the earth and animals, but a term to distinguish the collective life of man (that unique being who is subject to cause and effect as defined in modern science, but also a member of the world of freedom).

As a North American, living outside Europeanness, and yet inheriting from many sides of the European tradition, it is perhaps worth stating that by and large it has been the English thinkers who have insisted that we apply the word "history" to stones and birds as well as to man, while it has been the German and French thinkers who have insisted on the unique human situation, and who have used the distinction between nature and history to make that clear. To them, man alone should be called essentially historical, because he not only suffers history, but in freedom can make it.

Both these ways of looking at man and the world are but facets of modernity. Indeed these two languages are used together in the sermons preached by our journalists about the achievement of landing on the moon. These events are called another upward step in the march of evolution, one of the countless steps since life came out of the sea. Man and nature are seen together. On the other hand in the same sermons, there is talk of man in his freedom conquering nature, indeed transcending himself. In as archetypal an event for technological man as the space programme, it is right that the two languages should come together in the hymning of the achievement. The two languages come together as man is seen not only as a part of evolution, but as its spearhead who can consciously direct the very process from which he came forth. In such speaking, man is either conceived as the creator, who arose from an accidental evolution, or if evolution is itself conceived within a terminology about the divine, man is then viewed as a cooperator, a co-creator with God. This latter language is presently very popular in the United States, particularly among those who want to include Christian or Jewish theology within the liberal idealogy of their society.

However these two sides of the modern project may be put together, my purpose is to write about the word "history" as it is used about existence in time, not as it is used to describe a particular academic study. I am not concerned with historical inquiry, its proper purposes and methods, to what extent it is a science and if a science how it differs from physics or mathematics, to what extent we can have correct knowledge of the past, etc., etc. These are technical questions for those who earn their living by being historians, or philosophers of historiology, and want to think about how best to practise their profession. All such professions, be they practical arts or theoretical sciences or a mixture of both — physicists, historians, dentists — have their own trade papers in which the methods of their particular occupation are discussed. Such occupational matters are not my business. I am concerned with what it means to conceive the world as an historical process, to conceive time as history and man as an historical being.

Words such as "time" arise from the fact that existing is a coming to be and a passing away. Our doing and our making (perhaps even our thinking) occur within time's thrall. Because "has been," "is now," and "will be" make possible our purposes but also dirempt us of them, it is no wonder that through the ages men have tried to understand the temporality of their lives. In our age, astonishment about that temporality has been calmed by apprehending it above all as history. It is this conception of time as history that I wish to try to enucleate.

To enucleate means to extract the kernel of a nut, the seed of a tree. In the present case, there appears around us and in us the presence which western men have made — modern technical society. It has been made by men who did what they did out of a vision of what was important to do. In that vision is the conception of time as history. The word "enucleation" implies that I am not simply interested in describing the manifestations of that vision, for example the mastery of movement through space or the control of heredity. Rather I try to partake in the seed from which the tree of manifestations has come forth. But the metaphor fails because to extract a kernel may be to expose it as a dead thing rather than as a potential tree. In another age, it would have been proper to say that I am attempting to partake in the soul of modernity. When we are intimate with another person we say that we know him. We mean that we partake, however dimly, in some central source from which proceeds all that the other person does or thinks or feels. In that partaking even his casual gestures are recognized. That source was once described as the character of his soul. But modern knowing, in a strict sense, has excluded the conception of the soul as a superstition, inimical to scientific exactness. To know about human beings is to know about their behaviour and to be able to predict therefrom. But it is not about the multiform predictable behaviours of modern technical society that I wish to write. It is about the animating source from which those behaviours come forth.

What I am not doing is what is done by modern behavioural social science, which is not interested in essences. A leading behavioural political scientist, Mr. David Easton, said recently: "We could not have expected the Vietnam war." This was said by a man whose profession was to think about political behaviour in North America, and whose methods were widely accepted by other scientists. But not to have expected the Vietnam war was not to have known that the chief political animation of the United States is that it is an empire. My use of the word "enucleate" indicates that I do not wish to use a method which cannot grasp such animations.

To write of the conception of time as history and to think of it as an animator of our existence is not, however, to turn away from what is immediately present to all of us. When I drive on the highways around Hamilton and Toronto, through the proliferating factories and apartments, the research establishments and supermarkets; when I sit in the bureaucracies in which the education for technocracy is planned; when I live in and with the mechanized bodies and resolute wills necessary to that system; it is then that the conception of time as history is seen in its blossoming. An animating vision is not known simply in a retired academic thinking, but in the urgent experience of every lived moment. The words used to explicate "time as history" may seem abstract, but they are meant to illuminate our waking and sleeping hours in technical society.

II

Chapter Two

Those who study history are concerned with the occurrences of passed times; those who conceive time as history are turned to what will happen in the future. When we speak of the present historical situation we are oriented to the future, in the sense that we are trying to gather together the intricacies of the present so that we can calculate what we must be resolute in doing to bring about the future we desire. The accomplishments of modern society are every year more before us, not simply as they once were as hoped for dreams, but as pressing realizations. The magnitude of those modern accomplishments, as compared with those of other civilizations, lies in what they enable us to do by our mastery through prediction over human and non-human nature. These accomplishments were the work of men who were determined to make the future different from what the past had been; men oriented to that future in which greater events than have yet been, will be. They conceived time as that in which human accomplishments would be unfolded; that is, in the language of their ideology, as progress. Whatever differences there may have been between the three dominant ideologies of our century — Marxist communism, American liberalism, national socialism — they all similarly called men to be resolute in their mastery of the future. Four centuries ago, those who thought of mastering the future were a dreaming minority, forced to work subtly against those with some other account of time. Today such men are our unquestioned rulers, welcomed by the overwhelming majority in both east and west. To enucleate the conception of time as history must then be to think our orientation to the future together with the will to mastery. Indeed the relation between mastery and concentration on the future is apparent in our language. The word "will" is used as an auxiliary for the future tense, and also as the word which expresses our determination to do.

Men have always attempted to understand what is meant by the future and what knowledge or control we can have of it. Certainly we must make the limited statement that a future awaits, and in that sense is an inescapable presence for us. When young we must be turned to the future for the realization of our potentialities, and we are aware of the future even as it becomes slowly clear that eventually and inevitably there will be no future for us as individuals. We die in the knowledge that tomorrow's dawn will not be present for us. We may be so egocentric that in that dying we hardly care about its coming for others. But can we reach that pitch of solipsism in which we are able to think that our death is the end of the world? In these atomic days the end of the race as a whole can easily be imagined; but imagining includes the sun rising over a humanless planet. Whatever certain modern philosophers have meant by the mind making the object, they did not mean that we could deny a future in our imagining. Whatever the physicists may mean in showing us the increasing randomness of the elementary things, they are not asking us to think what it would be for nothing to be happening. Some theologians have conceived time as a creature. But to use that language sensibly (that is not as some extension from human making to explain our dependence upon God) it must be recognized that the language of creation leaves us always with the question: what does it mean to speak of the end of time? — certainly not, after time. The word "creativity" is only properly used about God and not about man. It is an abyss in which the human mind is swallowed up, and those of us who use it must recognize it as such a limit. It is not possible to imagine what it would be for nothing (or better for no event) to be occurring. To speak of the future as potential and not actual, does not deny its presence for us. Those of our contemporaries who, in their revolt against the doctrine of progress and its concentration on living for the future, assert that living is always in the present are saying something North Americans need to hear. But they distort the truth about time, if in so saying they assume that the future is not with us, although in a less articulated presentation.

Yet that which is there for us potentially can only be there in an undetailed way. In the public world, who would have guessed in the early 1960s that the Kennedy dynasty would move into the 1970s with an uncertain political future, while Mr. Nixon would be in the seat of political authority?

To deny all chance in the name of a predicting science may be logically possible but the nearer we get to the details of life, the more clearly it invalidates common sense. Yet the inscrutability and unpredictability of events must not be over-emphasized, in either the individual or the collective case. We can plan our lives so that within limits the future depends on what we have done and are doing. This is truer collectively than individually because of the greater ability of the collective to control the results of chance. The success of the planned moon landing did not fluctuate because of the assassination of the president who had made the decision that it was to be an imperial purpose. (Indeed the greater ability of collective than of individual purposes to be sustained against accidents is one of the reasons why, in an age given over to making the future, we all more and more truly exist in the collective, and less and less pursue purposes which transcend it.) Indeed our surrender to the oil cartels has taught us ecologically that the best laid schemes o' mice an' men gang aft a-gley. It would be however facile pessimism to carry the tag too far. Human purposive doing is both possible and potent. And the more complex that which we wish to accomplish, the more we have to envisage the future in which it will be accomplished.

The presence of the future in our imagining is one reason why men are so effective in their doing. It is not necessary to be able to define satisfactorily the difference between men and the other animals to recognize that human beings are able to accomplish more purposes than the members of other species. Both men and the other animals are in an environment in which their food and their shelter, their protection and their continuance, are not given to them without organization. They have to take continuing steps in arranging and using other parts of nature so that these ends can be achieved. (By way of parenthesis I would say that in the past at least, those nations and classes within nations who have come through generations of ease to take their food, shelter, and protection for granted, as given in the nature of things, have not long survived. Some now hope that this is no longer the case.) But men are so much more potent and therefore so much more violent than other animals in this using and arranging. Other species also have histories — for example, certain birds changed their migrations after the glacial age. But human beings have more history because they are capable of more differentiated doing, and this capability depends upon openness to an imagined future and the power to plan toward that future. Whatever is the correct use of the word "novelty," we can bring more novelty into the future than any other species. To deny novelty may be to speak in some true way which moderns cannot penetrate, but it is at least contradicted in common sense understanding, by many human projects.

The more we are concentrated on the future as the most fascinating reality, the more we become concentrated on that side of our existence which is concerned with making happen. The more we can make happen novel events which come forth in the potential future, the more properly can we be called historical beings. When we single out somebody as an historical individual, or a people as an historical people, we surely mean that those in question have been in their doing the makers of events. Thus the English were an historical people in harnessing new power to industry, and in beating their European rivals in taking it around the world. In our generation Chairman Mao is an historical individual in bringing European technology to the Chinese masses, by uniting Chinese and European politics. In this sense we can say that just as men are more historical than other animals, so in the last centuries western men have been more historical than the other civilizations still present, and than those civilizations we superseded geographically. Ours has been a dynamic civilization and that dynamism has been related to the fact that our apprehension of temporality was concentrated on the future. "Has been" and "is now" weakened in our consciousness compared with "will be." The concentration upon time as future and the dynamism of doing fed upon each other. As westerners found their hope in an imaginable future, they turned more and more to mastery; their concentration on mastery eliminated from their minds any partaking in time other than as future. Equally, the clarification of this conception of time by thinkers and the intensified making of novelty by practical men were mutually interdependent. As

Europeans achieved more and more mastery through their works, thinkers increasingly defined time as history. As words such as "progress" and "history" were placed in the centre of the most comprehensive thought, so practical men were encouraged thereby to justify their conquests as the crown of human activity. Also (as I have tried to describe elsewhere) we North Americans whose ancestors crossed the ocean were, because of our religious traditions and because this continent was experienced as pure potentiality (a tabula rasa), the people most exclusively enfolded in the conception of time as progress and the exaltation of doing which went with it.[1] We were to be the people who, after dominating two European wars, would become the chief leaders in establishing the reign of technique throughout all the planet and perhaps beyond it.

The accomplishments of masterful doing lead us to think about the language of willing. When we say that somebody has a strong will we mean that there is a resoluteness through time about his determination to carry out his purposes in the world. It says little about how much he may have deliberated about those purposes, nothing about their nobility. To state the obvious: in a university one knows many thoughtful people, irresolute in decision; in the political world one meets decisive men whose purposes are little deliberated. For example, in the regime of the Kennedys there was much rhetoric about decisiveness, but we may well ask (in the light of the results of their decisions, for example toward South East Asia or toward De Gaulle) whether there was sufficient deliberation on what it was important to be decisive about. The language surrounding the word "will" summons up human doing and distinguishes it from our thinking or feeling. I do not wish here to give a justification of what is currently described and abused as faculty psychology: the doctrine which speaks of a power of human beings to will, to think, to suffer, etc. We need, however, some language that catches the determination necessary to our doings, and distinguishes that from our other activities. When Shakespeare writes of the Macbeths' determination to be rulers, he puts into Lady Macbeth's mouth the following words to her husband at their decisive moment: "But screw your courage to the sticking-place, and we'll not fail." What is required of them is not further thought about their desire to rule, nor further calculation about the means to that end, but an unflinching "will" to carry out the deeds which she believes will realize what they want.

The language of will that summons forth for us the deeds of men is found in many civilizations — not only among people who conceive time as history. But the language of willing has been at the very core of western men's account of themselves. However, the reference of that language is often uncertain. Some have used it as if willing were simply a kind of thinking; others as if it were desiring. Neither seems to me satisfactory. Therefore, to approach the language of "willing" it is useful to relate it to our "desiring" and "thinking" and then to distinguish it therefrom.

What we are determined to do is clearly related to our thought about purposes and our calculating about the means to those purposes. But however long and beautifully men deliberate about purposes, however carefully they calculate, there comes the moment when they either bring about or do not bring about certain events. Willing is that power of determining by which we put our stamp on events (including ourselves) and in which we do some violence to the world. In willing to do or not to do we close down on the openness of deliberation and decide that as far as we are concerned, this will happen rather than that. Indeed, one strange ambiguity among human beings is that what seems required for the greatest thought is opposite to what is required for the greatest doing. If our thinking is not to be procrustean, we require an uncertain and continuous openness to all that is;

certainty in closing down issues by decision is necessary for great deeds. In thought about the most important matters there is nothing we need do, there is nothing we can wish to change.

It is more difficult to distinguish the language of willing from desiring, particularly because of the history of the English language. Indeed from the changes in the use of the word "will" can be seen the changes in what men thought they were. In its beginnings the word "will" is most often used synonymously with wishing or wanting or desiring, and yet also it is used in the sense of determining or making happen.[2] When we use the erotic language of wanting or desiring, we express our dependence on that which we need — be it food, another person, or God. The language of desire is always the language of dependence. Some English uses of "willing" are closely identified with this language of need. Yet as we enter the modern era the language of will comes more and more to be used about making happen what happens. Here it becomes the assertion of the power of the self over something other than the self, and indeed of the self over its own dependencies. The dependence of desire passes over into the mastery. In related language, Kant, who always so brilliantly expressed what it is to be a modern as against a classical man, made the modern use clear when he maintained that we cannot will a purpose without willing means to bring it about. "To wish" or "to want" can be casual when we are not serious about what happens in the world; "to will" means that we are serious about actualizing our purposes. To will is to legislate; it makes something positive happen or prevents something from happening. Willing is then the expression of the responsible and independent self, distinguished from the dependent self who desires.

Indeed as soon as we look at the modern era, we see how the language of willing has taken on a significance not present in other civilizations. On Marx's tomb at Highgate in London is inscribed his most famous aphorism: "The philosophers have only interpreted the world in various ways. The point, however, is to change it."[3] Here we are called to master the world through our doing and to make it as we want it. Greek heroes were summoned to be resolute for noble doing, but their deeds were not thought of as changing the very structure of what is, but as done rather for the sake of bringing into immediacy the beauty of a trusted order, always there to be appropriated through whatever perils. In the modern call, human wills are summoned to a much more staggering challenge. It is our destiny to bring about something novel; to conquer an indifferent nature and make it good for us. Indeed in that summons our wills come to be thought of as operating within a quite different context. Human willing is no longer one type of agent in a total process of natural agents, all of which are directed toward the realization of good purposes. We now see our wills as standing above the other beings of nature, able to make these other beings serve the purposes of our freedom. All else in nature is indifferent to good. Our wills alone are able, through doing, to actualize moral good in the indifferent world. It is here that history as a dimension of reality, distinguished from nature, comes to be thought. History is that dimension in which men in their freedom have tried to "create" greater and greater goodness in the morally indifferent world they inhabit. As we actualize meaning, we bring forth a world in which living will be known to be good for all, not simply in a general sense, but in the very details we will be able more and more to control. Time is a developing history of meaning which we make. The self-conscious animal has always been plagued by anxiety as to whether it is good to be in the world. But to modern man, though life may not yet be meaningful for every one, the challenge is to make it so. Upon our will to do has been placed the whole burden of meaning.

To distinguish the language of willing and thinking, and then to say that modern life has near its centre the will's challenge to itself to make the world, must in no way imply that the modern world is not made by reasoning. Such an implication would be absurd because it would disregard the chief mark of the modern era — the progress of the sciences. The systematic use of reasoning and experimenting in order to know objectively — that is for knowledge to be accumulated collectively by the race through the generations — has been and is increasingly the central achievement of our civilization. Indeed the idea of time as history was more shaped in response to the progressive sciences than by anything else. In the methodology by which the scientists of the last centuries carried out their activities, the race had at last found the sure and certain path which would guarantee that knowledge would increase among men, collectively. The belief in progress gained its power over the minds of intelligent men through this recognition, more than through anything else. The will to change the world was a will to change it through the expansion of knowledge.

This is how willing and reasoning have come together in the modern era. At a superficial level it is obvious that the ability of men to discover how the world works can be used to improve the conditions of man's estate. This relation between the discoveries of science and their use for human good has been the cause of the great public respect for the scientist. But leaving the matter there might imply that the modern relation between willing and reasoning is an external one, in which practical men simply turn into technology what the scientists happen to discover. Such a conception leads to the false view that the relation between technology and science is an external, not an intrinsic one. It leads to that popular falsehood, namely that scientists just find out what their pure curiosity leads them to, and that it is up to society to decide whether that knowledge be used for good or ill. Such statements must be denied, not because they might free scientists from responsibility for the results of their discoveries, but because they imply a false description of what scientists do.

The coming together of willing and reasoning lies essentially in the method which has made possible the successes of modern science. The world is a field of objects which can be known in their workings through the "creative" acts of reasoning and experimenting by the thinking subject who stands over them. This brings together willing and reasoning, because the very act of the thinking-ego standing over the world, and representing it to himself as objects, is a stance of the will. This statement could only be substantiated by a careful analysis of the work of the greatest modern scientists and philosophers; how they illuminated what they were doing in their science. It would require thinking through what they meant by such words as "object" and "subject," "representation" and "experiment," what the word "technique" has come to mean for us, and above all what is now meant by "mathematics."[4] I have not the time to do that here nor indeed the capability. But in turning from this question, I leave incomplete the enucleation of what we are thinking when we think time as history. However, as the methods of modern science are more and more applied to understanding human beings, in what are now called "the social sciences," it becomes easier to grasp what is meant by our science being a kind of willing, because in the social sciences the stance of the subject-scientist standing over against the object-society has very immediate and pressing consequences for us, since we are the objects.

When Marx wrote of changing the world, he still believed that changing was not an end in itself, but the means to a future society conducive to the good life for all. Overcoming the chances of an indifferent nature by technique and politics was an interim stage until conditions should be ripe for the realization of men's potential goodness. For all his denial of past thought, he retained from that past the central truth about human beings — namely, that there is in man a given humanness which it is our purpose to fulfill. So equally in the sentimentalized Marxism of Marcuse, the victory of the will over nature is not an end in itself, but simply a means to that time when men will find happiness in the polymorphous liberation of their instincts. The burden on the will to make the meaning of the world is thus limited by the belief that in some unspecified future the age of willing will be at an end. Even the traditional capitalist ideologists, who believed that changing the world was best achieved by sanctifying greed, had some vision of the fulfilled state of man (albeit a vulgar one) which transcended changing the world.

In the conceptions of history now prevalent among those "creative" men who plan the mastery of the planet, changing the world becomes ever more an end in itself. It is undertaken less simply to overcome the natural accidents which frustrate our humanity and more and more for the sheer sake of the "creation" of novelty. This movement inevitably grows among the resolute as the remnants of any belief in a lovable actuality disappear. We will, not so much for some end beyond will, but for the sake of the willing itself. In this sense, the challenge of the will is endless to the resolute, because there is always more "creation" to be carried out. Our freedom can even start to make over our own species.

As Hegel so clearly expounded, doing is in some sense always negation. It is the determination that what is present shall not be; some other state shall. But it is positive in the sense that in its negating of what is, it strives to bring forth its own novel "creations." In this sense the burden of "creation" itself is placed upon us. Resoluteness for that task becomes the key virtue for the history makers — a resoluteness which finds the sources of novelty in their own "values." They assert that meaning is not found in what is actually now present for us, but in that which we can yet bring to be.

III

Chapter Three

An obvious question is why the conception of time as history came to its flowering in the west, rather than in one of the other great civilizations. Why have western men come to think as they think and do as they do? Why was it our destiny to raise up "willing" and "orientation to the future" so that they have become universal ways of men's existing? As in the most hidden aspects of our lives we cannot come to know ourselves without recognizing our own familial histories, in all their idiosyncrasy, so equally we cannot know ourselves without recognizing how our enfolding civilization came to be what it is. Such a search for recognition must start from the truism that the two chief sources of modern "westernness" are the Bible and the relics of Greek civilization. However, care must be taken that this truism is not turned into the idea that the origins of our "rationality" are Greek, while we receive our "religion" from the Bible. This is a distortion of our origins, because both among the Greeks and in the Bible thought and reverence are sustained together. Also as these origins came out into the west they were held together in ways "too deep, too numerous, too obscure, even simply too beautiful for any ease of intellectual relation." Many of the deepest controversies in which western men have defined what they are have been centred around the proper ways of relating or distinguishing what was given to them from Athens and Jerusalem.

If we were searching for the origins of our present, we would first try to state what was given to men in Judaism or Christianity, and then seek out how this intermingled with the claims of universal understanding which were found in the heights of Greek civilization. As Christianity was the majoritarian locus in which that intermingling occurred, we would have to examine how it was that Christianity so opened men to a particular consciousness of time, by opening them to anxiety and charity; how willing was exalted through the stamping proclamations of the creating Will; how time was raised up by redemption in time, and the future by the exaltation of the "eschaton." But to recognize ourselves today, we cannot turn simply to our origins in Athens and Jerusalem, because those "aitia" are obscured for us by the massive criticism which the thinkers and scientists and scholars have carried on for the last centuries. That criticism so penetrates every part of our education that we cannot hope to reach back easily to make these origins present. Indeed even that penetrating criticism — which scholars hypostasize as the Enlightenment — is itself ambiguous in so far as it is penetrated by an acceptance of certain aspects of that which was being criticized. This is just the truism that the modern conception of progress may be characterized as secular Christianity. As in the relations of children and parents, the conception of time as history in its first optimistic and liberal formulation was at one and the same time a critical turning away from our origins and also a carrying along of some essential aspects of them. Even today as the liberal formulation of time as history disappears before the hammer blows of the twentieth century, we are left with a more frightening conception of time as history which holds within it that presence of anxiety and willing which came from our particular origins.

However, it is not possible in lectures such as these to sort out the complexity of the geneses of what we now are. Therefore I turn away from a search for the fundamentals of the western past to the thoughts of that writer where the conception of time as history is most luminously articulated.

Nearly a hundred years ago Nietzsche thought the conception of time as history more comprehensively than any other modern thinker before or since. He did not turn away from what he thought. That is, for good or ill, he accepted "*en pleine conscience de cause*" that temporality enfolds human beings and that they experience that temporality as history. Yet he also understood, better than any other thinker, the profundity of the crisis that such a recognition must mean for those who have accepted it. Therefore in trying to follow Nietzsche's thought, we can go further in thinking what it means to conceive that time is history. Moreover, in looking at the flowering tree at the height of its wildest blooming, we are not far from its seed and its seed bed.

There are certain difficulties which stand in the way of English-speaking people listening seriously to Nietzsche. The cataclysms of violence which have occurred between the English-speaking peoples and the Germans, in this century, make it hard for us to look at the German tradition without suspicion. Many English-speaking intellectuals write about Nietzsche in the tone of personal discrediting. This often has the mark of those who wish to inoculate themselves against thoughts they do not want to think by calumniating the author of those thoughts. Although we can exclude by such inoculation the thought of Nietzsche explicitly from our minds, we are still caught in its implicit presence. For example, modern sociology is central to our North American way of living. The chief founder of that sociology was Max Weber. And certainly Weber's sociology must be taken, more than anything else, as a commentary on his engrossed encounter with Nietzsche's writings.

In much writing in English, Nietzsche is spoken of as a second rate poet masquerading as a philosopher, or as an aphorist who did not face questions comprehensively, or as a romantic of the feelings who was not concerned with science. His thoughts are impugned by the fact that he retreated into madness (to use that ambiguous word). In the worst condemnation he is accused of being a fountainhead of National Socialism and open to what is called today anti-Semitism. (Anti-Judaism is a more accurate name for that baseness.)

To start from the worst of these accusations, Nietzsche's works are filled with his loathing of anti-Judaism and of his understanding of its particular danger in certain German circles. He clearly would have been disgusted by the Nazis, that union of a desperate ruling class, of romantic nationalism among the bourgeoisie, and the industrial gutter. As for romanticism, his deepest book is indeed in dramatic form, a conscious parody of the New Testament, which sometimes breaks into poetic utterance. But his other writings are in limpid prose which expounds difficult philosophic questions with breath-taking clarity. This picture of Nietzsche as a second rate romantic poet was partly created among the English by the absurd early translations of his work. His German was translated into a phoney Gothic English, filled with words such as "thou" and "spake." Above all, this obscured Nietzsche's great wit with a patina of pretentiousness. In fact, there are few works of modern comedy which could rank beside *The Case of Wagner*. As for modern science, nobody ever more emphasized its achievements, took these achievements to be the centre of the modern world, and pondered on the nature of that science. It shows a good understanding of the course of modern science to predict in the 1870s: "The dynamic interpretation of the world will shortly gain power over the physicists." He was, at twenty-four, a professor of philology at a great European university. It is indeed true that he spent the last years of his life in madness. One must remember, however, that he was the first thinker to bring out the very great difference in the use of the word "madness" in modern thought as compared to the traditional meaning of that term.

At a deeper level, I must say that in using the thought of Nietzsche to enucleate the conception of time as history, I in no sense imply that what he said is the best or highest word about what is. Nor do I imply that however much he would have loathed the Nazis, he is free from any responsibility for their power in Germany. The very clarity and force of his criticism of the European past liberated many Germans from the traditional religious and moral restraints of their tradition, so that they were opened to a barren nihilism which was a fertile field for the extremities and absurdities of National Socialism. Nor do I imply that his lucid but immoderate rhetoric is the best way to put forth one's thoughts. Indeed it might have been better for humanity if Nietzsche's works of high genius had never been written, or if written, published. But to raise this possibility implies that it is better, at least for most men, not to be told where they are. Nietzsche's words raise to an intensely full light of explicitness what it is to live in this era. He articulates what it is to have inherited existence as a present member of western history. His thought does not invent the situation of our contemporary existing, it unfolds it. He carries the crisis of modern thought further only in the sense that by the accuracy and explicitness of his unfolding, he makes it more possible for others to understand the situation of which they are the inheritors. But the inheritance of modern western man was something that Nietzsche took over as a given fate from what others had done and thought, made and felt before him. He made explicit what had been implicit. Therefore, to say that it would have been better for Nietzsche's words not to have been published, implies that some men can live better, if they know less where they are. From whom should some knowledge be hidden? How much is it good for any one person to know?

I raise this question to make clear that I do not intend to take up Nietzsche's words as journalists take up the thoughts of others on television. They call thoughts fascinating and controversial, and in so doing castrate them for themselves and for their audience by cutting off those thoughts from any connection with actuality. The work is done through the implication that no thought can rise above the level of opinion, and therefore be something more important than a source of entertainment. I would not want to trivialize Nietzsche, as if I wished to entertain the bored with a "controversial" figure. To speak about his thoughts on history implies that as the present situation is what it is in any case, it is better to know that situation for what it is, than to live in it without so knowing. Whether this is a correct judgement depends on a difficult argument in political philosophy.

Indeed some of what Nietzsche says will seem obvious today, so that the response may easily be: "what's so new?" In the century since he began to write, not only have his opinions filtered down unrecognized through lesser minds to become the popular platitudes of the age, but also what he prophesied is now all around us to be easily seen. Nevertheless, though his more obvious teachings have become the platitudes of such schools as positivism and existentialism, psychiatry and behavioural social science, the subtler consequences of extremity he draws necessarily from them are not much contemplated. Most men want it both ways in thought and in practice; the nobility of Nietzsche is that he did not.

In *Human, All Too Human* Nietzsche says: "Lack of historical sense is the inherited defect of all philosophers." Or again: "What separates us from Kant, as from Plato and Leibnitz, is that we believe that becoming is the rule even in the spiritual things. We are historians from top to bottom. . . . They all to a man think unhistorically, as is the age old custom among philosophers." Previous philosophers have taken their contemporaries as if they were man as he always is, and proceeded from their definition of that supposedly unchanging being to make generalizations about the meaning of human life, and even about the whole of which man is a part. But it has become evident that all species, human as much as non-human, can only be understood as continually changing, that is, as having histories. Darwin made this patently clear about the other animals. There are not types of animals that are always on earth; species come to be, are in continual change and pass away. The same is so about ourselves. What is fundamental about all human behaviour (including our understanding of it — itself a behaviour) is its historicity.

To repeat, this does not seem very new today. Every literate high school student would take a simple statement of this historicism for granted. We are taught early to use the language of values, to say that our values are dependent on our historical situation and that this generalization proceeds from any objective study of the past. Civilizations and individuals have lived by different values. As there is no way of judging between the value of these values, we are taught early a very simple historical relativism. As we go farther in our education, we are taught to express that historicism with greater sophistication. However, the almost universal acceptance of this relativism by even the semiliterate in our society is very recent. The belief that men are enfolded in their historicity, and the consequent historical relativism with its use of the word "values," only began to be the popular vocabulary in this century.

Nietzsche is the first thinker who shows how this historicity is to be recognized in the full light of its consequences, in every realm of existence. To repeat, most previous philosophers have shown their lack of historical sense by trying to insist, in some form or other, that there is something permanent in human beings, individually or collectively, which survives through change and in terms of which we can be defined. From that definition can be drawn out a scale of better and worse purposes for ourselves and others. But as Nietzsche says in *The Genealogy of Morals*: "All terms which semiotically condense a whole process elude definition; only that which has no history can be defined." We must give up about man (as much as about other animals) the thought that "species" is a definable term from which we can draw forth our proper purposes. Nietzsche uses the metaphor "bridge" to describe the human process. Men are a bridge between the beasts from which we came and what we may yet be, if we should overcome being simply men.

The historical sense is more precise than a general recognition of the change in and between the civilizations which make up that bridge. It is the apprehension that in the shortest moment we are never the same, nor are we ever in the presence of the same. Put negatively, in the historical sense we admit the absence of any permanence in terms of which change can be measured or limited or defined. In Nietzsche's ironic phrase, we are required to accept the finality of becoming. Belief in permanence in the world us arises from the different rhythms of change — for example, in roses, in birds, in stones. Belief in permanence in ourselves (for example, that we are "selves" or even "souls") arises from our desire to believe that there is some unifying purpose in our existing. The desire to assert some permanence is particularly pressing among those who have begun to be aware of the abysmal void of its absence, and who wish to turn away from such a cause of fright. The reasonable activities of scientists and philosophers are the attempt to impose some order, so that awareness of primal chaos may be mitigated whether through practical or contemplative ordering. The very language centring around the word "truth" dominated previous western history because it was the most disciplined attempt to sedate consciousness against the terror and pain of becoming. But when we examine that language scientifically we see that it is made up of a set of metaphors and metonyms which mitigate the chaos by imposing anthropomorphic explanations on everything. The use of the language of "truth" is an assertion of value about what we consider "good" and "evil," which we will to impose upon ourselves and others.

At the beginning of the nineteenth century the consequences to be drawn from the dawning historical sense had been alleviated for many by the belief in progress. Because they believed that the process of historical change manifested as a whole the growing power of rationality in the race, and because they assumed that rationality was "good," they could find in history the purpose of their existing. Scientists had increasingly been able to show that the non-human world could be fully explained without any idea of final purpose; but the idea of purpose was retained as the unfolding of rationality among the species, man. Nietzsche sees that just as natural science has shown that there is no need of the idea of purpose to understand the geneses and developments of the non-human species, so also there are no reasons to justify belief in the goodness of rationality as our given purpose. The belief that increasing rationality is good is just a survival left over from the centuries of Christianity, when men had seen human life grounded in the sovereignty of the divine wisdom, and so considered reason as more than an instrument. Those who had criticized this traditional perspective to death, in the name of modern science and philosophy, still wanted to keep from it the belief in good and evil. They maintained the idea of purpose through the belief in progressive rationality, while freeing themselves from the legacy of philosophy and theology. But can the exaltation of reasoning be maintained when the very meaning of the word "reason" has been changed in modern science? According to Nietzsche in the light of the historical sense men have to give up belief not only in the transcendent ground of permanence (God is dead), but also in the moral valuations which accompanied the former, particularly the idea that our existing has its crowning purpose in rationality.

Nietzsche turns with irony to the fact that the centuries of western belief in rationality as the highest for man, finally produced from itself that science which was to show that there is no reason for this belief. The first exaltation of rationality occurred in Platonism, (which according to Nietzsche took popular form in Christianity). It identified reason with virtue, and virtue with happiness, and grounded this identification in the primacy of the idea of the Good. Human existing was at its heart to be trusted as good. It therefore exalted truth-seeking as virtue, and the discipline necessary to that ascetic pursuit. From the long history of disciplined truth-seeking in Christianity, there came forth at last the great modern scientists who, in their pursuit of truth, showed that the human and non-human things can be fully understood without the idea of final purpose, or that human nature is properly directed toward rationality. The very greatness of Christianity was to produce its own grave-diggers.

While Nietzsche recognizes that the historical sense is the basis for all valuable science and philosophy, he affirms with equal force that it casts a blight upon living. Great living comes forth from those who are resolute in the face of chaos. Such resolution has been sustained by the horizons within which men lived. Horizons are the absolute presuppositions within which individuals and indeed whole civilizations do their living. He uses the metaphor "horizons" because everything which appears, appears to us within their limits. The lives of ordinary men are lived from within their horizons; the deeds of historical men, such as Caesar or Napoleon, come forth from the strength of their horizons. The greatest have been those such as Socrates, the Buddha, or Christ, who have themselves created horizons, within which the people of whole civilizations have henceforth lived.

The historical sense shows us that all horizons are simply the creations of men. In the past, men thought that their horizons were true statements about reality. For example, they affirmed that ultimate reality was reason or love. In terms of these statements which they considered "true," they thought they could know what human purposes were worth pursuing. For example, God being self-giving weakness, the highest human virtue is to give oneself away. But what the historical sense makes plain is that these horizons are not what they claimed to be; they are not true statements about actuality. They are man-made perspectives by which the charismatic impose their will to power. The historical sense teaches us that horizons are not discoveries about the nature of things; they express the values which our tortured instincts will to create.

Nietzsche affirms that once we know that horizons are relative and man-made, their power to sustain us is blighted. Once we know them to be relative, they no longer horizon us. We cannot live in an horizon when we know it to be one. When the historical sense teaches us that our values are not sustained in the nature of things, impotence descends. Nietzsche's most famous aphorism, "God is Dead," implies that God was once alive. He was alive in the sense that He was the horizon from which men could know what was worth doing and therefore be sustained in the resolute doing of it. When it is recognized that God is an horizon, He is dead, once and for all. Indeed the death of the Christian God in western civilization is not just the death of one horizon, it is the end of all horizons. The Christian God might be called the last horizon, because its formidable confidence in truth-seeking as the way of contending with the primal anguish brought forth that science and critical philosophy which have made evident that all horizons are man-made. Nietzsche does not take the death of God — the end of all horizons — as a moment to be taken lightly, as something after which we can get on with the business of making life cosy. He is not the American liberal described by Abbie Hoffman as saying: "God is dead and we did it for the kids." For Nietzsche, the end of horizons is not cosy, because we are still left with how to live when we have admitted chaos.

When Nietzsche writes "only that which has no history can be defined" it may seem that this has little importance outside the logic of definition, — an academic matter. Science does not need definitions except as instruments. But "to define" in a wider context includes stating the purpose of something. The definition of man as the rational animal asserted that our special purpose was rationality. To have been told that man is the creature of Trinity was to know that our highest activity was loving. To say that man has a history and therefore cannot be defined is to say that we can know nothing about what we are fitted for. We make ourselves as we go along. This is what Nietzsche means when he says that we are at the end of the era of rational man. We must live in the knowledge that our purposes are simply creations of human will and not ingrained in the nature of things. But what a burden falls upon the will when the horizons of definition are gone. This is the burden that Nietzsche sees the historical sense imposing on man. On the one hand, we cannot deny history and retreat into a destroyed past. On the other hand, how can we overcome the blighting effect of living without horizons? In his twenties Nietzsche saw the crisis with which the conception of time as history presented men. The great writings of his maturity were his attempt to overcome it.

IV

Chapter Four

In the last section of *Thus Spoke Zarathustra*, Nietzsche wrote: "The hour in which I tremble and in which I freeze; the hour which demands and demands and goes on always demanding: 'Who has enough courage for that, who deserve to be the masters of the earth?'" In the eighty years since Nietzsche stopped writing, the realized fruits of that drive to mastery are pressed upon us in every day of our lives. Capabilities of mastery over human and non-human beings proliferate, along with reactions by both against that mastering. The historical sense comes from the same intellectual matrix as does the drive to mastery. We have been taught to recognize as illusion the old belief that our purposes are ingrained and sustained in the nature of things. Mastery comes at the same time as the recognition that horizons are only horizons. Most men, when they face that their purposes are not cosmically sustained, find that a darkness falls upon their wills. This is the crisis of the modern world to Nietzsche. The capabilities for mastery present men with a more pressing need of wisdom than any previous circumstances. Who will deserve to be those masters? Who will be wise enough? What is wisdom when reason cannot teach us of human excellence? What is wisdom when we have been taught by the historical sense the finality of becoming? What is wisdom, when we have overcome the idea of eternity?

Till recently it was assumed that our mastery of the earth would be used to promote the values of freedom, rationality, and equality — that is, the values of social democracy. Social democracy was the highest political wisdom. It was to be the guaranteed culmination of history as progress. But to repeat: for Nietzsche progress was the doctrine which held men when the conception of history in western Christianity had been secularized by modern philosophy and science. Christianity was Platonism for the people. Platonism was the first rationalism. Its identification of rationality, virtue, and happiness was a prodigious affirmation of optimism. This identification was for the few who could reach it in the practice of philosophy. Christianity took this optimism and laid it open to the masses, who could attain it through trust in the creating and redeeming Triune God. It united the identification of reason, virtue, and happiness with the idea of equality, sustained in the fact that all men were created by God and sought by Him in redemption. By this addition of equality, the rationalism was made even more optimistic. In the modern era, that doctrine was secularized: that is, it came to be believed that this uniting of reason and virtue and happiness was not grounded beyond the world in the Kingdom of God, but was coming to be here on earth, in history. By saying that this union was to be realized here on earth, the height of optimism was reached.

In the last part of *Zarathustra* Nietzsche writes: "The masses blink and say: 'We are all equal. — Man is but man, before God — we are all equal.' Before God! But now this God has died." The modern movements which believe in progress toward social democracy assert the equality of all men and a politics based on it. But the same liberal movements have also at their heart that secularism which excludes belief in God. What kind of reason or evidence then sustains the belief that men are equal?

As for the expectations from the progress of knowledge — that is the belief that freedom will be given its content by men being open to the truths of science and philosophy — Nietzsche asserts that we have come to the end of the age of rational man. To repeat: the cause of this end is the ambiguity at the heart of science. For Nietzsche, modern science is the height of modern truthfulness and the centre of our destiny. But it is an ambiguous centre, because in the very name of "truthfulness" — itself a moral value — it has made plain that the values of rationalism are not cosmically sustained. The natural science of Darwin and Newton has shown us that nature can be understood without the idea of final purpose. In that understanding, nature appears to us as indifferent to moral good and evil. We can control nature; but it does not sustain virtue. As for the sciences of man, they have shown us that reason is only an instrument and cannot teach us how it is best to live. In openness to science we learn that nature is morally indifferent, and that reason is simply an instrument.

At the end of the era of "rational" man, the public world will be dominated by two types, whom Nietzsche calls the last men and the nihilists. The last men are those who have inherited the ideas of happiness and equality from the doctrine of progress. But because this happiness is to be realized by all men, the conception of its content has to be shrunk to fit what can be realized by all. The sights for human fulfillment have to be lowered. Happiness can be achieved, but only at the cost of emasculating men of all potentialities for nobility and greatness. The last men will gradually come to be the majority in any realized technical society.

Nietzsche's description of these last men in *Zarathustra* has perhaps more meaning in us and for us than it had for his contemporaries who read it in 1883. "They have their little pleasure for the day and their little pleasure for the night: but they respect health. 'We have discovered happiness,' say the last men and blink." Or again, "A little poison now and then: that produces pleasant dreams. And a lot of poison at last, for a pleasant death." Or again, "Formerly all the world was mad, say the most acute of the last men and blink. They are clever and know everything that has ever happened: so there is no end to their mockery. They still quarrel, but they soon make up — otherwise they might have indigestion" — our intellectuals. The central fact about the last men is that they cannot despise themselves. Because they cannot despise themselves, they cannot rise above a petty view of happiness. They can thus inoculate themselves against the abyss of existing. They are the *last* men because they have inherited rationalism only in its last and decadent form. They think they have emancipated themselves from Christianity; in fact they are the products of Christianity in its secularized form. They will be the growing majority in the northern hemisphere as the modern age unfolds. The little they ask of life (only entertainment and comfort) will give them endurance. This is the price the race has to pay for overcoming two millennia of Christianity.

The end of rational man brings forth not only last men but nihilists. These are those who understand that they can know nothing about what is good to will. Because of the historical sense, they know that all values are relative and man-made; the highest values of the past have devaluated themselves. Men have no given content for their willing. But because men are wills, the gong cannot give up willing.[1] Men would rather will nothing than have nothing to will. Nietzsche clearly has more sympathy for the nihilists than for the last men, because the former put truthfulness above the debased vision of happiness, and in this hold on to the negative side of human greatness. But he has little doubt of the violence and cataclysms which will come forth from men who would rather will nothing than have nothing to will. They will be resolute in their will to mastery, but they cannot know what that mastery is for. The violence of their mastery over human and non-human beings will be without end. In the 1880s he looked ahead to that age of world wars and continued upheavals which most of us in this century have tried to endure.

In parenthesis: if we look at the crises of the modern world through Nietzsche's eyes, and see them above all as the end of two millennia of rational man, we can see that those crises have come to North America later than to Europe. But now that they have come, they are here with intensity. The optimism of rational man was sustained for us in the expectations of the pioneering moment. It was also sustained by the fact that among most of our population our identification of virtue and happiness took the earlier and more virile form which came out of Biblical religion, rather than the soft definition of that identification in the liberalisms of the last men. Among the early majority this was above all Protestant; but its virility was sustained in the Catholicism and Judaism of the later immigrants. In the fresh innocence of North America these religions maintained their force, albeit in primitive form, longer than they did in the more sophisticated Europe. Because the identification of virtue and reason and happiness in these religions was not altogether immanent in its expectations, it held back many North Americans for longer from that banal view of happiness which is the mark of mass liberalism. As these religions provided some protection from the historical sense, they still provided horizons for our willing which saved the resolute from nihilism. At the height of our present imperial destiny, the crisis of the end of modern rationalism falls upon us ineluctably. In Nietzsche's words: "the wasteland grows." The last men and the nihilists are everywhere in North America.

For Nietzsche, there is no possibility of returning to the greatness and glory of pre-rational times, to the age of myth and cult. The highest vision of what men have yet been was unfolded in the early Greek tragedies. Here was laid forth publicly and in ordered form the ecstasy of the suffering and knowing encounter of the noblest men and women with the chaos of existing. The rationalism of Socrates smoothed away that encounter by proclaiming the primacy of the idea of the Good, and in so doing deprived men of the possibility of their greatest height. The optimism of philosophy destroyed the ecstatic nobility which had been expressed in the tragedies. But now that rationalism has dug its own grave through the truthfulness of science, there is no returning to that earlier height. The heritage of rationalism remains in its very overcoming. Its practical heritage is that through technique and experimental science men are becoming the masters of the earth. Its theoretical heritage is that men now know that nature is indifferent to their purposes and that they create their own values. Therefore the question for our species is: can we reach a new height which takes into itself not only the ecstasy of a noble encounter with chaos, but also the results of the long history of rationalism? Neither the nihilists nor the last men deserve to be masters of the earth. The nihilists only go on willing for the sake of willing. They assuage their restlessness by involvement in mastery for its own sake. They are unable to use their mastery for joy. The last men simply use the fruits of technique for the bored pursuit of their trivial vision of happiness. The question is whether there can be men who transcend the alternatives of being nihilists or last men; who know that they are the creators of their own values, but bring forth from that creation in the face of chaos a joy in their willing which will make them deserving of being masters of the earth.

It must be said that for Nietzsche this crisis is authentic, because there is no necessity about its outcome. This may be compared with another influential account of the modern crisis, that of Marx. For Marx also, industrial society is at a turning point. The achievements of capitalism have led to the stage where this form of social organization must now be transcended. For Marx, as for Nietzsche, this is a situation which produces widespread and terrible human suffering. But according to Marx, if we have knowledge of the forces now at work, we can know that the crisis will inevitably be transcended. In the midst of the suffering we have that enormous consolation and spur to effort. A net of inevitable success is put under the performers, so that their actions are guaranteed from the ultimate anguish. For Nietzsche there is no such net. The historical sense shows us that we must take seriously the idea that we create history, and that therefore there can be no inevitable outcome. We do not know whether beings will appear who will so overcome themselves that they will deserve to be masters of the earth; we do not know whether the last men will be in charge for centuries and centuries. To repeat: for Nietzsche the net of inevitable progress is a shallow secular form of the belief in God. Just as the historical sense has killed God, it kills the secular descendants of that belief. Indeed the first step in man's self-overcoming is to know that all such nets over chaos are simply comforting illusions. The historical sense teaches us that what happens now and what will happen is radically contingent. (I may be allowed to note that the absence of all nets is a truth that those of us who trust in God must affirm.)

Unfortunately, one of the key words in Nietzsche's answer has been killed amongst us by strangely diverse associations. Most of us on this continent grew up with the comic strips and film cartoons in which the bespectacled newspaper man, Clark Kent, turned into "Superman," who went zooming through the skies destroying gangsters and enemies of his country. To use the word "superman" is to think that image — an image from the comics and the Saturday matinee filled with screaming children and popcorn.

The other association is a debased one. The word "superman" was used by the propagandists of the most disgusting political regime that the western world has yet produced. The Nazis took over this part of Nietzsche's language, so that when people of my generation hear the word "superman" as used about reality, we conjure up images of those arrogant and sadistic maniacs sweeping their violence and vulgarity over Europe. Because of those events, the word "superman" has become revolting. Of course, without doubt, Nietzsche would have seen in the Nazis his worst predictions of nihilism and vulgarity combined — predictions which he made particularly about his own people — the Germans.

Indeed as I have watched Leni Riefenstahl's famous documentaries of the Nazi era, particularly her shots of Hitler speaking, I have been aware in Hitler of just that spirit which Nietzsche believes to be the very curse of mankind — the spirit of revenge, (that which in Nietzsche's language above all holds back men from becoming "supermen" — *übermensch*). As one watches Hitler speaking one sees that his effectiveness came from the uniting of his own hysterical self-pity with the same feelings present in his German audience. Life has been a field of pain and defeat for him both privately and publicly, as it has been for the Germans, and he summons up their *ressentiment*. In a political context, Hitler made specific demands; but behind anything specific one feels a demand more universal — a demand for unlimited revenge. This is what Nietzsche says is the very basis for the violence of nihilism. Indeed in his language, the supermen will be those who have overcome in themselves any desire for revenge. As he writes in *Zarathustra*: "That man may be delivered from revenge: that is for me the bridge to the highest hope."

(To make a parenthesis about Leni Riefenstahl's films: many people these days seem to place enormous confidence in the electronic media. They see in them the way by which enlightenment can be brought to the majority. Electronic enlightenment will overcome the old anal rationality of print and speech. Those who think this way should ponder these films of Leni Riefenstahl. The art of the film was there used in all its stunning magic. But these films were made to persuade men of the glory of the basest of political regimes. Indeed to watch them is to be presented with Nietzsche's very question: who deserves to be the master of electronics? The last men and nihilists from contemporary television journalism and politics? One would be happier about the McLuhanite cult, if its members dealt with such questions.)

Both because of the comic strip and because of the Nazis, the word superman cannot be used with seriousness amongst us. But that fact must not prevent us from looking at Nietzsche's question. Who is wise enough for this moment in history? Nietzsche takes the historical sense for granted. He does not speak of the race of men as if they had a nature which is unchanging through the course of history. Man is a bridge between the beasts and something higher than man. As he writes in *Beyond Good and Evil*: "Man is the as yet undetermined animal." It is now open to man in the future to become nobler than his past, so that some will come to deserve the present destiny of being masters of the planet. For this deserving, the essential condition is that men overcome the spirit of revenge. Therefore if one wants to understand what Nietzsche means by history, one must look at what he means by revenge.

Desire for revenge has come from the very conditions of human existence. As self-conscious animals men have lived in the chaotic world, experiencing as anguish all its accidents, its terrors, and its purposelessness. Most men have lived in a world in which our instincts are thwarted and twisted from the very moment we enter it. Our wills are continually broken on the wheel of the chaos which is the world. Our response to that brokenness is the will to revenge against others, against ourselves, against the very condition of time itself. "It is the body which has despaired of the body." From that despair comes forth the spirit of revenge. The more botched and bungled our instincts become in the vicissitudes of existing, the greater our will to revenge on what has been done us.

Nietzsche was the first to use consistently that description of man which Freud later employed for psycho-analysis. The elemental in man is an "it"; that is an impersonal chaos of instincts out of which comes forth as epiphenomena, reason and morality. It was once believed that the irrational in man existed to be subordinated to the rational. In Nietzsche this is denied. This does not, however, free us from thinking. It simply means that thinking is carried on over an abyss which it can never fathom. Philosophy is simply the highest form of "the will to power." As he writes in *Beyond Good and Evil*: "There is a point in every philosophy when the philosopher's 'conviction' appears on the stage — or to use the language of an ancient Mystery:

> *Adventavit asinus,*
> *Pulcher et fortissimus.*"

Nietzsche enucleates with black wit the many forms of revenge which make up for him the very substance of history. In the earliest societies, the victory of the strong over the weak is the victory of those with vigorous instincts over the majority of weak instinct. The weak bring forth from their condition of enslavement the spirit of revenge. The rules of justice come from that spirit. The creditor takes a quantum of revenge from the debtor who cannot meet his debts. As the infliction of pain gives pleasure, the creditor finds his satisfaction in that punishment. In the West, the greatest achievement of the spirit of revenge has been Christianity. In it, the priests, who are those among the ruling classes whose instincts have been most botched and bungled, and therefore desire the greatest revenge, get power by uniting with the weak majority against the strong. They produce a morality which exalts such virtues as altruism, humility, equality, etc. Those virtues necessary anyway for the weak majority are guaranteed to get them revenge, in the next world, if not in this. The priests teach an ascetic morality, telling men that the instincts should be repressed. In the name of this rationalist control, those of strong and noble instinct are held back from their proper authority for the sake of the weak and bungled majority.

Indeed, the will to revenge is turned inward by men against themselves. They punish themselves, not only others. The greed of the self teaches us that if we put aside full living in the name of humility and altruism and asceticism, we will gain an infinite extension of our wills in eternity. Those who transpose their will from this world to the beyond are expressing the most intense will to power from out of their desire for revenge at not being able to express it in this life. For Nietzsche the very idea of transcendence — that time is enfolded in eternity — is produced out of the spirit of revenge by those who because of their broken instincts are impotent to live in the world, and in their self-pity extrapolate to a non-existent perfection in which their failures will be made good. In the language I have used in these lectures, any belief that time cannot be identified with history comes from the broken instincts of men who cannot live greatly in history. For Nietzsche, Plato is the philosophic enemy, because he conceives time as an image, "the moving image of eternity." The reality of the "idea" was invented by Socrates, who wanted to overcome tragedy and who therefore posited that the immediate world was just the moving image of a real eternity. The greatness of Socrates was the greatness of his revenge on tragedy. But philosophy only provided revenge for the few. In Christianity the will to revenge is taken up into a transcendence opened to the majority. As Nietzsche puts it in *The Genealogy of Morals*: "Then suddenly we come face to face with that paradoxical and ghastly expedient which brought temporary relief to tortured humanity, that most brilliant stroke of Christianity: God's sacrifice of himself for man. God makes himself the ransom for what could not otherwise be ransomed; God alone has power to absolve us of a debt we can no longer discharge; the creditor offers himself as a sacrifice for his debtor out of sheer love (can you believe it) out of love for his debtor."

Now that Christianity has been secularized, the transcendence of progress has been substituted for the transcendence of God. The spirit of revenge is still at work among the last men and the nihilists. The last men want revenge against anything that is noble and great, against anything that threatens their expectations from triviality. The nihilists want revenge on the fact that they cannot live with joy in the world. Their revenge takes the form of restless violence against any present. As nothingness is always before them, they seek to fill the void by willing for willing's sake. There can be no end to their drive for mastery.

Indeed for Nietzsche revenge arises most deeply in our recognition that all our existing is subject to time's thrall. Everything is enfolded in "it was," "it is," "it will be." And as we recognize that inescapable temporality in every lived minute, we can will to batter against its inevitable consequences. That is the deepest cause of our revengings. At its simplest, we want revenge against what is present in our present. If we seek to overcome our present by bending our efforts to the building of a future to suit our heart's desire, when that future came we would still be subject to that thrall. At the deepest level, revenge is most engaged against the past. Consciousness always includes within itself "it was." Human life would not be possible without some memory. But the will can do nothing about the past. What has happened has happened, and we cannot change it. By the "it was" of time, Nietzsche means not only our personal past (with its defeats, its enslavements, its tortured instincts), but the past of the race which is opened to us in communal memory, and opened to us as never before by the historical sense. In *Zarathustra* Nietzsche writes: "To transform every 'it was' into 'this is what I wanted' — that alone I could call redemption." The height is for him *amor fati*. And that love must come out of having grasped into one's consciousness the worst that can be remembered or imagined — the torturing of children and the screams of the innocent.

To deserve to be masters of the earth will be to have overcome the spirit of revenge and therefore to be able to will and create in joy. Nietzsche's image for himself is the convalescent. He is recovering, step by step, from the spirit of revenge. The recovery from that sickness is not simply from the disasters of his own instincts, but the recovery from the long history of revenge in the race. In that history, the greatest revenge against time's "it was" took the form of belief in the transcendence of a timeless eternity. It pretended to be a redemption of time, but it was in fact an expression of revenge against time. To live on the earth, to be masters of the earth, to deserve to be masters because we can live in joy, requires the act of *amor fati*, held outside any assertion of timelessness. The love of fate has been asserted in the Greek tragedies, in Plato, and by certain Christians. But this fate was enfolded in a timeless eternity, in an ultimate perfection. For Nietzsche, the achievement of *amor fati* must be outside any such enfoldment. It must be willed in a world where there is no possibility of either an infinite or finite transcendence of becoming or of willing.

For Nietzsche, the possibility of that love of fate is related to his discovery of "the eternal recurrence of the identical." This "discovery" was that as the number of possible combinations of what exists is finite, yet time is infinite; there has already been and will be again an endless recurrence of the present state of affairs, and of every other state possible. As he writes in *Zarathustra*:

You do not know my abysmal thought — that thought which you could not endure.

Look at this gateway. — Two paths come together here and no one has ever reached their end.

This long path behind us goes on for an eternity. And that long path ahead of us — that is another eternity.—

On the gateway is written its name: "Moment." —

Must not all things that can run have already run along this path? Must not all things that can happen have already happened, been done, run past?

And if all things have been here before; what do you think of this moment? — Must not this gateway, too, have been here, before?

And are not all things bound inextricably together in such a way that this moment draws after it all future things? Therefore, draws itself too?

For all things that can run must also run once again forward along this long path.

And this slow spider that creeps along in the moonlight, and this moonlight itself and both of us at this gateway whispering together — must we not all have been here before

— and must we not return and run down that other path before us, down that long terrible path — must we not return eternally?

This is what I said and I said it more and more softly: for I was afraid of my own thoughts and reservations.

It is not my business to repeat here all that Nietzsche says about that "discovery." It can be found in *Zarathustra* and in his notebooks which have been published posthumously in English under the title *The Will to Power*. Nor is it my task to write here of the objections which have been made against "the eternal recurrence of the identical" — that is, to discuss the varied thoughts of those who claim that it is not a discovery. However, I can say that in the endurance of that "discovery" Nietzsche found the possibility of overcoming the spirit of revenge. In that thoughtful enduring was the movement toward the realization of *amor fati*. According to Nietzsche, when men know themselves beyond good and evil, the strong are moved to the violence of an undirected willing of novelty. But from his "discovery" Nietzsche's nihilism becomes therapeutic, so that he can begin to will novelty in joy. In the recognition of the dominance of time in which no past is past and no future has not yet been and yet in which there is openness to the immediate future — the conception of time as history reaches its height and yet is not hypostasized into a comforting horizon.

V

Chapter Five

I have brushed against the writings of Nietzsche because he has thought the conception of time as history more comprehensively than any other thinker. He lays bare the fate of technical man, not as an object held in front of us, but as that in which our very selves are involved in the proofs of the science which lays it bare. In thinking the modern project, he did not turn away from it. His critical wit about modern society might lead one to believe that he condemned its assumptions. Rather he expressed the contradictions and difficulties in the thought and life of western civilization, not for the sake of turning men away from that enterprise, but so that they could overcome its difficulties and fulfill its potential heights. In his work, the themes that must be thought in thinking time as history are raised to a beautiful explicitness: the mastery of human and non-human nature in experimental science and technique, the primacy of the will, man as the creator of his own values, the finality of becoming, the assertion that potentiality is higher than actuality, that motion is nobler than rest, that dynamism rather than peace is the height.

The simpler things that Nietzsche says (for example, that men must now live without the comfort of horizons) seem so obvious to most people today that they are hardly worth emphasizing. Everybody uses the word "values" to describe our making of the world: capitalists and socialists, atheists and avowed believers, scientists and politicians. The word comes to us so platitudinously that we take it to belong to the way things are. It is forgotten that before Nietzsche and his immediate predecessors, men did not think about their actions in that language. They did not think they made the world valuable, but that they participated in its goodness. What is comic about the present use of "values," and the distinction of them from "facts," is not that it is employed by modern men who know what is entailed in so doing; but that it is used also by "religious" believers who are unaware that in its employment they are contradicting the very possibility of the reverence they believe they are espousing in its use. The reading of Nietzsche would make that clear to them. Indeed even some of the deeper aspects of Nietzsche's thought increasingly become explicit in our world. If one listens carefully to the revolt of the noblest young against bourgeois America, one hears deeper notes in it than were ever sounded by Marx, and those are above all the notes of Nietzsche.

To repeat: the thought of great thinkers is not a matter for the chit-chat of television and cocktail parties; nor for providing jobs for academics in the culture industry. In it the fate of our whole living is expressed. In this sense, the thought of Nietzsche is a fate for modern men. In partaking in it, we can come to make judgements about the modern project — that enormous enterprise that came out of western Europe in the last centuries and has now become worldwide.

Nevertheless, as implied in the previous pages, the conception of time as history is not one in which I think life can be lived properly. It is not a conception we are fitted for. Therefore I turn away from Nietzsche and in so turning express my suspicion of the assumptions of the modern project. Yet this immediately produces a difficulty. Before speaking against Nietzsche, one must affirm the language one shares with him, even as one negates his use of it. To illustrate: Nietzsche clearly uses the same language as the tradition in its eternal truth, when he says that the height for human beings is *amor fati*. Yet the love of fate which he would call redemption is not in any sense a call to the passivity which some moderns falsely identify with words such as "fate" or "destiny." In him the love of fate is at one with his call to dynamic willing. The love of fate is the guarantee that dynamic willing shall be carried on by lovers of the earth, and not by those twisted by hatred and hysteria against existing (however buried that hysteria may be in the recesses of our instincts). Some Marxists have taken his love of fate as if it were a call to passivity as the height, and as if, therefore, he were an essentially nonpolitical writer. They have denied that love of fate (love of the injustices and alienations and exploitations of time) can be good. Is it not just a sufficiently deep and sustained hatred of these iniquities which brings men to fight and to overcome them? But Nietzsche's love of fate is not passive, but a call to dynamic political doing. He states explicitly that any philosophy must finally be judged in the light of its political recommendations. What he is saying beyond many Marxists is that the building of the potential height in modern society can only be achieved by those who have overcome revenge, so that what they accomplish comes forth from a positive love of the earth, and not simply from hatred of what presently is. Dynamic willing that has not overcome revenge will always have the marks of hysteria and hatred within it. It can only produce the technical frenzy of the nihilists or the shallow goals of the last men. It cannot come to terms with the questions: "what for, whither and what then?" However, against the complacency of any easy *amor fati*, Nietzsche makes clear that it must take into itself all the pain and anguish and ghastliness that has ever been, and also the loathing of that ghastliness and pain. Hatred against existence is, it would seem, limitless, and the more we are aware of the nervous systems of others, the more that hatred and hysteria must be actual or repressed for us. Only those of us who are not much open to others can readily claim that we think existing to be as we wanted it. *Amor fati* is then a height for men, not in the sense that it is easily achieved or perhaps ever achieved by any human being. The redemption that Nietzsche holds forth is not cheaply bought.

Yet having said this, I must state my simple incomprehension. How is it possible to assert the love of fate as the height and, at the same time, the finality of becoming? I do not understand how anybody could love fate, unless within the details of our fates there could appear, however rarely, intimations that they are illumined; intimations that is, of perfection (call it if you will God) in which our desires for good find their rest and their fulfillment. I do not say anything about the relation of that perfection to the necessities of existing, except that there must be some relation; nor do I state how or when the light of that perfection could break into the ambiguities and afflictions of any particular person. I simply state the argument for perfection (sometimes called the ontological argument): namely that human beings are not beyond good and evil, and that the desire for good is a broken hope without perfection, because only the desire to become perfect does in fact make us less imperfect. This means that the absurdities of time — its joys as well as its diremptions — are to be taken not simply as history, but as enfolded in an unchanging meaning, which is untouched by potentiality or change. So when Nietzsche affirms that *amor fati* comes forth from the contemplation of the eternity (not timelessness, but endless time) of the creating and destroying powers of man and the rest of nature, I do not understand how that could be a light which would free us from the spirit of revenge. It seems to me a vision that would drive men mad — not in the sense of a divine madness, but a madness destructive of good.

The preceding statements are not here proved or even argued. Indeed it is questionable how much it would be possible to argue them in the modern world. For all those statements are made from out of an ancient way of thinking. And to repeat: the core of the intellectual history of the last centuries has been the criticism of that ancient account of thought. As that criticism has publicly succeeded, what comes to us from that ancient thought is generally received as unintelligible and simply arbitrary. All of us are increasingly enclosed by the modern account. For example, central to my affirmations in the previous paragraph are the propositions: the core of our lives is the desire for perfection, and only that desire can make us less imperfect. Yet clearly that account of "morality" (to use a modern word) is quite different from what has been affirmed about morality in the last centuries. The attempt to argue for my propositions would require a very close historical analysis of how the use of such words as "desire" and "reason" have changed over the last centuries. It would require, for example, what the ancients meant by "passion." Whatever the differences between what has come to us from Plato and from Christianity, on this central point there is commonness. The height for man could only come forth out of a "passion." Yet in using such a word, the enormous difficulty of thinking outside the modern account can be seen. When we use the word "pathetic" we may be thinking of a defeated character in a movie, or the performance of the quarterback for the Hamilton Tiger

Cats football team this season. The word "passion" has come to be limited for us to little more than an emotion of driving force, particularly intense sexual excitement. To say that philosophy arises from the suffering of astonishment would bear no relation to our present understanding of thought, because the archetype of thought is now that science which frames instrumental hypotheses and tests them in experiment, a kind of willing. How can we think of "morality" as a desiring attention to perfection, when for the last centuries the greatest moral philosophers have written of it as self-legislation, the willing of our own values? Therefore my affirmations in the previous paragraph use language in a way that can hardly be appropriated.

Indeed, beyond this, there is a further turn of the screw for anybody who would assert that *amor fati* is the height, yet cannot understand how that height could be achievable outside the vision of our fate as enfolded in a timeless eternity. The destruction of the idea of such an eternity has been at the centre of the modern project in the very scientific and technical mastery of chance. As a great contemporary, Leo Strauss, has written in *What Is Political Philosophy*: "Oblivion of eternity, or, in other words, estrangement from man's deepest desire and therewith from the primary issues, is the price which modern man had to pay, from the very beginning, for attempting to be absolutely sovereign, to become the master and owner of nature, to conquer chance." And the turn of the screw is that to love fate must obviously include loving the fate that makes us part of the modern project: it must include loving that which has made us oblivious of eternity — that eternity without which I cannot understand how it would be possible to love fate.

To put the matter simply: any appeal to the past must not be made outside a full recognition of the present. Any use of the past which insulates us from living now is cowardly, trivializing, and at worst despairing. Antiquarianism can be used like most other drugs as mind contracting. If we live in the present we must know that we live in a civilization, the fate of which is to conceive time as history. Therefore as living now, the task of thought among those held by something which cannot allow them to make the complete "yes" to time as history, is not to inoculate themselves against their present, but first to enter what is thought in that present.

What has happened in the West since 1945 concerning the thought of Marx is an example of inoculation. Our chief rival empire has been ruled by men who used Marx's doctrine as their official language, while we used an earlier form of modernity, the liberalism of capitalist democracy. The thought of Marx, therefore, appeared as a threatening and subverting disease. The intellectual industry in our multiversities produced a spate of refutations of Marx. Most of these, however, were written with the purpose of inoculating others against any contagion, rather than with thinking the thoughts that Marx had thought. These books have not prevented the reviving influence of Marx's thought among many of the brightest young; anymore than the official Marxism of the East has been able to stop the influence of existentialism among its young élites. Men may have to attempt this inoculation if they are concerned with the stability of a particular society, but it is well to know when one is doing it that it is not concerned directly with philosophy but with public stability. And you will not even be successful at inoculating those most important to inoculate, if you pretend you understand Marx when you do not. To apply the comparison: when I state that I do not understand how Nietzsche could assert *amor fati* to be the height, while at the same time asserting the finality of becoming, my purpose is not to inoculate against Nietzsche. The task of inoculation is best left to those who write textbooks.

What then could be the position of those who cannot live through time as if it were simply history, who cannot believe that love of fate could be achieved together with the assertion of the finality of becoming, and yet must live in the dynamism of our present society? In that position there is a call to remembering and to loving and to thinking.

What I mean by remembering was expressed for me by a friend who died recently. He knew that he was dying, not in the sense that we all know that this is going to happen sometime. He knew it because a short term had been put upon his life at an early age, long before what he was fitted for could be accomplished. Knowing that he lived in the close presence of his own death, he once said shortly: "I do not accept Nietzsche." Clearly such a remark was not intended to express a realized refutation of Nietzsche. Neither he nor I saw ourselves capable of that magisterial task. He had collected (at a time when such collecting must have been pressed upon him) what had been given him about the unfathomable goodness of the whole, from his good fortune in having partaken in a tradition of reverence. In the inadequate modern equivalent for reverence and tradition, his remark might be called "religious."

In an age when the primacy of the will, even in thinking, destroys the varied forms of reverence, they must come to us, when and if they come, from out of tradition. "Tradition" means literally a handing over; or, as it once meant, a surrender. The man who was dying was in his remark surrendering to me his recollection of what had been surrendered to him, from the fortune that had been his, in having lived within a remembered reverence — in his case, Christianity. In the presence of death, he had collected out of that remembrance an assertion for me which stated how he transcended conceiving time as history.

By distinguishing remembering from thinking, I do not imply

that this collecting was unthoughtful, but that what this man had there collected could not have been entirely specified in propositions. For nearly everyone (except perhaps for the occasional great thinkers) there is no possibility of entirely escaping that which is given in the public realm, and this increasingly works against the discovery of any reverence. Therefore those of us who at certain times look to grasp something beyond history must search for it as the remembering of a negated tradition and not as a direct thinking of our present. Perhaps reverence belongs to man *qua* man and is indeed the matrix of human nobility. But those several conceptions, being denied in our present public thought, can themselves only be asserted after they have been sought for through the remembrance of the thought of those who once thought them.

Remembering must obviously be a disciplined activity in a civilization where the institutions which should foster it do not. One form of it may be scholarship, the study of what the past has given us. But scholarship of itself need not be remembering. The scholar may so hold out from himself what is given from the past (that is, so objectify it) that he does not in fact remember it. There are scholars, for example, who have learnt much of the detailed historical and literary background of the Bible, and yet who remember less of what was essentially given in those books than Jews or Christians untutored in such scholarship. This is no argument against the necessity of disciplined scholarship. It is simply the statement that modern scholarship has to hold itself above the great gulf of progressive assumptions, if it is to be more than antiquarian technique and become remembering.

It may also be said that "remembering" is a misleading word, because we should turn not only to our own origins in Athens and Jerusalem, but to those of the great civilizations of the East. Many young North Americans are learning from Asia, because of the barrenness of their own traditions. Indeed many have only

been able to look at their own past because they have first been
grasped by something in Asia. It is hardly necessary for a
member of a department of religion, such as myself, to assert
that it can be a great good for western people in their time of
darkness to contemplate the sources of thought and life as they
have been in the East. But that meeting will be only a kind of
esoteric game, if it is undertaken to escape the deepest roots of
western fate. We can only come to any real encounter with Asia,
if we come in some high recognition of what we inevitably are. I
use the word "remembering" because, wherever else we turn, we
cannot turn away from our own fate, which came from our original openings to comedy and tragedy, to thought and charity, to
anxiety and shame.

As remembering can only be carried on by means of what is
handed over to us, and as what is handed over is a confusion of
truth and falsity, remembering is clearly not self-sufficient. Any
tradition, even if it be the vehicle by which perfection itself is
brought to us, leaves us with the task of appropriating from it, by
means of loving and thinking, that which it has carried to us. Individuals, even with the help of their presently faltering institutions,
can grasp no more than very small segments of what is there. Nor
(to repeat) should any dim apprehensions of what was meant by
perfection before the age of progress be used simply as means to
negate what may have been given us of truth and goodness in this
age. The present darkness is a real darkness, in the sense that the
enormous corpus of logistic and science of the last centuries is
unco-ordinate as to any possible relation it may have to those
images of perfection which are given us in the Bible and in philosophy. We must not forget that new potentialities of reasoning and
making happen have been actualized (and not simply contemplated as mistrusted potentialities, as for example in Plato) and
therefore must be thought as having been actualized, in relation to

what is remembered. The conception of time as history is not to be discarded as if it had never been.

It may be that at any time or place, human beings can be opened to the whole in their loving and thinking, even as its complete intelligibility eludes them. If this be true of any time or place, then one is not, after all, trapped in historicism. But now the way to intelligibility is guarded by a more than usual number of ambiguities. Our present is like being lost in the wilderness, when every pine and rock and bay appears to us as both known and unknown, and therefore as uncertain pointers on the way back to human habitation. The sun is hidden by the clouds and the usefulness of our ancient compasses has been put in question. Even what is beautiful — which for most men has been the pulley to lift them out of despair — has been made equivocal for us both in detail and definition.

Nevertheless, those who cannot live as if time were history are called, beyond remembering, to desiring and thinking. But this is to say very little. For myself, as probably for most others, remembering only occasionally can pass over into thinking and loving what is good. It is for the great thinkers and the saints to do more.

Myth and Meaning

by
Claude Lévi-Strauss

Introduction

Although I am going to talk about what I have written, my books and papers and so on, unfortunately I forget what I have written practically as soon as it is finished. There is probably going to be some trouble about that. But nevertheless I think there is also something significant about it, in that I don't have the feeling that I write my books. I have the feeling that my books get written through me and that once they have got across me I feel empty and nothing is left.

You may remember that I have written that myths get thought in man unbeknownst to him. This has been much discussed and even criticized by my English-speaking colleagues, because their feeling is that, from an empirical point of view, it is an utterly meaningless sentence. But for me it describes a lived experience, because it says exactly how I perceive my own relationship to my work. That is, my work gets thought in me unbeknown to me.

I never had, and still do not have, the perception of feeling my personal identity. I appear to myself as the place where something is going on, but there is no "I," no "me." Each of us is a kind of crossroads where things happen. The crossroads is purely passive; something happens there. A different thing, equally valid, happens elsewhere. There is no choice, it is just a matter of chance.

I don't pretend at all that, because I think that way, I am entitled to conclude that mankind thinks that way too. But I believe that, for each scholar and each writer, the particular way he or she thinks and writes opens a new outlook on mankind. And the fact that I personally have this idiosyncracy perhaps entitles me to point to something which is valid, while the way in which my colleagues think opens different outlooks, all of which are equally valid.

I

THE MEETING OF MYTH AND SCIENCE

Let me start with a personal confession. There is a magazine which I read faithfully each month from the first line to the last, even though I don't understand all of it; it is the *Scientific American*. I am extremely eager to be as informed as possible of everything that takes place in modern science and its new developments. My position in relation to science is thus not a negative one.

Secondly, I think there are some things we have lost, and we should try perhaps to regain them, because I am not sure that in the kind of world in which we are living and with the kind of scientific thinking we are bound to follow, we can regain these things exactly as if they had never been lost; but we can try to become aware of their existence and their importance.

In the third place, my feeling is that modern science is not at all moving away from these lost things, but that more and more it is attempting to reintegrate them in the field of scientific explanation.

The real gap, the real separation between science and what we might as well call mythical thought for the sake of finding a convenient name, although it is not exactly that — the real separation occurred in the seventeenth and the eighteenth century. At that time, with Bacon, Descartes, Newton, and the others, it was necessary for science to build itself up against the old generations of mythical and mystical thought, and it was thought that science could only exist by turning its back upon the world of the senses, the world we see, smell, taste, and perceive; the sensory was a delusive world, whereas the real world was a world of mathematical properties which could only be grasped by the intellect and which was entirely at odds with the false testimony of the senses. This was probably a necessary move, for experience shows us that thanks to this separation — this schism if you like — scientific thought was able to constitute itself.

Now, my impression (and, of course, I do not talk as a scientist — I am not a physicist, I am not a biologist, I am not a chemist) is that contemporary science is tending to overcome this gap, and that more and more the sense data are being reintegrated into scientific explanation as something which has a meaning, which has a truth, and which can be explained.

Take, for instance, the world of smells. We were accustomed to think that this was entirely subjective, outside the world of science. Now the chemists are able to tell us that each smell or each taste has a certain chemical composition and to give us the reasons why subjectively some smells or some tastes feel to us as having something in common and some others seem widely different.

Let's take another example. There was in philosophy from the time of the Greeks to the eighteenth and even the nineteenth century — and there still is to some extent — a tremendous discussion about the origin of mathematical ideas — the idea of the line, the idea of the circle, the idea of the triangle. There were, in the main, two classical theories: one of the mind as a *tabula rasa*, with nothing in it in the beginning; everything comes to it from experience. It is from seeing a lot of round objects, none of which were perfectly round, that we are able nevertheless to abstract the idea of the circle. The second classical theory goes back to Plato, who claimed that such ideas of the circle, of the triangle, of the line, are perfect, innate in the mind, and it is because they are given to the mind that we are able to project them, so to speak, on reality, although reality never offers us a perfect circle or a perfect triangle.

Now, contemporary researchers on the neurophysiology of vision teach us that the nervous cells in the retina and the other apparatus behind the retina are specialized: some cells are sensitive only to straight direction, in the vertical sense, others in the horizontal, others in the oblique, some of them to the relationship between the background and the central figures, and the like. So — and I simplify very much because it is too complicated for me to explain this in English — this whole problem of experience versus mind seems to have a solution in the structure of the nervous system, not in the structure of the mind or in experience, but somewhere between mind and experience in the way our nervous system is built and in the way it mediates between mind and experience.

Probably there is something deep in my own mind, which makes it likely that I always was what is now being called a structuralist. My mother told me that, when I was about two years old and still unable to read, of course, I claimed that actually I was able to read. And when I was asked why, I said that when I looked at the signboards on shops — for instance, *boulanger* (baker) or *boucher* (butcher) — I was able to read something because what was obviously similar, from a graphic point of view, in the writing could not mean anything other than "bou," the same first syllable of *boucher* and *boulanger*. Probably there is nothing more than that in the structuralist approach; it is the quest for the invariant, or for the invariant elements among superficial differences.

Throughout my life, this search was probably a predominant interest of mine. When I was a child, for a while my main interest was geology. The problem in geology is also to try to understand what is invariant in the tremendous diversity of landscapes, that is, to be able to reduce a landscape to a finite number of geological layers and of geological operations. Later as an adolescent, I spent a great part of my leisure time drawing costumes and sets for opera. The problem there is exactly the same — to try to express in one language, that is, the language of graphic arts and painting, something which also exists in music and in the libretto; that is, to try to reach the invariant property of a very complex set of codes (the musical code, the literary code, the artistic code). The problem is to find what is common to all of them. It's a problem, one might say, of translation, of translating what is expressed in one language — or one code, if you prefer, but language is sufficient — into expression in a different language.

Structuralism, or whatever goes under that name, has been considered as something completely new and at the time revolutionary; this, I think, is doubly false. In the first place, even in the field of the humanities, it is not new at all; we can follow very well this trend of thought from the Renaissance to the nineteenth century and to the present time. But it is also wrong for another reason: what we call structuralism in the field of linguistics, or anthropology, or the like, is nothing other than a very pale and faint imitation of what the "hard sciences," as I think you call them in English, have been doing all the time.

Science has only two ways of proceeding: it is either reductionist or structuralist. It is reductionist when it is possible to find out that very complex phenomena on one level can be reduced to simpler phenomena on other levels. For instance, there is a lot in life which can be reduced to physicochemical processes, which explain a part but not all. And when we are confronted with phenomena too complex to be reduced to phenomena of a lower order, then we can only approach them by looking to their relationships, that is, by trying to understand what kind of original system they make up. This is exactly what we have been trying to do in linguistics, in anthropology, and in different fields.

It is true — and let's personalize nature for the sake of the argument — that Nature has only a limited number of procedures at her disposal and that the kinds of procedure which Nature uses at one level of reality are bound to reappear at different levels. The genetic code is a very good example; it is well known that, when the biologists and the geneticists had the problem of describing what they had discovered, they could do nothing better than borrow the language of linguistics and to speak of words, of phrase, of accent, of punctuation marks, and the like. I do not mean at all that it is the same thing; of course, it is not. But it is the same kind of problem arising at two different levels of reality.

It would be very far from my mind to try to reduce culture, as we say in our anthropological jargon, to nature; but nevertheless what we witness at the level of culture are phenomena of the same kind from a *formal* point of view (I do not mean at all substantially). We can at least trace the same problem to the mind that we can observe on the level of nature, though, of course, the cultural is much more complicated and calls upon a much larger number of variables.

I'm not trying to formulate a philosophy, or even a theory. Since I was a child, I have been bothered by, let's call it the irrational, and have been trying to find an order behind what is given to us as a disorder. It so happened that I became an anthropologist, as a matter of fact not because I was interested in anthropology, but because I was trying to get out of philosophy. It also so happened that in the French academic framework, where anthropology was at the time not taught as a discipline in its own right in the universities, it was possible for somebody trained in philosophy and teaching philosophy to escape to anthropology. I escaped there, and was confronted immediately by one problem — there were lots of rules of marriage all over the world which looked absolutely meaningless, and it was all the more irritating because, if they were meaningless, then there should be different rules for each people, though nevertheless the number of rules could be more or less finite. So, if the same absurdity was found to reappear over and over again, and another kind of absurdity also to reappear, then this was something which was not absolutely absurd; otherwise it would not reappear.

Such was my first orientation, to try to find an order behind this apparent disorder. And when after working on the kinship systems and marriage rules, I turned my attention, also by chance and not at all on purpose, toward mythology, the problem was exactly the same. Mythical stories are, or seem, arbitrary, meaningless, absurd, yet nevertheless they seem to reappear all over the world. A "fanciful" creation of the mind in one place would be unique — you would not find the same creation in a completely different place. My problem was trying to find out if there was some kind of order behind this apparent disorder — that's all. And I do not claim that there are conclusions to be drawn.

It is, I think, absolutely impossible to conceive of meaning without order. There is something very curious in semantics, that the word "meaning" is probably, in the whole language, the word the meaning of which is the most difficult to find. What does "to mean" mean? It seems to me that the only answer we can give is that "to mean" means the ability of any kind of data to be translated in a different language. I do not mean a different language like French or German, but different words on a different level. After all, this translation is what a dictionary is expected to give you — the meaning of the word in different words, which on a slightly different level are isomorphic to the word or expression you are trying to understand. Now, what would a translation be without rules? It would be absolutely impossible to understand. Because you cannot replace any word by any other word or any sentence by any other sentence, you have to have rules of translation. To speak of rules and to speak of meaning is to speak of the same thing; and if we look at all the intellectual undertakings of mankind, as far as they have been recorded all over the world, the common denominator is always to introduce some kind of order. If this represents a basic need for order in the human mind and since, after all, the human mind is only part of the universe, the need probably exists because there is some order in the universe and the universe is not a chaos.

What I have been trying to say here is that there has been a divorce — a necessary divorce — between scientific thought and what I have called the logic of the concrete, that is, the respect for and the use of the data of the senses, as opposed to images and symbols and the like. We are witnessing the moment when this divorce will perhaps be overcome or reversed, because modern science seems to be able to make progress not only in its own traditional line — pushing forward and forward but still within the same narrow channel — but also at the same time to widen the channel and to reincorporate a great many problems previously left outside.

In this respect, I may be subjected to the criticism of being called "scientistic" or a kind of blind believer in science who holds that science is able to solve absolutely all problems. Well, I certainly don't believe that, because I cannot conceive that a day will come when science will be complete and achieved. There will always be new problems, and exactly at the same pace as science is able to solve problems which were deemed philosophical a dozen years or a century ago, so there will appear new problems which had not hitherto been not perceived as such. There will always be a gap between the answer science is able to give us and the new question which this answer will raise. So I am not "scientistic" in that way. Science will never give us all the answers. What we can try to do is to increase very slowly the number and the quality of the answers we are able to give, and this, I think, we can do only through science.

II

"Primitive" Thinking and the "Civilized" Mind

The way of thinking among people we call, usually and wrongly, "primitive" — let's describe them rather as "without writing," because I think this is really the discriminatory factor between them and us — has been interpreted in two different fashions, both of which in my opinion were equally wrong. The first way was to consider such thinking as of a somewhat coarser quality, and in contemporary anthropology the example which comes to mind immediately is the work of Malinowski. I must say immediately that I have the greatest respect for him and consider him a very great anthropologist, and I'm not at all deriding his contribution. But nevertheless the feeling in Malinowski was that the thought of the people he was studying was, and generally speaking the thought of all the populations without writing which are the subject matter of anthropology was entirely, or is, determined by the basic needs of life. If you know that a people, whoever they are, is determined by the bare necessities of living — finding

285

subsistence, satisfying the sexual drives, and so on — then you can explain their social institutions, their beliefs, their mythology, and the like. This very widespread conception in anthropology generally goes under the name of functionalism.

The other fashion is not so much that theirs is an inferior kind of thought, but a fundamentally different kind of thought. This approach is exemplified by the work of Lévy-Bruhl, who considered that the basic difference between "primitive" thought — I always put the word "primitive" within quotes — and modern thought is that the first is entirely determined by emotion and mystic representations. Whereas Malinowski's is a utilitarian conception, the other is an emotional or affective conception; and what I have tried to emphasize is that actually the thought of people without writing is, or can be in many instances, on the one hand, disinterested — and this is a difference in relation to Malinowski — and, on the other hand, intellectual — a difference in relation to Lévy-Bruhl.

What I tried to show in *Totemism* and in *The Savage Mind*, for instance, is that these people whom we usually consider as completely subservient to the need of not starving, of continuing able just to subsist in very harsh material conditions, are perfectly capable of disinterested thinking; that is, they are moved by a need or a desire to understand the world around them, its nature and their society. On the other hand, to achieve that end, they proceed by intellectual means, exactly as a philosopher, or even to some extent a scientist, can and would do.

This is my basic hypothesis.

I would like to dispel a misunderstanding right away. To say that a way of thinking is disinterested and that it is an intellectual way of thinking does not mean at all that it is equal to scientific thinking. Of course, it remains different in a way, and inferior in another way. It remains different because its aim is to reach by the

shortest possible means a general understanding of the universe —
and not only a general but a *total* understanding. That is, it is a
way of thinking which must imply that if you don't understand
everything, you don't explain anything. This is entirely in contradiction to what scientific thinking does, which is to proceed step
by step, trying to give explanations for very limited phenomena,
and then going on to other kinds of phenomena, and so on. As
Descartes had already said, scientific thinking aimed to divide the
difficulty into as many parts as were necessary in order to solve it.

So this totalitarian ambition of the savage mind is quite different from the procedures of scientific thinking. Of course, the great
difference is that this ambition does not succeed. We are able,
through scientific thinking, to achieve mastery over nature —
I don't need to elaborate that point, it is obvious enough — while,
of course, myth is unsuccessful in giving man more material power
over the environment. However, it gives man, very importantly,
the illusion that he can understand the universe and that he *does*
understand the universe. It is, of course, only an illusion.

We should note, however, that as scientific thinkers we use a
very limited amount of our mental power. We use what is needed
by our profession, our trade, or the particular situation in which
we are involved at the moment. So, if somebody gets involved for
twenty years and even more in the way myths or kinship systems
operate, then he uses this part of his mental power. But we cannot
request that each of us be interested in exactly the same things; so
each of us uses a certain amount of our mental power for what is
needed or for what interests us.

Today we use less and we use more of our mental capacity than
we did in the past; And it is not exactly the same kind of mental
capacity as it was either. For example, we use considerably less of
our sensory perceptions. When I was writing the first version of
Mythologiques (*Introduction to a Science of Mythology*), I was

confronted with a problem which to me was extremely mysterious. It seems that there was a particular tribe which was able to see the planet Venus in full daylight, something which to me would be utterly impossible and incredible. I put the question to professional astronomers; they told me, of course, that we don't but, nevertheless, when we know the amount of light emitted by the planet Venus in full daylight, it was not absolutely inconceivable that some people could. Later on I looked into old treatises on navigation belonging to our own civilization and it seems that sailors of old were perfectly able to see the planet in full daylight. Probably we could still do so if we had a trained eye.

It is exactly the same with our knowledge about plants or animals. People who are without writing have a fantastically precise knowledge of their environment and all their resources. All these things we have lost, but we did not lose them for nothing; we are now able to drive an automobile without being crushed at each moment, for example, or in the evening to turn on our television or radio. This implies a training of mental capacities which "primitive" peoples don't have because they don't need them. I feel that, with the potential they have, they could have changed the quality of their mind, but it would not be needed for the kind of life and relationship to nature that they have. You cannot develop all the mental capacities belonging to mankind all at once. You can only use a small sector, and this sector is not the same according to the culture. That is all.

It is probably one of the many conclusions of anthropological research that, notwithstanding the cultural differences between the several parts of mankind, the human mind is everywhere one and the same and that it has the same capacities. I think this is accepted everywhere.

I don't think that cultures have tried systematically or methodically to differentiate themselves from each other. The fact is that for hundreds of thousands of years mankind was not very numerous on the earth; small groups were living in isolation, so that it was only natural that they developed characteristics of their own and became different from each other. It was not something aimed at. Rather, it is the simple result of the conditions which have been prevailing for an extremely long time.

Now, I would not like you to think that this in itself is harmful or that these differences should be overcome. As a matter of fact, differences are extremely fecund. It is only through difference that progress has been made. What threatens us right now is probably what we may call over-communication — that is, the tendency to know exactly in one point of the world what is going on in all other parts of the world. In order for a culture to be really itself and to produce something, the culture and its members must be convinced of their originality and even, to some extent, of their superiority over the others; it is only under conditions of under-communication that it can produce anything. We are now threatened with the prospect of our being only consumers, able to consume anything from any point in the world and from every culture, but of losing all originality.

We can easily now conceive of a time when there will be only one culture and one civilization on the entire surface of the earth. I don't believe this will happen, because there are contradictory tendencies always at work — on the one hand toward homogenization and on the other toward new distinctions. The more a civilization becomes homogenized, the more internal lines of separation become apparent; and what is gained on one level is immediately lost on another. This is a personal feeling, in that I have no clear proof of the operation of this dialectic. But I don't see how mankind can really live without some internal diversity.

Let us now consider a myth from western Canada about the skate trying to master or dominate the South Wind and succeeding. It is a story of a time that existed on earth before mankind, that is, of a time when animals and humans were not really distinct; beings were half-human and half-animal. All were extremely bothered by the winds, because the winds, especially the bad winds, were blowing all the time, making it impossible for them to fish and to gather shellfish on the beaches. So they decided that they had to fight the winds and compel them to behave more decently. There was an expedition in which several human animals or animal humans took part, including the skate, which played an important role in capturing the South Wind. The South Wind was liberated only after he promised not to blow all the time, but only from time to time, or at certain periods. Since that time, it is only at certain periods of the year, or one day out of two, that the South Wind blows; during the rest of the time, mankind can fulfill its activities.

Well, this story never happened. But what we have to do is not to satisfy ourselves that this is plainly absurd or just a fanciful creation of a mind in a kind of delirium. We have to take it seriously and to ask ourselves the questions: why the skate and why the South Wind?

When you look very closely at the mythical material exactly as it is told, you notice that the skate acts on account of very precise characteristics, which are of two kinds. The first one is that it is a fish like all flat fish, slippery underneath and rough on the back. And the other capacity, which allow the skate to escape very successfully when it has to fight against other animals, is that it is very large seen from above or below, and extremely thin when seen from the side. An adversary may think that it is very easy to shoot an arrow and kill a skate because it is so large; but just as the arrow is being aimed, the skate can suddenly turn or slip and show only its profile, which, of course, is impossible to aim at; thus it escapes. So the reason why the skate is chosen is that it is an animal which, considered from either one point of view or from the other, is capable of giving — let's say in terms of cybernetics — only a "yes" or "no" answer. It is capable of two states which are discontinuous, and one is positive, and one is negative. The use the skate is put to in the myth is — though, of course, I would not like to strain the simile too far — like the elements in modern computers which can be used to solve very difficult problems by adding a series of "yes" or "no" answers.

While it is obviously wrong and impossible from an empirical point of view that a fish is able to fight a wind, from a logical point of view we can understand why *images* borrowed from experience can be put to use. This is the originality of mythical thinking — to play the part of conceptual thinking: an animal which can be used as what I would call a binary operator can have, from a logical point of view, a relationship with a problem which is also a binary problem. If the South Wind blows every day of the year, then life is impossible for mankind. But if it blows only one day out of two — "yes" one day, "no" the other day, and so on — then a kind of compromise becomes possible between the needs of mankind and the conditions prevailing in the natural world.

Thus, from a logical point of view, there is an affinity between an animal like the skate and the kind of problem which the myth is trying to solve. The story is not true from a scientific point of view, but we could only understand this property of the myth at a time when cybernetics and computers have come to exist in the scientific world and have provided us with an understanding of binary operations which had already been put to use in a very different way with concrete objects or beings by mythical thought. So there is really not a kind of divorce between mythology and science. It is only the present state of scientific thought that gives us the ability to understand what is in this myth, to which we remained completely blind before the idea of binary operations become familiar to us.

Now, I would not like you to think that I am putting scientific explanation and mythical explanation on an equal footing. What I would say is that the greatness and the superiority of scientific explanation lies not only in the practical and intellectual achievement of science, but in the fact, which we are witnessing more and more, that science is becoming able to explain not only its own validity but also what was to some extent valid in mythological thinking. What is important is that we are becoming more and more interested in this qualitative aspect, and that sciences which had a purely quantitative outlook in the seventeenth to nineteenth centuries, is beginning to integrate the qualitative aspects of reality as well. This undoubtedly will enable us to understand a great many things present in mythological thinking which we were in the past prone to dismiss as meaningless and absurd. And the trend will lead us to believe that, between life and thought, there is not the absolute gap which was accepted as a matter of fact by the seventeenth-century philosophical dualism. If we are led to believe that what takes place in our mind is something not substantially or fundamentally different from the basic phenomenon of life itself, and if we are led then to the feeling that there is not this kind of gap which is impossible to overcome between mankind on the one hand and all the other living beings — not only animals, but also plants — on the other, then perhaps we will reach more wisdom, let us say, than we think we are capable of.

III

HARELIPS AND TWINS
The Splitting of a Myth

Our starting point here will be a puzzling observation recorded by a Spanish missionary in Peru, Father P. J. de Arriaga, at the end of the sixteenth century, and published in his *Extirpacion de la Idolatria del Peru* (Lima, 1621). He noted that in a certain part of Peru of his time, in times of bitter cold the priest called in all the inhabitants who were known to have been born feet first, or who had a harelip, or who were twins. They were accused of being responsible for the cold because, it was said, they had eaten salt and peppers, and they were ordered to repent and to confess their sins.

Now, that twins are correlated with atmospheric disorder is something very commonly accepted throughout the world, including Canada. It is well known that on the coast of British Columbia, among the Indians, twins were endowed with special powers to bring good weather, to dispel storms, and the like. This is not, however, the part of the problem which I wish to consider here. What strikes me is that all the mythographers — for instance, Sir James Frazer who quotes Arriaga in several instances — never asked the question why people with harelips and twins are considered to be similar in some respect. It seems to me that the crux of the problem is to find out: Why harelips? Why twins? And why are harelips and twins put together?

In order to solve the problem, we have, as sometimes happens, to make a jump from South America to North America, because it will be a North American myth which will give us the clue to the South American one. Many people have reproached me for this kind of procedure, claiming that myths of a given population can only be interpreted and understood in the framework of the culture of that given population. There are several things which I can say by way of an answer to that objection.

In the first place, it seems to me pretty obvious that, as was ascertained during recent years by the so-called Berkeley school, the population of the Americas before Columbus was much larger than it had been supposed to be. And since it was much larger, it is obvious that these large populations were to some extent in contact with one another, and that beliefs, practices, and customs were, if I may say so, seeping through. Any neighbouring population was always, to some extent, aware of what was going on in the other population. The second point in the case that we are considering here is that these myths do not exist isolated in Peru on the one hand and in Canada on the other, but that in between we find them over and over again. Really, they are pan-American myths, rather than scattered myths in different parts of the continent.

Now, among the Tupinambas, the ancient coastal Indians of Brazil at the time of the discovery, as also among the Indians of Peru, there was a myth concerning a woman, whom a very poor individual succeeded in seducing in a devious way. The best known version, recorded by the French monk André Thevet in the sixteenth century, explained that the seduced woman gave birth to twins, one of them born from the legitimate husband, and the other from the seducer, who is the Trickster. The woman was going to meet the god who would be her husband, and while on her way the Trickster intervenes and makes her believe that *he* is the god; so, she conceives from the Trickster. When she later finds the legitimate husband-to-be, she conceives from him also and later gives birth to twins. And since these false twins had different fathers, they have antithetical features: one is brave, the other a coward; one is the protector of the Indians, the other of the white people; one gives goods to the Indians, while the other one, on the contrary, is responsible for a lot of unfortunate happenings.

It so happens that in North America, we find exactly the same myth, especially in the northwest of the United States and Canada. However, in comparison with South American versions, those coming from the Canadian area show two important differences. For instance, among the Kootenay, who live in the Rocky Mountains, there is only one fecundation which has as a consequence the birth of twins, who later on become, one the sun, and the other the moon. And, among some other Indians of British Columbia of the Salish linguistic stock — the Thompson Indians and the Okanagan — there are two sisters who are tricked by apparently two distinct individuals, and they give birth, each one to a son; they are not really twins because they were born from different mothers. But since they were born in exactly the same kind of circumstances, at least from a moral and a psychological point of view, they are to that extent similar to twins.

Those versions are, from the point of view of what I am trying to show, the more important. The Salish version weakens the twin character of the hero because the twins are not brothers — they are cousins; and it is only the circumstances of their births which are closely parallel — they are both born thanks to a trick. Nevertheless, the basic intention remains the same because nowhere are the two heroes really twins; they are born from distinct fathers, even in the South American version, and they have opposed characters, features which will be shown in their conduct and in the behaviour of their descendants.

So we may say that in all cases children who are said to be twins or believed to be twins, as in the Kootenay version, will have different adventures later on which will, if I may say so, untwin them. And this division between two individuals who are at the beginning presented as twins, either real twins or equivalents to twins, is a basic characteristic of all the myths in South America or North America.

In the Salish versions of the myth, there is a very curious detail, and it is very important. You remember that in this version we have no twins whatsoever, because there are two sisters who are travelling in order to find, each one, a husband. They were told by a grandmother that they would recognize their husbands by such and such characteristics, and they are then each deluded by the Tricksters they meet on their way into believing that they are the husband whom each is supposed to marry. They spend the night with him, and each of the women will later give birth to a son.

Now, after this unfortunate night spent in the hut of the Trickster, the elder sister leaves her younger sister and goes visiting her grandmother, who is a mountain goat and also a kind of magician; for she knows in advance that her granddaughter is coming, and she sends the hare to welcome her on the road. The hare hides under a log which has fallen in the middle of the road, and when the girl lifts her leg to cross the log, the hare can have a look at her genital parts and make a very inappropriate joke. The girl is furious, and strikes him with her cane and splits his nose. This is why the animals of the leporine family now have a split nose and upper lip, which we call a harelip in people precisely on account of this anatomical peculiarity in rabbits and hares.

In other words, the elder sister starts to split the body of the animal; if this split were carried out to the end — if it did not stop at the nose but continued through the body and to the tail — she would turn an individual into twins, that is, two individuals which are exactly similar or identical because they are both a part of a whole. In this respect, it is very important to find out what conception the American Indians all over America entertained about the origin of twins. And what we find is a general belief that twins result from an internal splitting of the body fluids which will later solidify and become the child. For instance, among some North American Indians, the pregnant woman is forbidden to turn around too fast when she is lying asleep, because if she did, the body fluids would divide in two parts, and she would give birth to twins.

There is also a myth from the Kwakiutl Indians of Vancouver Island which should be mentioned here. It tells of a small girl whom everybody hates because she has a harelip. An ogress, a supernatural cannibal woman, appears and steals all the children including the small girl with the harelip. She puts them all in her basket in order to take them home to eat them. The small girl who was taken first is at the bottom of the basket and she succeeds in splitting it open with a seashell she had picked up on the beach. The basket is on the back of the ogress, and the girl is able to drop out and run away first. She drops out *feet first*.

This position of the harelipped girl is quite symmetrical to the position of the hare in the myth which I previously mentioned: crouching beneath the heroine when he hides under the log across her path, he is in respect to her exactly in the same position as if he had been born from her and delivered feet first. So we see that there is in all this mythology an actual relationship between twins on the one hand and delivery feet first or positions which are, metaphorically speaking, identical to it on the other. This obviously clears up the connection from which we started in Father Arriaga's Peruvian relations between twins, people born feet first, and people with harelips.

The fact that the harelip is conceived as an incipient twinhood can help us to solve a problem which is quite fundamental for anthropologists working especially in Canada: why have the Ojibwa Indians and other groups of the Algonkian-speaking family selected the hare as the highest deity in which they believed? Several explanations have been brought forward: the hare was an important if not essential part of their diet; the hare runs very fast, and so was an example of the talents which the Indians should have; and so on. Nothing of that is very convincing. But if my previous interpretations were right, it seems much more convincing to say: (1) among the rodent family the hare is the larger, the more conspicuous, the more important, so it can be taken as a representative of the rodent family; (2) all rodents exhibit an anatomical peculiarity which makes out of them incipient twins, because they are partly split up.

When there are twins, or even more children, in the womb of the mother, there is usually in the myth a very serious consequence because, even if there are only two, the children start to fight and compete in order to find out who will have the honour of being born first. And, one of them, the bad one, does not hesitate to find a short cut, if I may say so, in order to be born earlier; instead of following the natural road, he splits up the body of the mother to escape from it.

This, I think, is an explanation of why the fact of being born feet first is assimilated to twinhood, because it is in the case of twinhood that the competitive hurry of one child will make him destroy the mother in order to be the first one born. Both twinhood and delivery feet first are forerunners of a dangerous delivery, or I could even call it a heroic delivery, for the child will take the initiative and become a kind of hero, a murderous hero in some cases; but he completes a very important feat. This explains why, in several tribes, twins were killed as well as children born feet first.

The really important point is that in all American mythology, and I could say in mythology the world over, we have deities or supernaturals, who play the roles of intermediaries between the powers above and humanity below. They can be represented in different ways: we have, for instance, characters of the type of a Messiah; we have heavenly twins. And we can see that the place of the hare in Algonkian mythology is exactly between the Messiah — that is, the unique intermediary — and the heavenly twins. He is not twins, but he is incipient twins. He is still a complete individual, but he has a harelip, he is half way to becoming a twin.

This explains why, in this mythology, the hare as a god has an ambiguous character which has worried commentators and anthropologists: sometimes he is a very wise deity who is in charge of putting the universe in order, and sometimes he is a ridiculous clown who goes from mishap to mishap. And this also is best understood if we explain the choice of the hare by the Algonkian Indians as an individual who is between the two conditions of (*a*) a single deity beneficent to mankind and (*b*) twins, one of whom is good and the other bad. Being not yet entirely divided in two, being not yet twins, the two opposite characteristics can remain merged in one and the same person.

IV

WHEN MYTH BECOMES HISTORY

This topic presents two problems for the mythologist. One is a theoretical problem of great importance because, when we look at the published material both in North and South America and elsewhere in the world, it appears that the mythic material is of two different kinds. Sometimes, anthropologists have collected myths which look more or less like shreds and patches, if I may say so; disconnected stories are put one after the other without any clear relationship between them. In other instances, as in the Vaupés area of Colombia we have very coherent mythological stories, all divided into chapters following each other in a quite logical order.

And then we have the question: what does a collection mean? It could mean two different things. It could mean, for instance, that the coherent order, like a kind of saga, is the primitive condition, and that whenever we find myths as disconnected elements, this is the result of a process of deterioration and disorganization; we can only find scattered elements of what was, earlier, a meaningful whole. Or we could hypothesize that the disconnected state was the archaic one, and that the myths were put together in an order by native wise men and philosophers who do not exist everywhere, but only in some societies of a given type. We have exactly the same problem, for instance, with the Bible, because it seems that its raw material was disconnected elements and that learned philosophers put them together in order to make a continuous story. It would be extremely important to find out if, among the people without writing who are studied by the anthropologists, the situation is the same as with the Bible or is completely different.

This second problem is, though still theoretical, of a more practical nature. In former times, let's say in the late nineteenth century and early twentieth century, mythological material was collected mostly by anthropologists, that is, people from the outside. Of course, in many cases, and especially in Canada, they had native collaborators. Let me, for instance, quote the case of Franz Boas, who had a Kwakiutl assistant, George Hunt (as a matter of fact, he was not exactly Kwakiutl because he was born of a Scottish father and a Tlingit mother, but he was raised among the Kwakiutl, married among the Kwakiutl, and completely identified with the culture). And for the Tsimshian, Boas had Henry Tate, who was a literate Tsimshian, and Marius Barbeau had William Benyon, who was also a literate Tsimshian. So native co-operation was secured from the beginning, but nevertheless the fact is that Hunt, Tate, or Benyon worked under the guidance of the anthropologists, that is, they were turned into anthropologists themselves. Of course, they knew the best legends, the traditions belonging to their own clan, their own lineage, but nevertheless they were equally interested in collecting data from other families, other clans, and the like.

When we look at this enormous corpus of Indian mythology, such as, for instance, Boas's and Tate's *Tsimshian Mythology*, or the Kwakiutl texts collected by Hunt, and edited, published, and translated too by Boas, we find more or less the same organization of the data, because it is the one which was recommended by the anthropologists: for instance, in the beginning, cosmological and cosmogonic myths, and later on, much later on, what can be considered as legendary tradition and family histories.

It has so happened that this task, started by the anthropologists, the Indians are taking now up themselves, and for different purposes, for instance, to have their language and mythology taught in elementary schools for Indian children. That is very important, I understand, at the moment. Another purpose is to use legendary tradition to validate claims against the white people — territorial claims, political claims, and so on.

So it is extremely important to find out if there is a difference and, if there is, what kind of difference between traditions collected from the outside from those collected on the inside, though *as if* they were collected from the outside. Canada is fortunate, I should say, in that books about its own mythology and legendary traditions have been organized and published by the Indian specialists themselves. This began early: there is *Legends of Vancouver* by Pauline Johnson, issued before the First World War. Later on, we had books by Marius Barbeau, who was, of course, not Indian at all, but who tried to collect historical or semi-historical material and make himself the spokesman of his Indian informants; he produced, so to speak, his own version of that mythology.

More interesting, far more interesting, are books such as *Men of Medeek*, published in Kitimat in 1962, which is supposedly the verbatim account collected from the mouth of Chief Walter Wright, a Tsimshian chief of the middle Skeena river, but collected by somebody else, a white field worker who was not even a professional. And even more important is the recent book by Chief Kenneth Harris, who is also a Tsimshian chief, published in 1974 by himself.

So we can, with this kind of material, make a kind of experiment by comparing the material collected by anthropologists, and the material collected and published directly by the Indians. I should not say "collected," as a matter of fact, because instead of being traditions from several families, several clans, several lineages put together and juxtaposed to each other, what we have in these two books is really the history of one family or one clan, published by one of its descendants.

The problem is: where does mythology end and where does history start? In the case, entirely new to us, of a history without archives, there being of course no written documents, there is only a verbal tradition, which is claimed to be history at the same time. Now, if we compare these two histories, the one obtained on the middle Skeena from Chief Wright, and the one written and published by Chief Harris from a family up Skeena in the Hazelton area, we find similarities and we find differences. In the account of Chief Wright, we have what I would call the genesis of a disorder: the entire story aims at explaining why after their first beginning, a given clan or lineage or group of lineages have overcome a great many ordeals, known periods of success and periods of failures, and have been progressively led toward a disastrous ending. It is an extremely pessimistic story, really the history of a downfall. In the case of Chief Harris, there is a quite different outlook, because the book appears principally geared at explaining the origin of a social order which was the social order in the historical period, and which is still embedded, if I may say so, in the several names, titles, and privileges which a given individual, occupying a prominent place in his family and clan, has collected by inheritance around himself. So it is as if a diachronic succession of events was simultaneously projected on the screen of the present in order to reconstitute piece by piece a synchronic order which exists and which is illustrated by the roster of names and privileges of a given individual.

Both stories, both books are positively fascinating, and are, literarily speaking, great pieces; but for the anthropologist, their main interest is to illustrate the characteristics of a kind of history widely different from our own. History as we write it is practically entirely based upon written documents, while in the case of these two histories there are obviously no written documents or very few. Now, what strikes me when I try to compare them is that both start with the account of a mythical or perhaps historical — I don't know which, perhaps archaeology will settle the matter — time when on the upper Skeena, near what is now Hazelton, there was a big town the name of which Barbeau transcribed as Tenlaham and an account of what happened there. It is practically the same story in both books: it explains that the city was destroyed, that the remnants of the people went on the move, and started difficult peregrinations along the Skeena.

This, of course, could be a historical event, but if we look closely at the way it is explained, we see that the type of event is the same, but not exactly the details. For instance, according to the version, there can be at the origin a fight between two villages or two towns, a fight which originated in an adultery; but the story can be either that a husband killed the lover of his wife, or that brothers killed their sister's lover, or that a husband killed his wife because she had a lover. So, you see, we have an explanatory cell. Its basic *structure* is the same, but the *content* of the cell is not the same and can vary; so it is a kind of mini-myth if I may say so, because it is very short and very condensed, but it has still the property of a myth in that we can observe it under different transformations. When one element is transformed, then the other elements should be rearranged accordingly. This is the first aspect of these clan stories that interests me.

The second aspect is that they are histories which are highly repetitive; the same type of event can be used several times, in order to account for different happenings. For instance, it is striking that in the stories of the particular tradition of Chief Wright and of the particular tradition of Chief Harris, we find similar happenings, but they don't take place in the same spot, they don't affect the same people, and, very likely, they are not exactly in the same historical period.

What we discover by reading these books is that the opposition — the simple opposition between mythology and history which we are accustomed to make — is not at all a clear-cut one, and that there is an intermediary level. Mythology is static, we find the same mythical elements combined over and over again, but they are in a closed system, let us say, in contradistinction with history, which is, of course, an open system.

The open character of history is secured by the innumerable ways according to which mythical cells, or explanatory cells which were originally mythical, can be arranged and rearranged. It shows us that by using the same material, because it is a kind of common inheritance or common patrimony of all groups, of all clans, or of all lineages, one can nevertheless succeed in building up an original account for each of them.

What is misleading in the old anthropological accounts is that a kind of hodge-podge was made up of tradition and beliefs belonging to a great many different social groups. This makes us lose sight of a fundamental character of the material — that each type of story belongs to a given group, a given family, a given lineage, or to a given clan, and is trying to explain its fate, which can be a successful one or a disastrous one, or be intended to account for rights and privileges as they exist in the present, or be attempting to validate claims for rights which have since disappeared.

When we try to do scientific history, do we really do something scientific, or do we too remain astride our own mythology in what we are trying to make as pure history? It is very interesting to look at the way both in North and South America, and indeed everywhere in the world, in which an individual, who has by right, and by inheritance a certain account of the mythology or the legendary tradition of his own group, reacts when he listens to a different version given by somebody belonging to a different family or to a different clan or lineage, which to some extent is similar but to some extent too is extremely different. Now, we would think that it is impossible that two accounts which are not the same can be true at the same time, but nevertheless, they seem to be accepted as true in some cases, the only difference made is that one account is considered better or more accurate than the other. In other cases, the two accounts can be considered equally valid because the differences between them are not perceived as such.

We are not at all aware in our daily life that we are exactly in the same situation in relation to different historical accounts written by different historians. We pay attention only to what is basically similar, and we neglect the differences due to the fact that the way historians carve the data and the way they interpret them are not exactly the same. So if you take two accounts by historians, with different intellectual traditions and different political leanings, of such events as the American Revolution, of the French-English war in Canada, or the French Revolution, we are not really so shocked that they don't tell us exactly the same thing.

Thus my impression is that by studying carefully this history, in the general sense of the word, which contemporary Indian authors try to give us of their own past, by not considering this history as a fanciful account, but by trying extremely carefully, with the help of a type of salvage archaeology — excavating village sites referred to in the histories — and by trying to establish correspondences, inasmuch as this is possible, between different accounts, and by trying to find what really corresponds and what does not correspond, we may in the end reach a better understanding of what historical science really is.

I am not far from believing that, in our own societies, history has replaced mythology and fulfils the same function, that for societies without writing and without archives the aim of mythology is to ensure that as closely as possible — complete closeness is obviously impossible — the future will remain faithful to the present and to the past. For us, however, the future should be always different, and ever more different, from the present, some difference depending, of course, on our political preferences. But nevertheless the gap which exists in our mind to some extent between mythology and history can probably be breached by studying histories which are conceived as not at all separated from but as a continuation of mythology.

V

MYTH AND MUSIC

The relationship between myth and music on which I insisted so much in the initial section of *The Raw and the Cooked* and also in the final section of *L'Homme nu* — there is not yet an English title because it is not translated — was probably the topic which gave rise to most misunderstandings, especially in the English-speaking world, though also in France, because it was thought that this relationship was quite arbitrary. My feeling was, on the contrary, that there was not only one relationship but two different kinds of relationship — one of similarity and an other of contiguity — and that, as a matter of fact, they were actually the same. But that I did not understand right away, and it was the relation of similarity which struck me first. I shall try to explain it in the following way.

In regard to the similarity aspect, my main point was that, exactly as in a musical score, it is impossible to understand a myth as a continuous sequence. This is why we should be aware that if we try to read a myth as we read a novel or a newspaper article, that is line after line, reading from left to right, we don't understand the myth, because we have to apprehend it as a totality and discover that the basic meaning of the myth is not conveyed by the sequence of events but — if I may say so — by bundles of events even although these events appear at different moments in the story. Therefore, we have to read the myth more or less as we would read an orchestral score, not stave after stave, but understanding that we should apprehend the whole page and understand that something which was written on the first stave at the top of the page acquires meaning only if one considers that it is part and parcel of what is written below on the second stave, the third stave, and so on. That is, we have to read not only from left to right, but at the same time vertically, from top to bottom. We have to understand that each page is a totality. And it is only by treating the myth as if it were an orchestral score, written stave after stave, that we can understand it as a totality, that we can extract the meaning out of the myth.

Why and how does this happen? My feeling is that it is the second aspect, the aspect of contiguity, which gives us the significant clue. As a matter of fact, it was about the time when mythical thought — I would not say vanished or disappeared — but passed to the background in western thought during the Renaissance and the seventeenth century, that the first novels began to appear instead of stories still built on the model of mythology. And it was exactly at that time that we witnessed the appearance of the great musical styles characteristic of the seventeenth and, mostly, the eighteenth and nineteenth centuries.

It is exactly as if music had completely changed its traditional shape in order to take over the function — the intellectual as well as emotive function — which mythical thought was giving up more or less at the same period. When I speak here of music, I should, of course, qualify the term. The music that took over the traditional function of mythology is not any kind of music, but music as it appeared in western civilization in the early seventeenth century with Frescobaldi and in the early eighteenth century with Bach, music which reached its full development with Mozart, Beethoven, and Wagner in the eighteenth and nineteenth centuries.

What I would like to do in order to clarify this statement is to offer a concrete example, which I shall take from Wagner's tetralogy, *The Ring*. One of the most important musical themes in the tetralogy is the one which we call in French "*le thème de la renunciation à l'amour*" — the renunciation of love. As is well known, this theme appears first of all in the *Rhinegold* at the moment when Alberich is told by the Rhine maidens that he can conquer the gold only if he renounces all kind of human love. This very startling musical motif is a sign to Alberich, given at the very moment when he says that he takes the gold but he renounces love once and for all. All this is very clear and simple; it is the literal sense of the theme: Alberich *is* renouncing love.

Now the second striking and important moment when the theme reappears is in the *Valkyrie* in a circumstance which makes it extremely difficult to understand why. At the moment when Siegmund has just discovered that Sieglinde is his sister and has fallen in love with her, and just when they are going to initiate an incestuous relationship, thanks to the sword which is buried in the tree and which Siegmund is going to tear away from the tree — at that moment, the theme of the renunciation of love reappears. This is some kind of a mystery, because at that moment Siegmund is not at all renouncing love — he's doing quite the opposite and knowing love for the first time of his life with his sister Sieglinde.

The third appearance of the theme is also in the *Valkyrie*, in the last act when Wotan, the king of the gods, is condemning his daughter Brunhilde to a very long magical sleep and surrounding her with fire. We could think that Wotan is also renouncing love because he is renouncing his love for his daughter; but this is not very convincing.

Thus you see that we have exactly the same problem as in mythology; that is, we have a theme — here a musical theme instead of a mythological theme — which appears at three different moments in a very long story: once at the beginning, once in the middle, and once at the end, if for the sake of the argument we limit ourselves to the first two operas of *The Ring*. What I would like to show is that the only way of understanding this mysterious reappearance of the theme is, although they seem very different, to put the three events together, to pile them up one over the other, and to try to discover if they cannot be treated as one and the same event.

We can then notice that, on the three different occasions, there is a treasure which has to be pulled away or torn away from what it is bound to. There is the gold, which is stuck in the depths of the Rhine; there is the sword, which is stuck in a tree, which is a symbolic tree, the tree of life or the tree of the universe; and there is the woman Brunhilde, who will have to be pulled out of the fire. The recurrence of the theme then suggests to us that, as a matter of fact, the gold, the sword, and Brunhilde are one and the same: the gold as a means to conquer power, the sword as a means to conquer love, if I may say so. And the fact that we have a kind of coalescence between the gold, the sword, and the woman is, as a matter of fact, the best explanation we have of the reason why, at the end of the *Twilight of the Gods*, it is through Brunhilde that the gold will return to the Rhine; they have been one and the same, but looked at through different angles.

Other points of the plot are also made very clear. For instance, even though Alberich renounced love, he will later on, thanks to the gold, become able to seduce a woman which will bear him a son, Hagen. It is thanks to his conquest of the sword that Siegmund also will beget a son, who will be Siegfried. Thus the recurrence of the theme shows us something never explained in the poems, that there is a kind of twin relationship between Hagen the traitor and Siegfried the hero. They are in a very close parallelism. This explains also why it will be possible that Siegfried and Hagen, or rather Siegfried first as himself and then under the disguise of Hagen, will at different moments of the story conquer Brunhilde.

I could go on like this for a very long time, but perhaps these examples are sufficient to explain the similarity of method between the analysis of myth and the understanding of music. When we listen to music, we are listening, after all, to something which goes on from a beginning to an end and which develops through time. Listen to a symphony: a symphony has a beginning, has a middle, it has an end, but nevertheless I would not understand anything of the symphony and I would not get any musical pleasure out of it if I were not able, at each moment, to muster what I have listened to before and what I am listening to now, and to remain conscious of the totality of the music. If you take the musical formula of theme and variations, for instance, you can only perceive it and feel it only if for each variation you keep in mind the theme which you listened to first; each variation has a flavour of its own, if unconsciously you can superimpose it on the earlier variation that you have listened to.

Thus there is a kind of continuous reconstruction taking place in the mind of the listener to music or the listener to a mythical story. It's not only a global similarity. It is exactly as if, when inventing the specific musical forms, music had only rediscovered structures which already existed on the mythical level.

For instance, it is very striking that the fugue, as it was formalized in Bach's time, is the true-to-life representation of the work-

ing of some specific myths, of the kind where we have two characters or two groups of characters. Let's say one good, the other one
bad, for instance, though that is an over-simplification. The story
unrolled by the myth is that of one group trying to flee and to
escape from the other group of characters; so you have a chase of
one group by the other, sometimes group A rejoining group B,
sometimes group B escaping — all as in a fugue. You have what we
call in French "*le sujet et la réponse.*" The antithesis or antiphony
continues through the story until both groups are almost confused
and confounded — an equivalent to the *stretta* of the fugue; then
a final solution or climax of this conflict is offered by a conjugation
of the two principles which had been opposed all along during the
myth. It could be a conflict between the powers above and the
powers below, the sky and the earth, or the sun and subterranean
powers, on the like. The mythic solution of conjugation is very
similar in structure to the chords which resolve and end the musical piece, for they offer also a conjugation of extremes which, for
once and at last, are being reunited. It could be shown also that
there are myths, or groups of myths, which are constructed like a
sonata, or a symphony, or a rondo, or a toccata, or any of all the
musical forms which music did not really invent but borrowed
unconsciously from the structure of the myth.

There is a little story I would like to tell you. When I was writing *The Raw and the Cooked*, I decided to give each section of the
volume the character of a musical form and to call one "sonata,"
another "rondo," and so on. I then came upon a myth, the structure of which I could very well understand, but I was unable to
find a musical form which would correspond to this mythical
structure. So I called my friend the composer, René Leibowitz,
and explained to him my problem. I told him the structure of the
myth: at the beginning two entirely different stories, apparently
without any relationship with each other, progressively become

intertwined and merge, until at the end they make up only one theme. What would you call a musical piece with the same structure? He thought it over and told me that in the whole history of music there was no musical piece he knew of with that structure. So there is no name for it. It was obviously quite possible to have a musical piece with this structure; and a few weeks later he sent me a score which he had composed and which borrowed the structure of the myth I had explained to him.

Now, the comparison between music and language is an extremely tricky one, because to some extent the comparison is extremely close and there are, at the same time, tremendous differences. For example, contemporary linguists have told us that the basic elements of language are phonemes — that is, those sounds that we represent, incorrectly, by the use of letters — which have no meaning in themselves, but which are combined in order to differentiate meaning. You could say practically the same thing of the musical notes. A note — A, B, C, D, and so on — has no meaning in itself; it is just a note. It is only the combination of the notes which can create music. So you could very well say that, while in language we have phonemes as elementary material, in music we would have something which in French I would call *"soneme"* — in English perhaps "toneme" would do. This is a similarity.

But if you think of the next step or the next level in language, you will find that phonemes are combined in order to make words; and words in their turn are combined together to make sentences. But in music there are no words: the elementary materials — the notes — are combined together, but what you have right away is a "sentence," a melodic phrase. So, while in language you have three very definite levels — phonemes combined to make words, words combined to make sentences — in music you have with the notes something of the same kind as phonemes from a logical point of view, but you miss the word level and you go directly to a sentence.

Now you can compare mythology both to music and to language, but there is this difference: in mythology there are no phonemes; the lowest elements are words. So if we take language as a paradigm, the paradigm is constituted by, first, phonemes; second, words; third, sentences. In music you have the equivalent to phonemes and the equivalent to sentences, but you don't have the equivalent to words. In myth you have an equivalent to words, an equivalent to sentences, but you have no equivalent to phonemes. So there is, in both cases, one level missing.

If we try to understand the relationship between language, myth, and music, we can only do so by using language as the point of departure, and then it can be shown that music on the one hand and mythology on the other both stem from languages but grow apart in different directions, that music emphasizes the sound aspect already embedded in language, while mythology emphasizes the sense aspect, the meaning aspect, which is also embedded in language.

It was Ferdinand de Saussure who showed us that language is made up of indissociable elements which are on the one hand the sound and on the other the meaning. And my friend Roman Jakobson has just published a little book which is entitled *Le Son et le Sens*, as the two inseparable faces of language. You have sound, the sound has a meaning, and no meaning can exist without a sound to express it. In music, it is the sound element which takes over, and in the myth it is the meaning element.

I have always dreamed since childhood about being a composer or, at least, an orchestra leader. I tried very hard when I was a child to compose the music for an opera for which I had written the libretto and painted the sets, but I was utterly unable to do so because there is something lacking in my brain. I feel that only music and mathematics can be said to be really innate, and that one must have some genetic apparatus to do either. I remember quite well how, when I was living in New York during the war as a refugee, I had dinner once with the great French composer, Darius Milhaud. I asked him, "When did you realize that you were going to be a composer?" He explained to me that, when he was a child in bed slowly falling to sleep, he was listening and hearing a kind of music with no relationship whatsoever to the kind of music he knew; he discovered later that this was already his own music.

Since I was struck by the fact that music and mythology were, if I may say so, two sisters, begotten by language, who had drawn apart, each going in a different direction — as in mythology, one character goes north, the other south, and they never meet again — then, if I wasn't able to compose with sounds, perhaps I would be able to do it with meanings.

The kind of parallelism I have tried to draw — I have said it already but I would like to emphasize it once again — applies only, as far as I am aware, to western music as it developed during the recent centuries. But now we are witnessing something which, from a logical point of view, is very similar to what took place when myth disappeared as a literary genre and was replaced by the novel. We are witnessing the disappearance of the novel itself. And it is quite possible that what took place in the eighteenth century when music took over the structure and function of mythology is now taking place again, in that the so-called serial music has taken over the novel as a genre at the moment when it is disappearing from the literary scene.

DANGERS & OPTIONS
The Matter of World Survival

by
WILLY BRANDT

FOREWORD

I welcome the opportunity to recommend to thoughtful people everywhere this timely and astute volume of Willy Brandt's thoughts about the basic challenge of our times: global survival. His analysis and recommendations are not designed to comfort the complacent, to strengthen illusions, or to excuse inaction. On the contrary, this is a book about harsh global realities, described with the keen insight and forthright language one would expect from a man who is profoundly committed to peace and justice in the world.

It will be difficult for anyone to escape the conclusion, after reading these pages, that interdependence is the dominant fact of life in our era — that we are all responsible for each other's well-being, and that we must learn to live together or face the prospect of perishing together.

Despite the dangers represented by the international crises which he describes in such compelling and forceful language,

Willy Brandt is not a man without hope. Indeed, realistic confidence in man's capacity to build a better world for all is the very foundation of his thought.

The dangers are very real. Every day we see evidence of the worldwide economic upheaval which has beset our planet during the past decade. We are alarmed by the increasing military rivalry between East and West. We are appalled by the human misery resulting in large part from the imbalance in wealth and opportunity among rich and poor countries.

But the hopeful options are just as real. While there may be room for debate about Mr. Brandt's specific suggestions, there can be no quarrel with his conviction that progress toward stability and justice is not only possible, not only urgently necessary, but is also to the advantage of every person on earth.

As Chancellor of the Federal Republic of Germany, and more recently as chairman of the Independent Commission on International Development Issues, Willy Brandt has been in the forefront of seminal thinkers on the great and pressing issue of global cooperation for survival. His ideas, as expressed in these Massey Lectures, are required reading for anyone who believes, as I do, that each of us is responsible for helping to create our common future.

PIERRE ELLIOTT TRUDEAU

I

DANGERS AND OPTIONS

Three years ago when I was spending a summer holiday in Valais in Switzerland, I received a visit from a retired political leader of that country. When he questioned me about the purpose of my new Secretariat in Geneva, I said it housed the staff appointed to help me and my Independent Commission to complete our North-South Report. "Ah, yes," replied my visitor, "these Italians and their eternal problems . . ."

And indeed, factual problems are often compounded by semantic ones. I am sure you will understand that while using the term "North-South", I am going to deal with relations between industrialized and developing nations. This, of course, was the difficult subject dealt with at the first North-South summit meeting, which was held in Cancun, Mexico, in October, 1981.

That meeting, where Pierre Trudeau, Prime Minister of Canada, acted as co-chairman, did not bring about any sensational, from my point of view not even satisfactory, results. But it still produced a certain atmosphere of moderate optimism. And that's better than nothing.

In July 1981, when the economic conference of the seven leading industrial countries had taken place in Ottawa, no one could say even with the best will in the world that mankind had found the path leading to a bright new existence. Various economic schools of thought were represented in Ottawa and the same old, familiar suggestions about safeguarding peace were restated. Only in regard to relations with the developing countries did one gain the impression of even the most cautious opening.

A fortnight before, during the opening days of July, I had undertaken an information-gathering journey to Moscow. There I found that although the Soviets were indulging in polemics against Western terminology and misinterpretations of their intentions, they in fact seemed to have come closer to the point where it could make sense to jointly discuss North-South issues. But I must admit that this still remains a hope.

In any case, the period we are going through is certainly full of drama and confusion. What we are experiencing is not a process of measurable change, but a series of wide-ranging upheavals in science and technology, in economic affairs and in international relations.

Numerous crises in many parts of the world provide ample evidence of this radical change. It would, however, be quite wrong to allow ourselves to be hypnotized by that suggestive word "crisis." There is no hope of things simply righting themselves and returning to "normal." We will always be facing radical change and having to find adequate solutions. Not to do so could be fatal.

To my way of thinking, worldwide change is necessary today for three chief reasons. First, there is the need for a profound restructuring of the world economy to increase world productivity and to provide jobs. Second, there is the persistent East-West rivalry and arms build-up. And last, but not least, are the completely unsatisfactory North-South relations between the industrialized states on the one hand and the developing nations on the other.

Let us consider the *first* factor, the profound change in the pattern of the world's economy. The period of persistent economic growth — on the scale which we experienced in the fifties and sixties — would seem to be over for the foreseeable future. This holds true for the whole world. In western industrialized countries, in the eastern industrial societies and in the developing countries as a group — wherever we look there is now much slower economic progress or no progress at all. In some parts we even see output declining.

The economic climate of the present age is clouded by inflation and unemployment; by expensive raw materials including energy and food, and costly environmental control measures; by high balance-of-payments deficits and an international monetary system whose shortcomings have become clear to many laymen.

We do not need to look far for the social and political consequences. For many years, it was possible to offset social tensions in western democratic societies because there was enough economic growth to go around for all, or almost all. As a result, even the broad masses of our nations derived benefit from a steadily rising level of affluence. Whenever divergent interests met head-on, a material compromise was at hand.

Today, this sort of compromise is available only on a somewhat limited scale. In most of our countries, the pace of social strife has quickened, even if everyone may not yet be aware of it.

It will require a considerable amount of imagination and sensitivity to balance the various interests in our modern industrial societies within the limits to further growth which are now visible, and at the same time to maintain a smoothly functioning political process. Our democracies will not remain what they have been if our elected leaders leave the field uncontested to rival, extremist groups or simply stand aside to make way for all-powerful bureaucracies.

If a new balance among the various factions and interests is not achieved, there will be an acceleration of a trend already noticeable in certain places: a loss of confidence in those in political office along with a dwindling faith in the viability of modern democracy. I see the possibility of an ever more widespread alienation — alienation of the sort expressed by many of the younger people — an escapism inspired by a blend of political weariness and anxiety about modern civilization. Misgivings about the whole purpose of technical progress might combine with a dangerous nostalgia for the apparent peacefulness and tranquillity of former times — a peacefulness and tranquillity which never really existed.

I consider it to be a remarkable coincidence that two different forms of conservatism have now become so influential in the two world powers, the United States and the Soviet Union. At the same time, we can see how previously aligned countries are asserting themselves more than in the past — countries which might not so much be questioning the alliances themselves as insisting on the expression of their own ideas and interests.

Poland has demonstrated this on the Eastern side, while corresponding cases may be cited in Western Europe. In Britain, a new political party is emerging which could soon gain considerable influence; in France, the election of Mitterrand's socialists might have dramatic results; in my own country the ecologists are gaining support, and a peace movement is growing stronger.

Let me now turn to the *second* factor likely to determine the fate of all of us: relations between East and West, and the attendant arms race. Our new decade did not make a very promising start. The precarious relationship between the superpowers, marked for years by ups and downs, once more deteriorated. Even the slightest increase in unpredictable behaviour or ideological influencing, any further lack of caution could have brought the whole of humanity to the brink of catastrophe at several times.

The arms race has not only continued apace, it has assumed dimensions which can no longer be grasped by the human mind. Every minute the world spends over one million dollars for military purposes; we stockpile more explosives than food, and we are more concerned with military security than with hunger and malnutrition, which in the end may pose an even greater threat. Every warning seems to have fallen on deaf ears. All efforts to achieve concrete arms limitation seem to be frustrated by the feeling of a growing threat from the other side. Sometimes, warnings miscarry because the overall situation becomes unstable. And regional conflicts expand. It is small wonder that many people are beginning to ask whether the policy of *détente* ever really existed, and if it did whether or not it has failed definitely, and if it has what alternative there might be.

It is still my feeling that the ideas underlying the efforts to reduce tension at the end of the sixties and the beginning of the seventies have not been futile, but they do not take us any further for the time being. In my view, these ideas did not flow from illusions, but from the pragmatic desire to supplement defence with a political dimension for safeguarding peace, producing attempts to help evolve a common interest in arms limitation. That remains indispensable. And it has, as we know, led to a reopening of talks between the two superpowers.

The concept of *Ostpolitik* — a concept which is in part, linked to my name — involved, at a level below that of peace and war, the normalization of interstate contacts, the implementation of different forms of practical cooperation and the possibility of an alleviation of hardships for humanitarian reasons. For individual human beings, small steps forward are nearly always worth more than fine words or political rhetoric. For the citizens of West Berlin, for example, it meant a lot when after many years they could again cross the border, pass through the Wall, and see their relatives in East Berlin. The reopening of telephone lines alone made life easier for many people in both East and West.

There can hardly be a return to the situation existing in the fifties. The risks have multiplied. The potential for destruction available today poses an even more immense threat. There are far too many regional crises capable of becoming major conflagrations.

The further commitment of valuable resources to even more gigantic arms projects — the inevitable outcome of another Cold War — would render it impossible to devote one's attention to the great problems which exist side by side with the arms race, with equally frightening possibilities. And we may well fool ourselves when we see security as purely a military problem, as if population growth and hunger, the limited resource base of our earth and the abuse of the environment were risks of a lesser category.

Still, let us not get discouraged. However painful setbacks may be, they don't give us an excuse for simply turning our backs. The important thing is to learn from mankind's mistakes and to stay on course for peace and cooperation without illusions, but with steadfastness.

The *third* factor in the global changes taking place and hence the third new task for this decade consists in reshaping relations between industrialized and developing countries — "North and South," as it is called in international discussions.

In point of fact, this much used term "North-South" inadequately conveys the complexity of highly different levels of development and gravely imbalanced relations between rich and poor peoples, richer and poorer nations. But it is certainly no exaggeration when I say that I regard this as *the* social challenge of our times — a challenge to all people with a sense of responsibility.

Today, one-fifth of humanity suffers from hunger and malnutrition in the developing countries. The majority of these men and women live in South and South-east Asia and the sub-Saharan regions of Africa. During the last decade, many countries in these regions have been able to make but little progress. If no fundamental changes take place, then this decade cannot be expected to bring any improvements either. It might well mean more under-development.

By the year 2000, the world's population will have grown to over six billion people; this means about two billion more people than today. Eighty-five percent of this total will be living in what we call the developing countries. Even if birth rates decline, a country like Tanzania will have more inhabitants by the end of the century than Canada with its vast expanse of land and abundance of resources.

For another thirty years or so we will have to live with a still-growing world population. With great efforts and a variety of measures we may succeed in stabilizing the total number of people living on earth. Success or failure in this respect will have tremendous consequences: it may mean the difference between ten billion or twenty billion people by the middle of the twenty-first century.

So you can see that a reduction in population growth is one of the first steps in halting the disastrous depletion of the world's natural resources. Yet, population control alone will not be enough. Nor is it just a technical problem for experts who advise on family planning methods. We have learned that there is a close link between poverty and the number of children people have, with children often seen, rightly or wrongly, as a source of support for parents in their old age. Fighting poverty in itself thus contributes to slower population growth.

Along with population control, there must be revision and reformation in the structural pattern of worldwide economic relations. The conditions for the historic and unparalleled growth of the last thirty years were created at a time before most of the developing countries had even gained their independence. And as many young emergent states have meanwhile found out, formal political independence in itself is no guarantee for any real freedom. Freedom of decision is hard to achieve as long as traditional poverty and economic dependence remain.

Therefore, it is perfectly understandable that the developing nations have been calling for fundamental reforms in the world economy for something like two decades. However, as in the case of domestic reforms in our own countries, the scope for international reforms has narrowed considerably.

The picture I have just drawn is not a very happy one, but it does reflect the real situation. Under these circumstances, we must try to implement adequate policies. It seems clear to me that employment policy and the structural policy accompanying it cannot be left solely to the oft-invoked "self-healing forces" of the market economy. Anyone who has held a position of responsibility in West Germany in recent years will never be tempted to underestimate the thrust of the market-economy system. Nevertheless, experience at home and abroad, especially in less developed countries, leads me to believe that an important role must be played by public authorities in a number of sectors. Energy problems have demonstrated, both on the domestic and the international scenes, that there must be a certain degree of public responsibility in many fields of activity.

At the same time, everyone with a knowledge of the current situation in the public sector, and in large private enterprises as well, will realize the importance of avoiding bureaucratic excesses. In any case, gross materialism cannot be the sole *raison d'état* in a

democracy. I am not pleading the virtue of high-minded renunciation; I am pleading the case of justice, solidarity and fair treat-
ment, both within states and between states. In a period of rapid
and deep-rooted change, we shall only survive if individual interests are embedded within an overall framework of social solidarity.

From this flows the perception that government decisions must
be taken with the closest possible involvement of the people
concerned and affected by such measures. In my own experience
this approach has brought good results in fields like city-planning
and the environment.

Those men and women, the citizens, to whom the measures
apply should be aware that a democratic society needs their special
knowledge and it depends on their cooperation. A successful
economic and social policy requires as much cooperation as possible among institutions, government, management and trade
unions. In Europe, there is a growing feeling that labour's co-
determination might be the proper instrument to promote
economic democracy.

The holders of political office must remain receptive to fresh
ideas, whether they themselves are able to develop them or not. In
my view, the search for alternative lifestyles, either for the individual or for the group, must not simply be dismissed as either idle
fancy or as a sinister attack on the established political order.

Those who believe that many things cannot continue as they
have in the past must be taken seriously. Have we not all been
emulating the mistaken United States model of a society based on
super-abundance and built-in obsolescence? Should we not be
mounting a more active search for solutions which correspond to
the economic and ecological requirements of our time in order to
establish, wherever possible, a stable equilibrium?

So what is the plan of action? First and most important, the
leaders of the two superpowers must discharge their specific

responsibilities toward other nations. They must do what has to be done in order to create that minimum of confidence without which predictability is impossible. Otherwise, there will be no end to the arms race, and without an end to the arms race, *détente* cannot survive; and without *détente* there can be only a fragile security.

Europe has long ceased to be the hub of the world. Nevertheless, it remains of great importance for the whole of mankind that we in Europe prove capable of maintaining peace and thereby furnish an example of how differing interests can be reconciled without explosive conflicts. We must not succumb to the paralyzing alternative: to do nothing if *détente* is not yet possible everywhere. It is my firm belief that we need *détente* in order to safeguard peace *and* to find the strength for balancing the interests of North and South.

My conclusion derives from lifelong experience — a life marked by ups and downs, disappointments and encouragements. What humanity needs is not less *détente*, but more negotiations and cooperation. We need this above all in the relations between the superpowers. And wherever that is possible, we must help them to achieve it. We can do so by acting as both loyal and independent partners in the Western Alliance.

If the western industrial states systematically and definitely overcome the legacy of the past, that is bound to produce positive consequences for others. In any event, the developing nations are now speaking up more forcefully than they did even a few years ago, telling the industrialized states of both East and West what they expect of them. They also expect something more from the affluent oil-producing countries.

For us in the western world, it is not history but future that matters. In addition to humanitarian and idealistic challenges, there is a good deal of legitimate self-interest involved. Peace is not only good for others. More exchange will be to our own advantage as well as to that of others. The jobs of many of our young people, and even more so, of their children, will depend upon speeding up the process of development and exchange.

I hope it is clear that I am not talking about the decline of the West and I have no intention of creating an atmosphere of hysteria. I want to discuss what we must jointly seek to accomplish: a sense of reality about the world in which we live, and the hard work necessary to find answers to the questions now besetting us.

It looks as if during the foreseeable future we shall be afflicted with more problems than can be quickly resolved. The objective of all those who carry and feel responsibility must therefore be to prevent the gap between rich and poor, within countries and between nations, from growing wider and to concentrate on particularly significant sectors.

We must carefully examine how the international economy works. And we must make changes wherever there are built-in disadvantages for the developing nations: in the monetary system, in trade of manufactured goods and raw materials, in research and technology. We must also not forget that the industrialized countries have not reached their present position only through their own efforts. Foreign capital and technical assistance, the influx of educated and well-trained people have always played an important role.

In my opinion, many political debates and many election campaigns simply bypass discussion of the crucial issues. Our democracies will be judged by many citizens in terms of their ability to shape the future actively and constructively. If the impression were to continue that traditional politics merely reacts to external events instead of shaping them, then it would hardly be surprising if unconventional or dangerous ideas were to spread.

The experience gained during recent years has pointed to the dimension of the challenges now drawing near. Today, we must recognize that international security is not just a question of military power, and act accordingly. Questions of social peace, an equitable balance of interests are equally important. And that applies to domestic as well as foreign policy.

That was the motivation for the activities carried out by the Independent Commission on International Development Issues, which worked for two years under my chairmanship and published its report in early 1980. We called it *North-South: A Program for Survival*. And "survival" will be my next theme.

II

SURVIVAL

It is not only the competition for power and exaggerated ideological conflicts that pose a threat to peace, and by that to survival. There loom ahead of us potential threats in the form of economic collapse, mass hunger, population explosion and ecological catastrophe.

As I mentioned earlier, it has become customary — and the Brandt Report also follows this custom — to use the geographical terms "North" and "South" as synonyms for the industrialized states and the developing states respectively. "North-South" has thus come to be a euphemism for the blatantly unequal levels of development and the alarming lack of balance in the relations between industrial and developing states.

The significance of this problem can hardly be overestimated. I would like to emphasize again that I consider the issues implicit in the expression "North-South" to be *the* social challenge of our time — a challenge to all responsible-minded people in the North *and* South, in the West *and* East of the world.

In 1978 and 1979 when I served as chairman of the Independent Commission on International Development Issues, I often found myself considering such categories as "global responsibility" and "mutual interest." The suggestion about setting up such a commission came from Robert McNamara, who was then president of the World Bank, where he remained until the summer of 1981. From the beginning, I decided it was important to arrange for complete technical and financial independence from all existing organizations, even the one responsible for the creation of the study. Upon the completion of our report, the first copy was presented to the Secretary-General of the United Nations.

This was one way in which our commission differed from the one which Lester Pearson directed for the World Bank ten years earlier. Another difference was that I appointed a majority of colleagues from the developing countries as members of the commission. My purpose was to rule out any possibility that they could be outvoted.

Of course, we soon found out that despite our common ground on many matters, individual colleagues adopted different approaches in answering the questions. After all, it came as no great surprise to find Eduardo Frei, Christian Democrat and former president of Chile, choosing a different set of priorities from those of our left-wing socialist colleague Layachi Yaker from Algeria, who again would not always agree with the Indian Governor Jha or Mr. Dakouré from Upper Volta. The same applied to the Conservative Edward Heath, the Social Democrat Olof Palme, Peter Peterson from Wall Street, or Joe Morris from Canada, who in a way represented the international trade union movement and who brought along great experience from the International Labor Organization in Geneva.

It was by no means my goal to produce a unanimous report. With the benefit of hindsight, however, it seems to be a good example for others that we were in fact able to uncover sufficient common ground to reach a consensus on our judgements and recommendations without any dissenting votes.

My colleagues and I remain certain of one thing. If we wish to raise the relations between North and South to a level of fruitful cooperation and thus to create worldwide conditions for reducing the immense gap between rich and poor, it will call for nothing short of a fundamental, underlying commitment to global co-responsibility. In these days of critical developments in international relations, that might sound utopian. Some people even claim that it is of minor importance, given the other dangerous trend toward military disaster.

I do not share their view. Naturally, the foremost task must be to bring acute conflicts under control and thus avoid a global conflagration. By the same token, however, we cannot afford simply to return to the sterile confrontation of the past. A continued process of *détente* and of more concrete cooperation between East and West must for some time to come provide the basis, in a wide measure, of North-South policies. Otherwise, we would risk outbursts of violence in the Third World at even shorter intervals, outbursts that would eventually drag us all in.

That is why I believe we could hardly commit a greater error than to push aside North-South issues until relations between the world powers and their alliances have once more improved. It would be equally wrong to revert to the habit of considering relations with the Third World first and foremost from what certain quarters regard as a strategic standpoint.

We need *détente* to safeguard peace *and* to find the strength necessary to bring about a balance between industrial and developing countries. We need a brake on world armaments to prevent the world from literally arming itself to death, *and* also to enable us to use the resources released in this way for development purposes. We need a just and stable international order so that people in the North *and* in the South can feel confident about their future and their chances of survival.

And I do not mean simply what the rich countries can do to help the poor countries. The issue is what rich and poor can do together to make human survival more probable. There are mutual interests in peace, justice and jobs.

My sketch of living conditions in the Third World is not intended to conjure up apocalyptic visions. Its purpose is to depict real dangers which affect life in the North too. These are dangers, moreover, which bring into question whether our capacities of anticipation and imagination will be sufficient to help us find peaceful solutions and strategies for the world.

As we know, the population of the world will have grown by another two thousand million people by the end of the present century. Even if the birth rate drops, a country like Bangladesh, one of the poorest nations in the world, could eventually equal the United States in population.

One-fifth of all people in the South are already suffering from hunger and malnutrition.

One of the great services performed by Robert McNamara during his term as president of the World Bank, was his constant reminder that even now as many as six hundred million or even eight hundred million people live in absolute poverty.

These people eke out a miserable existence without employment. They spend their lives in primitive housing without electricity and with inadequate sanitary facilities; without medical care and without educational opportunities.

The majority of these poorest of the world's citizens live in Africa south of the Sahara and in South Asia. In most of these countries the average annual income is less than two hundred fifty dollars per person, and in many of them the growth in agricultural production cannot keep pace with the increase in population.

In my opinion, it is our duty to help our fellow humans by doing everything we can to overcome hunger and to ensure that everyone's fundamental needs are satisfied — their needs for food, health, housing and elementary education.

If anybody thinks this sounds too idealistic, then let me assure you that *it is an illusion to believe that islands of prosperity and safety can in the long run survive in a sea of poverty.* Our own interest in survival is involved. And while it is obvious for me that world hunger increases the dangers of instability and eventually war, it is also obvious that development could become a catalyst for peace.

Of course, the "South" does not present a picture of uniform poverty. The countries of the Third World possess very different economic structures. There is even a growing group of states whose development has advanced so far that their manufactured products are making their impact felt in international markets.

Consumers in the North are already familiar with industrial goods from Singapore, South Korea, Brazil or Colombia. But the economic growth of these countries has not always benefited the broad masses of the population. In Latin America alone, where conditions as a whole are not quite as bad as in large parts of Africa and Asia, about one hundred million people still live in absolute poverty.

The facts of rapid and uneven development do not excuse pressure for "buy at home" policies in more developed countries. We must accept competition from these newly industrializing countries if we do not want to stop their development. By stopping it, if we could, we would hurt our own interests as far as exchange is concerned. If they are not allowed to sell to us, they will also be unable to buy from us or pay back our loans. Trade, we must always remember, is not a one-way street. And we would all lose potential new jobs which would result from speeding-up international cooperation.

What my friends from emerging countries say they want, and I have no reason not to believe them, are external trade accords which result "not in welfare, but work; not handouts, but jobs."

Some of the oil-exporting countries have managed to amass immense wealth in recent years. But these countries too face great development problems. And the densely populated ones, like Indonesia or Nigeria, are anything but affluent.

One thing simply cannot be denied: world markets have often operated in ways that have been very unfavourable to the countries of the Third World. It is thus understandable that the 120 developing nations belonging to what is called the "Group of 77" have, since the first United Nations Conference on Trade and Development (UNCTAD) in 1964, demanded the abolition of unequal exchange between North and South.

They have drawn up a list of demands in various areas in which they wish to see world economic reform implemented. From all these demands and objectives, there emerged what came to be known in the "Group of 77" and the United Nations as the New International Economic Order. This new International Economic Order is meant to replace the present system of unequal exchange and calls for reform of the existing institutions.

The international community, to which reference is made so often, consists of some 150 nation states, about three times as many as in 1945 when most of the international institutions were created. Thus, the international community is governed by institutions and rules that have not changed much since they were designed. This holds true, among others, for the International Monetary Fund and the World Bank, and the General Agreement on Tariffs and Trade (GATT).

It is thus understandable that the newly independent countries seek a revision of these systems to take into account their interests and their concerns. We are not simply concerned with the so-called transfer of resources. Rather, we need to review the sharing of power and of responsibility among the countries of the world.

This New International Economic Order includes the stabilization of commodity prices or their indexation so that they would move in line with the more quickly increasing prices of industrial goods. It also includes the demand that the developing countries should have easier access to more advanced technology. Because such access concerns in part the role of the big transnational corporations, it has led to differing and wide-ranging proposals with respect to their rights and duties.

Reforms since 1964 have not come easily. Common positions of the developing countries were indeed not always very realistic, while those of the industrialized countries often showed that they were unwilling to give up any major privilege. In negotiations, their representatives defended the existing status, and were often unwilling to even admit that there might be a problem. Official development aid gained some importance, but it stayed well below the level promised at successive international conferences.

Then, in the course of the seventies, the incipient recession in the industrial states turned into a full-blooded economic crisis on a scale not experienced for decades. Now there were millions of unemployed in the North, too, as more and more economies suffered the paralysis of stagflation — a low rate of growth combined with simultaneous inflation.

The enormous increases in the price of oil, the lifeblood of industrial societies, reinforced the largely negative response to Third World demands. In the view of many governments the scope for international and national reforms alike became even more restricted than before, while others argued that such reforms had now become more important and urgent.

In the wake of the oil-price shock in 1973–74, collective action by the Organization of Petroleum Exporting Countries (OPEC) seemed to imply one thing at least: some of the Third World countries had acquired a better bargaining position. In the meantime, both sides have begun to realize that North-South relations have become deadlocked. Yet there is no lack of people, including governments, who argue that North and South must find a common approach in this highly interdependent world of ours if we are jointly to survive.

Let me illustrate this with an example. If more and more people in the poorest regions of the world are forced to cut down their forests to have enough firewood for cooking purposes, that is bound to cause soil erosion and a reduction in the supply of food. It would also have far-reaching consequences for the climate in other parts of the world.

Similarly, there is no need for me to spell out the consequences for the Third World of a nuclear war between East and West. By the same token, however, a further impoverishment of the southern hemisphere and a spread of chaotic conditions would be certain to engender a much greater number of armed conflicts.

The current crises in the Middle East and elsewhere should have finally opened our eyes to the close interrelationship between North-South problems on the one hand and East-West conflicts on the other, and to the highly explosive mixture which it represents.

More than one country confronts us with not only the economic but also the cultural problems of development. There are obviously limits to aid and not merely to growth. There are perhaps avenues of approach to a new type of partnership, but these avenues are difficult to open.

We in the West should make it clear beyond suspicion and doubt that we are interested in strong and healthy partners abroad. And that we respect their non-alignment. More thought and attention ought to be given to arriving at a clear statement of the various interests, including the mutual ones, between developing countries and industrial states. That would make it easier to work on sensible compromises without having to feel that one can simply sweep the real, and in part, profound differences between North and South under the carpet.

I find it encouraging that leading representatives of the Third World have repeatedly stressed their interest not in separation from, but in integration within a world economy based on a division of labour. Needless to say, such an orientation must be backed in many individual countries by energetic national efforts to overcome mass poverty.

In my Commission's report we discussed a series of measures in trade, finance and monetary reform which would provide a basis for international discussion and a framework for working toward a new order of international economic relations over the next few decades. But perhaps I should rather concentrate on what we proposed for the immediate future.

My colleagues and I felt, and still feel, that four main objectives ought to have priority, and indeed must be achieved during the next five years. And I appreciate that these priorities were discussed, even if only to a smaller degree agreed upon, at the Cancun summit meeting in October 1981.

There must first be substantially improved financial flows. Second, we need an agreed international energy strategy and assured global supply of energy. Third, mass hunger must be overcome. Finally, work must begin on a structural reform of international organizations and institutions which influence the world's economic system. Let me explain what these four points mean.

First: The poorest countries and the poverty belts of Africa and Asia are the countries hardest hit in the present economic crisis. They need an influx of resources. The basic conditions must be created so that these regions can develop an economic dynamism of their own and start the process of sustained growth.

Most industrial countries have already promised to contribute 0.7 percent of their gross national product for official development aid. We think they should follow the example of the Scandinavians and the Dutch, who give more than 0.7 percent and who also lead in terms of per capita contributions, providing more than twice the amount per person than does, for example, Canada or Federal Germany. And they should immediately commit themselves to a firm timetable for reaching this target. That would make an additional thirty billion dollars a year available.

If the rich oil-producing countries and the industrialized states in the East and even some of the middle-income countries were also to make larger contributions, we would begin to see significant improvements in the most desperate human conditions.

Energetic aid programs should not be seen as a burden, but as a worthwhile investment in a healthier world community. Since we published our report in 1980, the debt situation of quite a number of countries has become, to put it mildly, even more serious. Now many countries are facing state bankruptcy. Banks, governments and international institutions will have to concern themselves with the need for debt rescheduling.

But in addition to such acute and transitional measures, financial flows must be promoted. For instance, oil money surpluses might move through the international banking system by co-financing and other appropriate measures for spreading risks, by the use of the International Monetary Fund's gold reserves, or a strengthening of the investment opportunities for the World Bank and the Regional Development Banks.

In the longer run, methods of modest international levies or taxation might prove not only to be effective, but also of mutual advantage. With this in mind, the experts ought to be encouraged to continue their examination of this field.

The *second* objective refers to the energy sector in general and oil in particular. Here, the important thing is to combine in a rational manner the need for regular oil supplies at more predictable prices with the demand for energy conservation and the development of alternative energy sources. That in turn presupposes a partnership between the oil-producing and the oil-consuming countries.

This is all the more important in that we must now brace ourselves for a critical transition period when we move away from oil. The waste of energy must come to an end. We must push ahead on a global scale to invest in alternative and, if possible, renewable sources of energy. We must do so without watching our national economies become paralyzed by abrupt rises in the price of oil.

Interestingly enough, the oil-producing countries themselves have recently displayed great interest in promoting research and their own activities in producing alternative sources of energy. After a visit to Saudi Arabia some time ago, I came away with the particularly pronounced impression of that country's interest in taking part in the most advanced developments for the post-oil era.

Another point is the need for joint efforts to use such sources of energy in less developed countries as have hitherto not been used or have remained entirely undiscovered: for example, coal and water power in Africa and indeed the growing importance of hydro-electric power in general. Here the proposal for a financing institution, in connection with the World Bank, deserves general support.

Due consideration must also be given to the interest of developing countries that import oil, by providing guarantees on deliveries and financial aid. Otherwise, the oil bills will thwart their growth completely. In this context, it is interesting to note the arrangements into which Mexico and Venezuela have entered with some of the countries in Central America and the Caribbean, as have Arab oil countries with some Arab non-oil countries. These arrangements mean either loans or a reduction of price, below that on the world market.

The *third* objective is to a certain extent linked with the transfer of resources: the need to produce more food in all those countries where the conditions exist but where they have become increasingly dependent on imports in recent years. They need irrigation schemes, technical equipment and the production of fertilizers and many other measures designed to step up productivity.

But what is also needed for some time to come is a greater volume of food aid. An international grains arrangement might make it possible to check the inflationary trends in the international markets for food products.

A *fourth* short-term objective should be to start wholehearted moves toward reforming the structure of those international organizations which deal with money and finance. This applies to the international monetary system and to the operations of institutions responsible for development financing and trade. We should review the system and change it with the goal of obtaining a greater right to a say by the users, a fairer sharing of power if you will. We should also support measures for the stabilization of commodity prices, and in spite of the difficulties deriving from the ongoing depression, a progressive liberalization of international trade. But, as I said before, international reforms must effectively be backed up in the developing countries by means of appropriate efforts of their own.

We must also look at the existing United Nations machinery, and our experience with huge international conferences. One of my Third World friends thought that dialogue, if that is the right word, was becoming "ritualistic, technocratic, and indeterminate."

No doubt various international arrangements ought to be restructured, so that they become more effective, with more balanced responsibilities and a greater capability to develop consensus — the first step in really getting things done.

This is by no means a complete list of everything we shall have to confront in the years ahead. An emergency program is not a substitute for, nor must it be in any way inconsistent with longer-term needs and reforms. But one thing is certain: if we achieve these four short-term, urgent objectives, it would present a fair deal for the world and one capable of removing the North-South dialogue from the blind alley in which it has been sadly stuck in recent years.

In our epoch, interdependence is the new fact of life, and without any spirit of solidarity there is no certainty that mankind will survive.

III

Development and Disarmament

When I convened my Independent Commission on International Development Issues at the end of 1977, I was often asked why I had not selected any members from countries with Communist governments. Well, the reason for this certainly did not lie in any prejudice on my part, but in my belief that the time was not opportune for such a widening of our deliberations.

While my colleagues and I were at work on the report, our staff remained in touch with Soviet experts and they travelled to Moscow and Peking. Our experts and those on the Soviet side reached a wide measure of agreement on the relevant data as well as on their assessment of the looming dangers. I gathered my own first-hand impressions in the many talks I have had over the past three years with leading public figures in the Eastern European states.

They all showed a great interest in the questions we put to them. As one of them expressed it: "It cannot be a matter of indifference to us when the issue concerns the future conditions of world trade; or the components of a new monetary system; or the international aspects of supplies of energy and foodstuffs."

The leaders of the Soviet Union were more cautious and they argued more along ideological lines. They refused to accept the legacy of colonialism and rejected any attempt to place them on a par with "capitalist" industrial states where responsibilities toward the developing countries were concerned. In the Third World, such arguments meet with growing skepticism. Those representing the developing nations point out with increasing frequency: "We do not want to waste time on this matter of historical guilt, but instead to tackle the immediate problems of the future. In order to master these problems, we expect the industrialized North as a whole to do something about them and not merely the western part of the North."

In early July 1981 when I went on my information-gathering journey to Moscow, I was able to satisfy myself about the genuine interest of the academics with whom I spent an afternoon at the Moscow Institute for International Relations. The group consisted of some seventy professors and fifty or sixty of their assistants.

As was only to be expected, they were critical, but not impervious to the argument about the growing significance of issues over and above the differences between the West and the East — what I call the "system-bridging" problems. These include, for example, the population explosion; world hunger; non-renewable raw materials, or hazards to the natural environment; and, of course, the arms race and what it may lead to.

The professors in Moscow were undoubtedly more advanced than most officials in their government, although this may well also be the case in parts of the world other than the Eastern bloc. The Soviet leaders give the impression of being rather conservative;

they also have a natural inclination to feel much more independent than the governments of their allied states.

To my surprise, Secretary-General Brezhnev revealed less reserve than one might have expected. At our meeting, he took the initiative in broaching the subject, but he raised some of the old arguments, which he described as fundamental, about not lumping the Communist countries together with "capitalist" colonial powers. Nor was he very keen on the term "North-South," about which he thought quite a lot could be said. Mr. Brezhnev also thought that the West was quoting misleading statistics in regard to Soviet contributions to Third World countries. One could not simply leave out countries like Cuba and Vietnam. Then came his surprising reference to the thought being given by the Soviet leaders as to whether or not they should participate in some way or other in the conference organized by Mexican President José Lopez Portillo together with Austrian Chancellor Bruno Kreisky. (It happened that the Austrian chancellor could not go to Cancun because he was ill, and Prime Minister Trudeau — well-qualified by his involvement in Third World matters — had to take over as co-chairman at the Cancun summit meeting in October.)

We did not discuss details while I was in the Soviet Union. Our talks were dominated by Euro-strategic weapons and other military matters, and not least the forthcoming negotiations between the nuclear superpowers. In the end, the Soviets did not participate in the Cancun summit meeting. It must have been a difficult decision for them to stay out while China was in. Soviet leaders might also have increasing problems in defending their doctrinaire position vis-à-vis large parts of the Third World.

It is my impression that in large parts of the Third World there is a growing fear of becoming victims of another cold war. If, on the other hand, there should be some progress in arms-reduction talks, they hope this might improve the prospects of constructive measures in the area of development.

In Moscow, as indeed elsewhere, I described the unsolved North-South issues not simply as a challenge in practical and in humanitarian terms, but as a horrendous time bomb. There was and still is every reason to speak up explicitly about the disproportion between development and armament.

The bad relations prevailing between the superpowers and the alliances in East and West, as well as the increasingly acute conflicts in various regions of the world have resulted in the spending of ever-mounting sums of money on weapons, with a correspondingly smaller amount available for the struggle against world hunger.

Only serious negotiations can avoid the emergence of new rounds in the global arms race. By 1980, annual military expenditure had topped the enormous amount of five hundred billion U.S. dollars while official development assistance came to about twenty-five billion dollars. Now the fate of mankind will depend upon whether or not the persistent arms race can be brought to an end.

This arms race has assumed dimensions hardly comprehensible to the human mind. The sum of money spent on armaments for 1981 was considerably more than the sum I mentioned for 1980. Let me repeat that figure: more than five hundred thousand million dollars.

The industrial states in East and West alone annually spend almost four hundred dollars per capita on armaments, a sum well above the average annual income in many developing countries. And a number of the developing countries themselves spend more on arms than on education and health care for their own people. Some ninety billion dollars in 1979 alone. One should, however, add in all fairness that a very great part of that sum is accounted for by the rich oil states.

In some ways, developing countries seem to imitate the bad example which the industrial states have given them. At the same time, we have to admit the fact that some of the countries in the West are trying to alleviate their economic problems with increased arms exports to the Third World.

A few years ago, the United States and the Soviet Union embarked upon preparatory negotiations in order to determine how they could limit their arms exports to developing countries. These negotiations did not make much progress and the problem has since become even greater. Every warning of the dangerous consequences of the arms race seems to have fallen on deaf ears. Every effort to achieve concrete limitation arrangements seems to be frustrated by the feeling of a growing threat from the other side, or by general distrust and confusion.

The history in the seventies of the SALT negotiation process — on strategic, intercontinental nuclear weapons — demonstrates this very clearly. It took years and years to reach an agreement on a SALT II Treaty and this was then not ratified by the U.S. Senate.

For some time, the only hope was that the two world powers would continue to behave as if SALT II had been ratified by both sides. However, the critical discussions about regional balance of power and especially about Euro-strategic nuclear weapons show that it is not enough simply to proceed on the basis of "as if." There must be negotiations — serious negotiations — and the necessary agreements must be reached, the sooner the better.

It is clearly necessary to make the non-proliferation of nuclear weapons a more serious aspect of international politics. It is therefore to be welcomed that the United States and the Soviet Union have started their talks in Geneva. And there is every reason to encourage both governments to widen the area of subjects to be discussed: strategic and medium-range — *and why not also so-called tactical* — nuclear machines of destruction.

Other events should be mentioned in this context. Much of what is taking place today must be seen as a trend toward a militarization of foreign policy. Afghanistan has furnished one of the worst examples. Central America must not be allowed to become the next one. Therefore, every effort should be made to bring about, for example, a political solution in a country like El Salvador. But there are a number of dangerous spots in Africa, too, with a growing involvement of foreign influences. And in the Middle East the traditional and by now well-known controversies might suddenly be aggravated by a more distinct confrontation between the superpowers.

On the one hand, there is a considerable lack of effort to solve those North-South problems which are capable of an objective solution, especially since this would also correspond with the industrial world's enlightened self-interest. On the other hand, new conflicts are arising in the relations between East and West and these have a tendency to complicate regional problems of a different nature, but most of which have a potential to produce dangerous crises.

It is a small wonder that many people ask whether the policy of *détente* will get another chance or what the alternative may be. I can only reiterate: it may be that a policy of reducing tensions and bringing about more cooperation, will not survive in the eighties. This would then be a result of the attitude of the major powers concerned, and perhaps already of the increasingly less controllable influences of modern weaponry and strategic computer-thinking. In the case that negotiations were to fail the only probable alternative would be some form of catastrophe.

Let me refer to what I discussed earlier. The further commitment of valuable resources to even more gigantic arms projects will render it impossible to devote our attention to the real, great problems of the future.

In my opinion, we in Europe and America, together with our partners in other parts of the world, will be able to cope with the difficulties — even those of unemployment and world hunger and the dangers to our natural environment — if we agree on intelligent measures and begin to act soon. But time is short.

As far as Europe is concerned, it seems to me that our old continent perhaps once more could find the strength to contribute to a balanced and stable peace in the world. Nobody can replace America and the Soviet Union. They have to take the lead as far as the world's peace and mutual security are concerned. But we in Europe would be unwise if we behaved as if we did not exercise any influence on the course of events. In point of fact, we could become, on a much more intensive scale and at a much earlier time than others, the real theatre of war, in the worst case for a nuclear holocaust.

This, of course, is the background for certain expressions of fear in various parts of Europe. They include an important element of skepticism about the superpowers. But it would be a serious mistake to interpret it as if one had to deal with any kind of old-fashioned or primitive anti-Americanism.

As far as my own country is concerned, our non-nuclear contribution to western defence is considerable, as would the French and British say about their specific part in the alliance. And the Western European contribution to world trade is significant. On the other hand, Europe's political influence must not and should not lag as far behind as has hitherto been the case.

Observers abroad have sometimes wondered why European unification makes as little progress as it does. Part of the answer is that the peoples of Europe want to maintain their national identity and still develop a political structure within which they can deal with those important matters which affect them as a community. While this is such a difficult and even disappointing process, one should not overlook the fact that a European consciousness has reappeared, and is growing slowly, even in the Communist-ruled eastern parts of the continent.

To accomplish an active role necessitated by the growing dangers, Europe must certainly do more to overcome its persistent inner strife. I appreciate only too well that many will smile somewhat wearily when I mention the unification of Europe. They may feel inclined to point to the many years during which this has been discussed and to the very modest achievements to date.

And yet I must insist on this point. The ten western countries of the European Community have made substantial progress toward coordinating their foreign policy, quite apart from the Common Market and some coordination of economic policies. Moreover, as I just indicated, the experience of the last few years did demonstrate more than once that European governments in West and East see some common interest, despite all the loyalty toward their respective alliances, in not being subjected to undue burdens as a result of deteriorating relations between the world powers. There has been a reference in this context to a slow "Europeanization of Europe."

I would not be surprised if the Europeans, or many of them, were more willing now than in the past to attempt to exercise not only a moderating influence on the superpowers and their arms race, but also on crisis-stricken regions. No doubt Europe has a role to play in Africa. No doubt many of the Latin American countries do not want less, but more cooperation with Europe. No doubt Europe cannot behave as if it did not have a high degree of interests in the Middle East, closely linked to that region as it is, after all.

In this period of change, a close and productive relationship between North America and Europe remains indispensable to peace. Naturally, these relations are also subject to dynamic movements.

The pattern of power no longer corresponds to what it was immediately after World War II. And not all the experience which the United States has meanwhile gathered would seem to us in Europe worthy of imitation. What we need today is an all-round willingness to continue to develop well-tried forms of cooperation and at the same time to take altered circumstances into account. Americans should be aware that there is a growing desire of the Europeans to decide for themselves and not just to listen to what others might have to say.

In any case, one thing is certain whether I look at it as a European or as a citizen of the world. We need arms limitation both to prevent a nuclear war *and* to be able to use the resources thus made available for development purposes in the not too distant future.

That strikes me as being the true "linkage" in political terms. We shall only be able to avoid a worldwide catastrophe if, in the face of our mutual interest in survival, we conclude serious agreements on arms limitation, and we must conclude these agreements not at some indefinite time in the future, but in this decade.

When this comes about, all the states positively affected by agreements on arms reduction will have goals to reach with the help of those funds which otherwise flow into the arms build-up. Yet it must, in fact, be possible to set aside part of such funds for use on international development schemes. For example:

- The military expenditure of only half a day would suffice to finance the whole malaria eradication program of the World Health Organization, and less would be needed to conquer river-blindness, which is still the scourge of millions.
- A modern tank costs about one million dollars; that amount could improve storage facilities for 100,000 tons of rice and thus save 4,000 tons or more annually — one person can live on

just over a pound of rice a day. The same sum of money could provide 1,000 classrooms for 30,000 children.

- For the price of one jet fighter (20 million dollars) one could set up about 40,000 village pharmacies.
- One-half of 1 percent of one year's world military expenditure would pay for all the farm equipment needed to increase food production and approach self-sufficiency in food-deficit low-income countries by 1990.

The planning of future steps ought not be delayed any longer; *nor should the requisite enlightening of public opinion.* Nor should we neglect what must be done now while the arms race is still going on.

The next few years will certainly engender a closer mental association between those two equally alarming problems: the world arms build-up and world hunger. Moreover, large numbers of the young people now see themselves face to face with a moral challenge and a threat to their own very existence.

The experience gained during recent years has pointed to the dimension of the challenges now drawing near. In future, we must bear in mind better than we have in the past that international security is not only a question of military power: it is also becoming more and more a question of peace with those who have been hungry so long, and of an equitable balance of interests, at home as well as abroad.

We live in an interdependent world marked by a coming shortage of resources and an accelerating growth in the problems confronting us. Our most precious assets are human inventiveness and social responsibility. And it is these qualities which the peoples of the world must call to mind as they become fully aware of their mutual dependence.

IV

Our Own Interest

After World War II, as we all know, the process of organizing peace was less successful than many people had hoped it would be. Still, the various organizations of the "un family" thrown up by the attempt at a new world order have become an important framework within which to discuss problems of international cooperation. And sometimes even to agree upon what has to be done.

On the economic scene, cooperation between the United States and Western Europe had a special role to play at the end of the Second World War. What we remember as the "Marshall Plan" became an impressive example of how to turn national interest to mutual advantage.

In that case, it was the link between a Western Europe devastated by war and a United States endowed with excess capacity. Though admittedly in very different circumstances, we again find ourselves in a situation marked by the need for new solutions. And without drawing over-simplistic parallels between then and now, the need today is again one of promoting peaceful relations *and* creating basic material conditions without which there obviously cannot be a well-functioning and relatively stable system of states.

Here is an example of what I mean: Africa needs harbours, roads and irrigation facilities while on the other hand Europe has surplus capacity. Why then can one not bring together the requirements of the one side and the potential of the other side? Admittedly, the question comes in highly simplified form, but that does not make it wrong. The problem simply is that the African countries cannot pay for what they need unless they earn more from their exports or they receive financial assistance from abroad. Thus, the needs are evident; the capacity to satisfy such needs exists; and even the required capital is there in the form of foreign exchange reserves in a number of countries, or could come from some relatively small reduction in consumption in the rich countries — not to speak of even a modest limitation on military expenditures. Obviously, these problems remain open to a solution as the Marshall Plan demonstrated.

I spoke of Africa because she is Europe's neighbouring continent. And I should certainly add to my observations and mention the Lomé Convention. This is a cooperation agreement between the European Community and some sixty countries in Africa, the Caribbean and in the Pacific, mostly former colonies of European states. The Convention was signed in 1976 and renewed and expanded in 1979. It covers various fields of economic relations: aid, trade relations, capital transfers. A special feature is the so-called Stabex system which guarantees the developing countries a minimum level of export earnings from almost all their agricultural exports and iron ore. They thus have a kind of insurance against losses when export earnings drop following some adverse local event like a drought or a hurricane, or when export earnings fall as a result of declining demand following a downturn in the European Community's economic situation.

I consider the Lomé Convention to be not only welcome as it stands, but also capable of further expansion. What it lacks is the dimension to which I referred earlier: a large-scale combination between the capacity of the one side and the development potential of the other so as to create or to promote markets from which both can benefit.

As the development of present-day industrial states has shown, the massive purchasing power of the workers formed one of the prerequisites for the advance of their economies. In a similar way, the industrial states ought to be taking a keen interest in expanding markets in the developing countries. This would mean a significant increase in jobs both there and here, not just immediately but in the years ahead. Economic history has taught us that developed and diversified economies are the best partners for each other and everything seems to indicate that this will continue to be so in future. This certainly adds another dimension to the humanitarian argument.

If we wish to raise the relations between North and South to a level of fruitful cooperation and thus to create worldwide conditions for narrowing the immense gap between rich and poor, internationally *and* nationally, that will call for nothing short of a consensus on the major aspects of a new order. It would be absolutely wrong to revert to the habit of considering North-South relations first and foremost from an outmoded strategic standpoint.

The future is not simply about what the rich countries can do to help the poor countries. It is about what rich and poor nations can do *together* to make human survival more probable. There is a mutual interest in peace, in jobs and, I hope also, in greater justice.

The total number of people living in absolute poverty is rising instead of falling. I consider it feasible that scientists will develop chemical food substitutes. Still, I do not feel that this will give mankind the license to continue to multiply as much as it wants, and we must not rely on an imagined scientific breakthrough over which we have no control.

As we know too well, growth without any accompanying social goals neither guarantees a reduction in poverty and blatant inequalities nor creates an adequate level of employment within a measurable space of time.

The economic growth in recent years in some of the Asian or Latin American countries has not — or not sufficiently — benefited the broad masses of the population. In various cases, industrial development has remained confined to small dynamic areas within these countries while the rural regions have been simultaneously neglected. And the exodus to urban slums has reached critical levels.

The often justifiable criticism of this uneven development should not be quoted in the North to condone protectionist policies. Industrial countries have a right and even the duty to look after their own backward regions to protect them against excessive external pressure. Yet they do not help them in the longer term if they erect protectionist barriers in favour of today's jobs. The conditions in Western Europe between the wars showed that if each nation pursues its own short-term self-interest by a wrong route — in this case by increasing its protectionist barriers and "buy-at-home policies" — the result is not the good of all but the ruin of each.

On the whole, it accords with the real interests of the industrialized countries that the other countries should develop and become major partners, if only in some cases for the next generation.

Liberalized trade is surely one of the achievements of the postwar era, and it must be expanded even further in the interest of both South and North. But, as we all know, protectionism is taking root both in trade with the Third World as well as in trade among industrial countries themselves.

If the South cannot export to the North, then it will prove unable to pay for the North's exports. And we should be aware of one simple fact: Western Europe, North America and Japan sell more than one-third of their exports to the Third World. In 1980, for example, the United States sold 39 percent of all exports of goods and services to the developing countries, which is more than was purchased by the European Community, Eastern Europe, Japan and Australia combined.

There are people who hold the extraordinary view that it is tantamount to throwing money away when financial institutions or governments or international organizations such as the World Bank use government contributions, the taxpayers' money, to overcome poverty elsewhere in the world and to create the basic conditions for jobs. In reality, these activities represent an opportunity for us, they safeguard jobs in the industrial countries as they create new ones.

Many people only see the adjustment difficulties faced by the North when it imports industrial products from the Third World. The impression is often aroused that the North appears to be inundated with finished products from a number of developing countries. In point of fact, the imports of finished products from the Third World altogether account for less than 2 percent of consumption in the industrialized states.

Nevertheless, there can be no doubt about the fact that economically weaker regions in the North can be hard hit. Or that the movement of labour out of declining industries becomes all the more difficult, the less one bothers about opportunities for retraining. Seamstresses in the clothing industry will not easily be able to accept jobs as lathe operators or assembly workers that engineering or electronic firms may offer in entirely different parts of a country, not even in a buoyant economy with full employment. In times of rising unemployment this adjustment creates difficult political and social problems which call for sensitive and imaginative handling by governments. A forward-looking structural policy will thus become even more important. The solution in the long run is not to protect outmoded structures if we believe, or have to believe, in an international division of labour marked by dynamic change.

It is also really necessary to point out, and even to facilitate, the opportunities inherent in South-South cooperation. What I have in mind is not only the beneficial transfer of experience within the same region, but also the possibility of, for example, India and Nigeria being able to sell each other products unlikely to find a market in the industrialized world.

What we need in our parts of the world are more effective policies of positive adjustment through regional planning, retraining schemes and so forth. In my own country we had, and still have, to restructure large parts of the Ruhr area and our textile industry, to facilitate economic progress. This process of adjustment in the North, of course, will operate less smoothly in a recession than during a boom when alternative jobs are available.

At the same time, I agree with the International Labour Organization that "the competitiveness of new imports from developing countries should not be achieved to the detriment of fair labour standards." As the report of my Commission stated:

> Exports that result from working conditions which do not respect minimum social standards relevant to a given society are unfair to the workers directly involved, to workers of competing Third World exporting countries and to workers of importing countries whose welfare is undermined.

In my opinion, it is fair to expect that trade unions should play an important role in developing countries and that they exercise solidarity with labour in the industrialized states. "Runaway industries" that have located in the Third World should be forced to make a positive contribution to development, and to face some of the normal risks involved. In other words, they should not be allowed to move their production to countries where labour is cheap and just reap all the benefits they receive as a result of the move. They should also share benefits with the host country, whether in the form of reinvestment of profits, or taxes or otherwise.

In this context, it will certainly be an advantage if an effective code of behaviour could be used to link the interests of transnational corporations with those of the host and home countries. This could also supplement national and international efforts to transfer technology at a reasonable cost.

Transnational corporations are not, by nature, either good or bad. As past experience has taught us, they may well act as instruments for economic advancement. None the less, they must accept the laws and heritage of the given developing country and invest the bulk of their profits in the country concerned. This is no mere "pie in the sky"; it is the logical conclusion of a large number of cases drawn from everyday commercial practice.

Where transnationals try to create their own secluded enclaves they will eventually be forced to pay a price. Their properties will be taken over, there will be losses that could have been avoided. British investment in railways in Argentina, United States mining companies in Chile, French companies in Algeria and even German projects in Iran all provide examples for what I am talking about.

It is quite usual to find Third World countries attaching importance to being supported by adapted technologies, for example, as an aid to development. Third World countries need the support of imported technology, properly adapted. Their own research and technology are far from sufficient to support their development. And the developing countries have come to recognize that cooperation under agreed rules provides the best opportunities. They also know that private investment is indispensable — official development assistance would never be large enough to do the job, even if all targets were met overnight.

But the social dimension of change ought not to be lost sight of, either. International reforms are a necessity, because one thing simply cannot be denied: world markets in many ways operate to the disadvantage of Third World countries. When the ground rules of our international economic system were established a generation ago, little thought was given to the conditions prevailing in a country like Mali on the fringes of the Sahara. And the problem today in the many Malis of the world is to link old structures with modern facilities such as irrigation plants, solar energy plants and cooperatives for peasants and fishermen, not to mention, of course, the modest foundations of educational and health systems.

Let us not fool ourselves — we cannot, out of our own experience, measure their difficulties. Our countries developed under conditions of great if not maximum convenience. Our countries were neither overpopulated nor lacking in natural resources. And we had sufficient time to make the transition.

It is different in Mali. And instead of recounting the stories of errors and ill-conceived development projects, the cases of waste and corruption, we must see how many countries survive against all odds. There is progress in Mali and our Commission saw it on the spot. It is slow sometimes and difficult all the time. But there are water pumps powered by solar energy. And they work.

And as such projects work, we could make the international system work to serve all nations. North and South must find a joint approach in this highly interdependent world of ours. Nothing would seem to be more sensible than to identify those mutual interests which link us together in what is called North and South, and to demand joint action wherever this is feasible. There will continue to be plenty of criticism about the systems which have evolved in our countries. And I also think we must feel free to criticize corruption and other unacceptable behaviour, whether it exists in our parts of the world or with power-élites in Third World countries.

I believe that in our epoch there will remain little room in international affairs for national narrow-mindedness or the exclusive quest for political power. I am also convinced that North-South relations transcend the mere economic dimension. They include major cultural and religious aspects.

In recent years we have seen examples of what happens if non-economic factors are neglected. The focus has to be on people, not on machines and institutions. People, as we all know but tend to forget, do not live by bread alone.

Only when the will to bring about change is borne by major social groups and only when governments feel the requisite push from the grass roots will the urgently needed reforms prove to be feasible and effective, both nationally and internationally.

Let us cite an example from one part of the world. After the appropriate climate of public opinion had been created in Sweden, there was virtually no opposition to the introduction of a high ratio of public development aid. And their outstanding commitment has been fulfilled in good years and in years of recession; they are at the top of the league (with 0.93 percent in 1979, the last year with definite figures).

After the Scandinavians had shown in suitable regions of East Africa how one can dig wells, this inspired a movement, a whole movement of well-digging by the developing country itself.

At last year's annual meeting of the International Monetary Fund and World Bank, Robert McNamara drew particular attention to the following features of the new situation: the impact on the developing countries of the explosive rise in oil prices; the reduced importing capacity of the industrial countries; and the calamitous state of some countries' balance of payments. Look at the non-industrial members of the Commonwealth, and you will find this confirmed almost everywhere.

McNamara came to the following conclusion. Although the implementation of essential development measures had never been an easy matter, it was now seriously in jeopardy. This description is quite true, but it was not meant to make us capitulate in the face of the difficulties. On the contrary, he advised us to swim against the current. And I agree with him. My own experience has taught me there is no such thing as a hopeless situation unless you accept it as such.

I have gained the impression in the industrialized countries that there are now growing numbers of young people who appreciate one simple fact: their future jobs and those of their children, and of course the conditions of peace, depend on relations with other parts of the world. I do not mean that there exists no room for the more conventional solutions like charity. On the contrary, voluntary groups and associations can never do enough. In the final analysis, however, it is more than charity we are concerned with: it is survival and international cooperation.

And there are quite a few people who sense that mass hunger and world peace may well be more closely interconnected in future. Mass hunger constitutes a moral challenge and at the same time a danger to mankind, even in those places where people have enough to eat or, indeed, more than enough. To ignore this problem would not only be profoundly immoral; it would also impair our own legitimate interests and inevitably breed a danger to world peace. Where hundreds of millions die of hunger, peace stands on shaky foundations.

This fact in itself amounts to a great deal more than traditional humanitarian and more concrete development aid. What it is all about, is the common future, and our own role in it — if there is in fact to be a future of mankind.

Last year, in the United States, the *Global 2000 Report to the President* aptly observed that "an era of unprecedented cooperation and commitment is essential." All those in positions of responsibility in the Americas should enlist the impressive dynamic energy of their continent in the service of organizing peace.

V

SUMMITRY

There are some international conferences which, to be quite honest, are best forgotten. Along come two or three thousand members of the delegations together with their staff, a few hundred interpreters and secretaries, plus well over a thousand journalists. Yet nothing really happens. No genuine discussions take place; there are no proper negotiations and thus no results of any substance.

Let us take a closer look at such conferences. A minister and his staff fly thousands of kilometres in order to rattle off a speech which he hastily put together at home and re-edited on the plane. He shows his face at a few cocktail parties, invites guests to a dinner, often squeezes in another engagement not related to the conference, and then flies back to his capital. He leaves behind him a ministerial official or diplomat without any real brief to conduct negotiations, just as do the other ambassadors and officials. That is often, much too often, the scenario for these international conferences.

Too often the discussion on serious international matters has been a dialogue of the deaf. The air has been thick with alibis for doing precisely nothing. This applies to all sides. We judge ourselves by our good points and the other side by their failings. The result is frustration and deadlock.

Despite this, my colleagues in our Commission and I have not been discouraged from making a number of suggestions about the content of negotiations and their form.

A friend of mine from the Caribbean raised the question as to whether one could create, as he put it, "a more productive negotiating environment under the umbrella of the United Nations system." We tried to come up with an answer. And at the end of 1979 when we reached the conclusions set out in our North-South Report, we found there were good reasons to propose and organize an international meeting at the highest level, perhaps to be followed by others, in order to discuss questions of acute concern. If possible, the participants would try to reach agreements, as concrete as possible, on how to turn certain mutual interests into creative partnerships, both for the immediate future and the longer term.

When we debated the summit idea in my Commission we wanted to make it quite clear that North and South cannot proceed with business as usual, merely adding a few bits here and there. What, we thought, was required was intellectual reorientation, serious steps toward structural change, and increased practical cooperation. A more relaxed climate of negotiations ought to eliminate any wish for rhetorical jousting or unjustified expressions of distrust.

We were in agreement that global negotiations, comprehensive both in regard to the participating states and the subjects under discussion, need the platform of the United Nations. That is irreplaceable, but it is nevertheless capable of improvement.

Therefore, the United Nations system as such should of course be reviewed and reformed. Its shortcomings are well known and hard to overcome. Yet it is the only system we have. Our summit proposal thus was not directed against the United Nations — it intended to give an impetus to the negotiations at the United Nations.

I was grateful that this idea was taken up by José Lopez Portillo, the Mexican President, and Bruno Kreisky, the Austrian Chancellor, and that they both accepted the co-chairmanship for the summit held at Cancun in October 1981. In the event, Chancellor Kreisky was unable to participate and Pierre Trudeau, Prime Minister of Canada, served as co-chairman instead. He had been deeply involved in the preparations for the summit and, presumably, his initiative and a joint recommendation from him and the Mexican President convinced President Reagan to go to Cancun.

The Cancun summit in my view could have produced better results, but still it was a partial success. It vindicated our Independent Commission in various ways and it created a basis to move ahead toward global negotiations. There was insufficient time to deal with the main subjects we had suggested, but I think Cancun was a first, and even if considered small by some, an important step forward.

It built on the Ottawa summit of the seven leading industrial countries held in July 1981, where a significant agreement had been concluded in connection with the North-South theme. At Cancun, "The Heads of State and Government confirmed the desirability of supporting at the United Nations, with a sense of urgency, a consensus to launch Global Negotiations on a basis to be mutually agreed and in circumstances offering the prospect of meaningful progress." Those are carefully chosen and diplomatic words, but they mark a movement in the right direction.

It is important that governments and international organizations now move ahead in the spirit of Cancun and exploit all avenues for progress on procedural and substantive issues.

For example, the need for increased energy investment, from both private and official sources, in developing countries was stressed at Cancun. The establishment of an institution for this purpose, possibly within, or closely linked to, the World Bank, seems only a matter of some months' work.

At Cancun the participants also dealt with the efficiency of international organizations, particularly those dealing with problems of food and agriculture. That is a point which I made in my initial observations. And it is a point made in the complaints, many of them by no means exaggerated, about the lack of efficiency in international bureaucracies.

Member states have tolerated the excessive growth of an international bureaucracy, and only they can reverse the trend. But their difficulties in containing the growth of their own domestic bureaucracies are not reassuring. There is not only a need to review the state of international organizations; in some areas the existing ones may need to be restructured and others to be supplemented in order to be able to meet emerging concerns. International cooperation in the monetary and financial areas should in any case become more universal, and serious efforts must be made to include those countries still on the outside.

North-South summitry might advance the efforts of the international community to deal with at least some of the most urgent problems. But a summit meeting of course can include only a limited number of heads of state and government. It seems therefore all the more important to maintain good contacts with the major regional groupings and the United Nations as a whole.

There are, of course, world conferences which need a great number of participants and depend upon much publicity, but serious deliberations cannot take place at meetings with thousands of people participating.

Even for a limited conference such as the one in Cancun, it is important to forgo the custom of sending huge delegations and to limit them to a handful of aides. Prime ministers, foreign secretaries, and others would be well advised *not* to deliver prepared speeches on such occasions and to dispense with prefabricated, long-winded communiqués. What we need is a working style which matches the subject and the situation.

Needless to say, a summit conference with twenty instead of one hundred fifty main participants does not in itself provide any guarantee of success. The experience gathered to date with such a procedure has varied. I have personal experience of the summit conferences of the European Community, now known as the "European Council," a body which still possess no clear-cut terms of reference but which has nevertheless proved a success in practice. These conferences cannot be compared with a pan-European conference such as the one staged in Helsinki in 1975; it included on the one hand the Soviet Union and, on the other hand, the United States and Canada. That conference had more of a ceremonial character, the final document having been agreed upon beforehand.

The meetings of the heads of state and government of seven western industrial countries including Japan, held every summer during the last few years, have by and large proved useful. But as the recent meetings demonstrated, expectations should not be pitched too high. Economic power does not guarantee success in fighting a depression.

A much wider-ranging affair is a summit meeting of the non-aligned nations, in former times bearing to a pronounced degree a personal stamp of men like Nehru, Tito and Nasser. Meetings of the non-aligned had, and still have, their demonstrative importance and furnish a forum for many bilateral and multilateral discussions.

Despite its shortcomings, the movement of non-aligned nations possesses some political weight in the maintenance of peace. These countries are almost, though not exactly, the same as those in the Group of 77 which has meanwhile expanded and consists of some 120 countries. The goal pursued by the Group of 77 has been to reduce to a common denominator the development policy and the economic demands of the Third World. However, the results obtained have not always been dramatic.

The first selective North-South summit, held in Mexico in October 1981, did not have a strict agenda. And it should remain clear that the views expressed at such a conference could not commit the international community. But decisions could be prepared and the appropriate attendance might provide the necessary climate for binding decisions in other forums. Global questions require global answers; and as there is now a risk of humanity destroying itself, this risk must be met by new methods.

Perhaps I might add what I think is necessary in the field of international organization in addition to the occasional use of limited summit meetings in order to advance the cause of consensus and change. My colleagues and I think that policies, agreements, and institutions in the field of international economic, financial and monetary cooperation should be guided by the principle of universality. The United Nations' system, which faces ever expanding tasks, needs to be strengthened but also to be made more efficient. This calls for more coordination of budgets, programs and personnel policies to avoid duplication of tasks and wasteful overlapping. The performance of the various multilateral organizations in the field of international development should be regularly monitored by a high level advisory body. There needs to be a review of the present system of negotiations to see whether a more flexible, expeditious and result-oriented procedure can be introduced without detracting from cooperation within established groups. And increased attention should be paid to educating public opinion and the younger generation about the importance of international cooperation.

When I recently met with my fellow-Commissioners, we welcomed the decision to hold a summit meeting of North-South leaders which we had proposed in our report. Naturally, we also took a look at the response evoked by our report. From the standpoint of the international political situation and the world's economy, we had not chosen a particularly auspicious time for publication. Our North-South Report was completed just before the Russian move into Afghanistan and the outbreak of war between Iran and Iraq. And many people asked how one could talk of common interests in the light of these and other serious events. But I strongly believe that global issues are a challenge we must address in any case. They will come to the forefront when local or regional conflicts are being contained. Moreover, the degree of interest varied greatly from one country to another. The report attracted an almost rapturous reception in Great Britain and also among people in other parts of Europe.

Our report managed to reach out farther and to do so with greater speed than Lester Pearson had achieved with his report in 1969 for the World Bank. Our report was in a way a follow-up to his in that we systematically tried to show how development aid must become development policy. By now, our report has been translated into nineteen languages, including Chinese, Polish and Romanian.

The response of the various governments to our recommendations ranged from lukewarm to conventional and friendly. A number of developing countries and international bodies took a more positive line on the report. Some of our suggestions were taken up by the International Monetary Fund and the World Bank even before we had published our findings. Both institutions introduced new types of lending to developing countries, which meet their needs, at least to a certain degree, to finance food imports and the adjustment of their economies to new circumstances.

Journalists in various countries displayed a highly encouraging open-minded approach mixed with an incredibly conservative type of criticism. That was particularly noticeable in England among the ranks of those whose dogmas have forfeited much of their appeal for the British. Greater importance must be assigned to the criticism of people, some of them from among these same journalists, who condemn the failure to carry out clear-cut reforms in various developing countries, agrarian reform in particular, and who fear the possibility of the North's development policy fizzling out if it is not matched by action in the South.

The miserable circumstances in the developing countries, and of the world economy in general, have deteriorated even more rapidly than our report had foreseen, especially in the areas of debt, food and energy. Moreover, the situation is aggravated by the competing expenditure on armaments by East and West. The current crisis calls for bold and courageous responses to the problems that threaten all the world's people, in order to produce a new climate for cooperation. The long-term structural changes must not delay urgent action to face the crisis already at hand. The existing emergency in the world economy requires an immediate and direct response.

Rising unemployment, persistent monetary instability, exorbitant interest rates, intolerable payments deficits and unprecedented debts all point to the need for international negotiations based on cooperation. Many individual nations appear to be retreating into short-term national solutions which can only worsen their own long-term prospects.

Together with my fellow-Commissioner Mr. Ramphal, the Commonwealth Secretary-General, I appealed to the world leaders before they assembled at Cancun, urging them to seize this unique chance for candid and direct discussion to release new opportunities for international cooperation. We suggested that they should point the way forward to those four areas I dealt with earlier namely:

1. A global food program to stimulate world food production and to overcome world hunger;
2. A global energy strategy to accommodate the need for security among producers and consumers alike;
3. Additional financial flows to ensure the stability of national economies strained by precarious balance of payments, and mounting debts;
4. Reforms to bring about broader participation in international financial institutions and more balanced conditions for world trade.

Reforms in these areas would provide important benefits for both North and South, and point the way forward to breaking the existing deadlock and stimulating the world's economy.

If some people argue that this represents a reformist approach, that is something which I cannot deny. I myself am unaware of any better way of tackling the problem. We must learn to cope with grave problems in a world marked by differing ideologies and opposing interests. And yet it is a world in which we have to learn to live with each other if we are not all to perish together.

That applies in particular when we think of the dangers attendant upon the arms race. Or when the matter at stake is the starvation of millions of people and the desperate need for a more just international order.

The shaping of our common future is much too important to be left to experts and governments alone. Therefore, my appeal again goes out to the young people of the world, to women's and labour movements, to political, intellectual and religious leaders, to scientists and educators, to technicians and managers, to members of the rural and business communities. May you all try to understand and to conduct your affairs in the light of the these new challenges.

Everybody is called upon to make a contribution. The leaders at Cancun have made a start. They must act on their expressed intentions. We must support them and press them to produce results which improve the prospects of the world economy and give hope to all. We must open our minds to the difficult problems of others in all parts of the world. And we must realize that together we might survive — or we will not survive at all.

NOTES

The Image of Confederation
by FRANK H. UNDERHILL

CHAPTER 1: *The New Nationality*

1. What British North American newspapers were saying about the project of Confederation from 1864 to 1867 is brilliantly analyzed in P. B. Waite's *The Life and Times of Confederation 1864–1867* (Toronto: University of Toronto Press, 1962).

2. *Parliamentary Debates on the Subject of the Confederation of the British North American Provinces* (Quebec, 1865).

3. A. T. Galt, *Speech on the Proposed Union of the British North American Provinces, delivered at Sherbrooke, C. E., November 23, 1864* (Montreal, 1864).

4. This book was published in London, England, in 1861. It is mainly a reprint of the dispatches that Woods sent home to his paper while on the tour. These dispatches were reprinted in

many Canadian papers at the time, a fact that shows how important English opinions were to the British Americans of the 1860s.

5. *The Globe*, August 2, 1864.

CHAPTER II: *The First Fine Careless Rapture*

1. Two accounts of Canada First by men who were active in the movement are: (i) G. T. Denison, *The Struggle for Imperial Unity* (Toronto: MacMillan & Co. Ltd., 1909); (ii) *Canada First: A Memorial of the Late William A. Foster, Q.C.* by W. A. Foster with an introduction by Goldwin Smith (Toronto: Hunter, Rose & Co., 1890). This volume contains the text of some of Foster's speeches and articles, and the Address of the Canadian National Association to the People of Canada.

2. On Goldwin Smith, there is a comprehensive and interesting study by Elisabeth Wallace titled *Goldwin Smith: Victorian Liberal* (Toronto: University of Toronto Press, 1957). See also the articles in my collection of essays, *In Search of Canadian Liberalism* (Toronto: MacMillan & Co. Ltd., 1961): "Goldwin Smith, Political Ideas of the Upper Canada Reformers 1867–1878," and "The Conception of a National Interest."

3. On Edward Blake in this period of the 1870s, see my articles: "Edward Blake" in C. T. Bissell, ed., *Our Living Tradition* (Toronto: University of Toronto Press, 1957); "Edward Blake, the Supreme Court Act, and the Appeal to the Privy Council, 1875–1876," in *The Canadian Historical Review*, September, 1938; "Edward Blake and Canadian Liberal Nationalism" in R. Flenley, ed., *Essays in Canadian History* (Toronto: MacMillan & Co. Ltd., 1931).

4. *The Globe*'s comment on the Canada First platform is in its issue of January 9, 1874.

5. *The Canadian Monthly*, July, 1872.

6. *The Canadian Monthly*, July, 1873.

7. *The Canadian Monthly*, November, 1874.

8. *The Nation*, February 26, 1875.

CHAPTER III: *History Against Geography*

1. Quoted in O. D. Skelton, *Life and Letters of Sir Wilfrid Laurier*, vol. i, p. 273 (Toronto: McClelland & Stewart, 1921).

2. Quoted in E. M. Saunders, *Life and Letters of Sir Charles Tupper*, vol. ii, p. 253 (Toronto: Cassell & Co. Ltd., 1916).

3. Laurier to Blake, December 29, 1891. Quoted in my article, "Laurier and Blake, 1891–1892," *The Canadian Historical Review*, June, 1943.

4. Goldwin Smith, *Lecture Before the Boston Fraternity*, 1864 (published as a pamphlet in Manchester, 1865).

5. Goldwin Smith, *The Empire: A Series of Letters Published in the Daily News, 1862, 1863* (London: J. Henry and J. Parker, 1863).

6. The case for commercial union had been presented at length in 1888 in a volume, *Handbook of Commercial Union*, edited by G. Mercer Adam, and with an Introduction by Goldwin Smith.

7. Goldwin Smith, *Canada and the Canadian Question*, p. 267 (Toronto: Hunter, Rose & Co., 1891).

8. On Grant, see the biography, *Principal Grant* by W. L. Grant (his son) and F. Hamilton (Toronto: Morang & Co. Ltd., 1904). See also, D. D. Calvin, *Queen's University in Kingston, 1841–1941* (Kingston: Queen's University Press, 1941).
   On Parkin, see the biography, *Sir George Parkin* by Sir John Willison (London: MacMillan & Co. Ltd. 1929).

9. G. M. Grant, *Canada and the Canadian Question: A Review*, a pamphlet published in 1891 by the Imperial Federation League in Canada; originally printed in two articles in *The Week*, May 1 and 15, 1891.
   The last sentence in this quotation is from a later controversy of

Grant with Smith, in *The Canadian Magazine*, November 1896.

10. George R. Parkin, *Imperial Federation: The Problem of National Unity*, p. 47 (London: MacMillan & Co. Ltd., 1892).

Parkin published a second book on Canada in 1895: *The Great Dominion: Studies of Canada* (London: MacMillan & Co. Ltd., 1895). This was based on a tour of Canada that he made as a special correspondent of the London *Times*. In the same year he became principal of Upper Canada College in Toronto, and in 1902 he became the first administrator of the Rhodes scholarships in Oxford.

11. See the article by K. A. MacKirdy on "The Loyalty Issue in 1891," in *Ontario History*, September 1963.

CHAPTER IV: *Canada's Relations with Britain*

1. For Principal Grant on the Boer War, see his notes on Current Events in *The Queen's Quarterly*: April and October 1897, July 1899; January and April 1900.

2. J. W. Dafoe, *Laurier: A Study in Canadian Politics*, p. 74.

Dafoe in this passage is quoting from a speech of Chamberlain in Toronto in 1887 and from Sir John Seeley's *Expansion of England*. The text of Chamberlain's speech, which is one of the finest expositions ever given of the case for closer imperial union, is to be found in Sir Willoughby Maycock's *With Mr. Chamberlain in the United States and Canada* (Toronto: Burns & Cockburn, 1914).

3. See Elisabeth Wallace, *Goldwin Smith: Victorian Liberal*, p. 119 (Toronto: University of Toronto Press, 1896).

4. David Mills, *The English in Africa* (Toronto: Morang & Co., 1900).

James Cappon, *Britain's Title in South Africa* (Toronto: MacMillan & Co. Ltd., 1901).

5. Sir Joseph Pope, *Correspondence of Sir John Macdonald*, p. 337,

March 12, 1885 (Toronto: Oxford University Press, 1921).

6. Canada, Debates, House of Commons, 1900, March 13, p. 1793.

7. Canada, Debates, House of Commons, 1900, March 13, p. 1837.

8. For two contemporary books on Canada's experience in the Boer War see:

    (i) T. G. Marquis, *Canada's Sons on Kopje and Veldt* (Toronto: Canada's Sons Publishing Co., 1900). This volume has a shrewd introductory chapter by Principal Grant of Queen's, entitled "Imperial Significance of the Canadian Contingents."

    (ii) W. Sanford Evans, *The Canadian Contingents and Canadian Imperialism* (Toronto: The Publishers' Syndicate Ltd., 1901).

9. Stephen Leacock, "Greater Canada, an Appeal," *The University Magazine*, June 1907.

10. Stephen Leacock, "The Psychology of American Humour," *The University Magazine*, February 1907.

Chapter v: *French-English Relations in Canada*

1. André Siegfried, *Canada: An International Power*, p. 224 (London: Jonathan Cape, 1947).

2. Laurier's long fight with the ultramontanes, who came to be nicknamed the Castors, is dealt with in the Skelton and Willison biographies. For contemporary comment by English-Canadians on the dangers of ultramontane ambitions, see Goldwin Smith, *Canada and the Canadian Question*, chap. ii, "The French Province" (Toronto: Hunter, Rose & Co., 1891); and Charles Lindsey, *Rome in Canada* (Toronto: Lovell Brother, 1877).

3. André Siegfried, *The Race Question in Canada*, p. 50 (London: Eveleigh Nash, 1907).

4. Ibid. p. 52.

5. André Siegfried, *The Race Question in Canada*, p. 52 (London: Eveleigh Nash, 1907).
6. Ibid. p. 141.

Chapter VI: *Conclusions*
1. W. L. Morton, *The Kingdom of Canada*, p. 443 (Toronto: McClelland & Stewart, 1963).
2. James Morris in *The Manchester Guardian Weekly*.

Time as History
by George Grant

Chapter One
1. It is often said that our concentration on history comes from our Biblical origins. The Biblical God of history is compared with the philosophical God of nature. Whatever use there may be in so distinguishing the traditions that come to us from philosophy and from the Bible, it first must be insisted that there are no words in the Bible which should serve as synonyms for what we mean by "nature" or "history."
2. This section of Kant's first Critique has generally been neglected by English-speaking commentators. Indeed the British have in their commentaries on Kant generally tried to turn that genius into one of their own. To put the matter simply, they neglect the fact that Kant paid an even greater tribute to Rousseau than he did to Hume.

Chapter Two
1. See *Technology and Empire*, House of Anansi, Toronto, 1969.
2. The philological question is complicated by the fact that the word "will" has its origin in two distinct old English verbs

"willan" and "willian." It is therefore difficult to follow the development of its use.

3. It is interesting for Canadians that Marx's tomb is close to Lord Strathcona's — the man who more than any other was responsible for the actual building of the C.P.R., a noble deed making possible the possibility of Canada.

4. This has been thought most illuminatingly by Heidegger.

CHAPTER THREE

1. Who ever more agreed with St. Augustine's dictum "Quid sumus nisi voluntates?"

FURTHER READING

The Image of Confederation
by FRANK H. UNDERHILL

No attempt is made in this list to include the more important histories of Canada, or biographies or memoirs of leading Canadians — though such books are likely to throw much light on the image of Canada in the minds of particular individuals or particular generations. The books included in the list are generally those devoted to discussion and argument about Canadian policies and purposes. Even within these limitations, the list is not a comprehensive one. It is weak on French-Canadian writing, and is a rather arbitrary compilation of the books that the author of these lectures has found most interesting and suggestive. Much of the best reading on the topics treated in these lectures is to be found in periodicals and newspapers.

Books by British authors are indicated by an *.
Books by American authors are indicated by a †.

I. ON THE PERIOD 1860–1900

Brebner, J. B. *North Atlantic Triangle*. New York: Columbia University Press, 1949.

Clark, S. D. *Church and Sect in Canada*. Toronto: University of Toronto Press, 1948.

Denison, George T. *The Struggle for Imperial Unity*. Toronto: MacMillan & Co. Ltd., 1909.

*Dilke, Sir Charles. *Problems of Greater Britain* (two volumes). London: MacMillan & Co. Ltd., 1890.

Fleming, Sanford. *England and Canada*. Montreal: Dawson Brothers, 1884.

Foster, W. A. *Canada First: A Memorial of the Late William A. Foster*. Toronto: Hunter, Rose & Co., 1890. Includes an Introduction by Goldwin Smith.

Galt, Sir Alexander. *Civil Liberty in Lower Canada*. Montreal: D. Bentley, 1876; *Church and State*. Montreal: Dawson Brothers, 1876.

Grant, G. M. *Ocean to Ocean*. Toronto: Coles Publishing Company, 1873.
An account of Grant's trip with Sandford Fleming in exploration of the Yellowhead route to the Pacific.

Grant, G. M. *Picturesque Canada* (two volumes). Toronto: Belden Brothers, 1882.

Lindsey, Charles. *Rome in Canada*. Toronto: Lovell Brothers, 1877.
Galt and Lindsey were two English Canadians who were alarmed at the pretensions of the French Catholic Church in politics.

Macoun, John. *Manitoba and the Great North-West*. Guelph: The World Publishing Company, 1882.

Parkin, George R. *Imperial Federation: The Problem of Imperial Unity*.

London: MacMillan & Co. Ltd., 1892; *The Great Dominion*. London: MacMillan & Co. Ltd., 1895.

Both of Parkin's books were written primarily for an English audience. The second consists of letters which he originally wrote as a special correspondent for the London *Times*.

*Russell, W. H. *Canada, Its Defences, Condition, and Resources*. Boston: Bradbury & Evans, 1865.

Sissons, C. B. *Church and State in Canadian Education: An Historical Survey*. Toronto: Ryerson Press, 1959.

Smith, Goldwin. *Canada and the Canadian Question*. Toronto: Hunter, Rose & Co., 1891.

*Smith, Goldwin. *The Empire*. London: John Henry & James Parker, 1863.

*Trollope, Anthony. *North America*. London: Chapman & Hall, 1862. (There is a modern edition, edited by D. Smalley and B. A. Booth, New York: DaCapo Press, 1951).

These four books are all by Englishmen about Canada as it was just before Confederation. Smith had not yet visited North America. Russell was the famous war correspondent of the London *Times* who made his name reporting the Crimea, and who was so frank about the early battles of the American Civil War that he had to leave the United States. Woods accompanied the Prince of Wales on his tour of British America in 1860. Trollope's book is mostly about the United States.

Waite, P. B. *The Life and Times of Confederation*. Toronto: University of Toronto Press, 1963.

A modern analysis of newspaper discussion of the Confederation project during the years 1864–1867.

Dilke has a discussion of Canada in his first volume which is much more optimistic than that of Goldwin Smith.

Wallace, Elisabeth. *Goldwin Smith: Victorian Liberal*. Toronto: University of Toronto Press, 1957.

†Warner, Donald. *The Idea of Continental Union: Agitation for the Annexation of Canada to the United States.* Lexington: University of Kentucky Press, 1960.

*Woods, N. A. *The Prince of Wales in Canada and the United States.* London: Bradbury & Evans, 1861.

II ON THE PERIOD 1900–1919

L'Action Nationale. "La pensée de Henri Bourassa." Montreal: 1952.

Bourassa, Henri. *Great Britain and Canada.* Montreal: C. O. Beauchemin & Fils, 1902; *Independence or Imperial Partnership?* Montreal: 1916.

The second book is a review of Curtis's book, *The Problem of the Commonwealth.*

Bourassa, Henri. *Que devons-nous à l'Angleterre?* Montreal: 1915; *Hier, aujourd'hui, demain.* Montreal: 1916.

*Brooke, Rupert. *Letters from America.* Toronto: McClelland, Goodchild & Stewart, 1916.

These were letters published while Brooke was on a trip across Canada in 1914.

*Bryce, James. *Modern Democracies* (two volumes). London: MacMillan & Co. Ltd., 1922.

Bryce's account of Canada here is based on his observations when ambassador to the United States before 1914.

*Curtis, Lionel. *The Problem of the Commonwealth.* Toronto: MacMillan & Co. Ltd., 1916.

Le Devoir. "Hommage à Henri Bourassa." Montreal: 1952.

Ewart, J. S. *The Kingdom of Canada.* Toronto: Morang, 1908; *Kingdom Papers.* Ottawa: 1912–1917.

*Hall, H. Duncan. *The British Commonwealth of Nations.* London: Methuen & Co., Ltd., 1920.

Jebb's book is an exposition of the Chamberlain policy of imperial preferences, which he presents as a great Liberal policy of "mutual aid in living." Curtis argues for imperial federation. Hall sets forth the point of view of the Borden-Smuts settlement at the end of the war.

*Hobson, J. A. *Canada To-Day*. London: T. Fisher Unwin, 1905.

*Jebb, Richard. *The Britannic Question*. London: Longmans, Green & Co., 1913.

Miller, J. O. (ed.). *The New Era in Canada*. Toronto: J. M. Dent & Sons Ltd., 1917.

Moore, W. H. *The Clash!: A Study in Nationalities*. Toronto: J. M. Dent & Sons, Ltd., 1918.

Rumilly, R. *Henri Bourassa*. Montreal: Éditions Chantecler ltée., 1953.

Siegfried, André. *The Race Question in Canada*. London: Eveleigh Nash, 1907.

III ON THE PERIOD 1918–1939

Brady, Alexander. *Canada*. London: Ernest Benn, Ltd., 1932.

†Chamberlain, W. H. *Canada: Today and Tomorrow*. Boston: R. Hale, 1942.

Cook, Ramsay. *The Politics of John W. Dafoe*. Toronto: University of Toronto Press, 1963.

Corbett, P. E. and Smith, J. A. *Canada and World Politics*. Toronto: MacMillan & Co. Ltd., 1928.

Dafoe, J. W. *Canada: An American Nation*. New York: Columbia University Press, 1935.

Flenley, R. (ed.). *Essays in Canadian History*. Toronto: MacMillan & Co. Ltd., 1931.

Groulx, Abbé Lionel. *Pour quoi nous sommes divisés*. Montreal: Éditions de l'Action nationale, 1943; *Nos luttes constitutionelles*. Montreal: Imprimé au Devoir, 1915–16; *La confédération canadienne, ses origines*. Montreal: Imprimé au Devoir, 1918; *Notre maître, le passé* (three volumes). Montreal: Libraire Granger Frères, ltée., 1937–1944.

King, William Lyon Mackenzie. *Industry and Humanity.* Toronto: Thomas Allen, 1918.

Leacock, Stephen. *Economic Prosperity in the British Empire.* Toronto: MacMillan & Co. Ltd., 1930; *My Discovery of the West.* Toronto: Thomas Allen, 1937.

League for Social Reconstruction. *Social Planning for Canada.* Toronto: Thomas Nelson, 1935.

†MacCormac, John. *Canada: America's Problem.* New York: Viking, 1940.

Maheux, Abbé Arthur. *Pour quoi sommes-nous divisés?* Quebec: Radio-Canada, 1943.

Morton, W. L. (ed.). *The Voice of Dafoe.* Toronto: MacMillan & Co. Ltd., 1945.

Morton, W. L. *The Progressive Party in Canada.* Toronto: University of Toronto Press, 1950.

Scott, F. R. *Canada Today.* London: Oxford University Press, 1939.

Siegfried, André. *Canada.* London: Jonathan Cape, 1949.

*Teeling, W. *England's French Dominion?* London: Hutchison & Co., 1932.

Williams, John R. *The Conservative Party of Canada 1920–1949.* Durham: Duke University Press, 1956.

IV SINCE 1939

Aitchison, J. (ed.). *The Political Process in Canada.* Toronto: University of Toronto Press, 1963.

Blishen, B., Jones, F. E., Naegele, K. J., Porter, J. *Canadian Society: Sociological Perspectives.* New York: Free Press of Glencoe, 1961.

Brady, A. *Democracy in the Dominions* (Third edition). Toronto: University of Toronto Press, 1958.

Brady, A., Corry, J. A., Lower, A. R. M., Scott, F. R., Soward, R. *Evolving Canadian Federalism*. Durham: Duke University Press, 1958.

Brunet, Michel. *La présence anglaise et les canadiens*. Montreal: C. O. Beauchemin & Fils, 1958.

†Chapin, Miriam. *Contemporary Canada*. New York: Oxford University Press, 1959.

Clark, Robert M. (ed.). *Canadian Issues: Essays in Honour of Henry F. Angus*. Toronto: University of Toronto Press, 1961.

Clark, S. D. *The Developing Canadian Community*. Toronto: University of Toronto Press, 1962.

Corry, J. A. and Hodgetts, J. E. *Democratic Government and Politics*. Toronto: University of Toronto Press, 1960.

Dawson, R. M., revised by Norman Ward. *The Government of Canada*. Toronto: University of Toronto Press, 1963.

Eayrs, James George. *Northern Approaches*. Toronto: MacMillan & Co. Ltd., 1961.

Falardeau, Jean Charles. *Roots and Values in Canadian Lives*. Toronto: University of Toronto Press, 1961.

Fowke, V. C. *The National Policy and the Wheat Economy*. Toronto: University of Toronto Press, 1957.

Fox, Paul (ed.). *Politics, Canada, Recent Readings*. Toronto: McGraw-Hill, 1962.

Hutchison, Bruce. *The Unknown Country*. New York: Coward-McCann Inc., 1942.

Johnson, Harry G. *Canada in a Changing World Economy*. Toronto: University of Toronto Press, 1962; *The Canadian Quandary*. Toronto: McGraw-Hill, 1963.

These two books contain devastating criticisms of the economic policies of both the Liberal and Conservative governments since 1957.

Lipset, S. M. *Agrarian Socialism*. Berkeley: University of California

Press, 1950; *Political Man*. New York: Doubleday, 1960; *The First New Nation*. New York: Basic Books, 1963.

The first of the Lipset books is the classical history of the rise of the C.C.F. movement in Saskatchewan. The two later books are about the conditions in which democratic politics are carried on in modern countries. They have many enlightening comments on Canadian politics.

Lyon, Peyton. *The Policy Question*. Toronto: McClelland & Stewart, 1963.

Two discussions of contemporary foreign policy.

MacKinnon, Frank. *The Politics of Education*. Toronto: University of Toronto Press, 1960.

Massey, Vincent. *On Being Canadian*. Toronto: Dent, 1948; *Canadians and Their Commonwealth*. Oxford: Clarendon Press, 1961.

Minifie, J. M. *Peacemaker or Powder-Monkey*. Toronto: McClelland & Stewart, 1960.

Morton, W. L. *The Canadian Identity*. Toronto: University of Toronto Press, 1961.

Neatby, Hilda. *So Little for the Mind*. Toronto: Clarke, Irwin & Co. Ltd., 1953.

Oliver, M. J. (ed.). *Social Purpose for Canada*. Toronto: University of Toronto Press, 1961.

†Park, Julian (ed.). *The Culture of Contemporary Canada*. Ithaca: Cornell University Press, 1957.

Pierce, Lorne. *A Canadian Nation*. Toronto: Ryerson Press, 1960.

A Carlylean denunciation of the country.

Quinn, H. F. *The Union Nationale*. Toronto: University of Toronto Press, 1963.

Report of the Royal Commission of Inquiry on Constitutional Problems. Province of Quebec: 1956. (The Tremblay Report.)

Ross, Malcolm (ed.). *Our Sense of Identity*. Toronto: Ryerson Press, 1954.

Scott, F. R. *Civil Liberties and Canadian Federalism*. Toronto: University of Toronto Press, 1959.

Seeley, J., Sim, R., and Looseley, E. *Crestwood Heights*. Toronto: University of Toronto Press, 1956.

Thorburn, Hugh (ed.). *Party Politics in Canada*. Toronto: Prentice-Hall, 1963.

Underhill, F. H. *The British Commonwealth of Nations*. Durham: Duke University Press, 1956; *In Search of Canadian Liberalism*. Toronto: MacMillan & Co. Ltd., 1961.

†Viner, Jacob. *Canada and Its Giant Neighbour*. Ottawa: Carleton University Press, 1958.

†Wade, Mason. *The French-Canadian Outlook*. New York: Viking, 1946; *The French Canadians*. Toronto: MacMillan & Co. Ltd., 1955; (ed.) *Canadian Dualism: Studies of French-English Relations*. Toronto: University of Toronto Press, 1960.

*Watkins, Ernest. *Prospect of Canada*. London: Secker & Warburg, 1954.

About the Lectures
and the Lecturers

The Massey Lectures were created in honour of the Right Honourable Vincent Massey, former Governor General of Canada, and were inaugurated by the CBC in 1961 to enable distinguished authorities to communicate the results of original study or research on a variety of subjects of general interest. The Massey Lectures are today co-sponsored by CBC Radio, House of Anansi Press, and Massey College at the University of Toronto.

The Rich Nations and the Poor Nations is the very first Massey Lecture ever to be delivered, and was broadcast on CBC Radio in the spring of 1961. The series was arranged by the CBC Department of Public Affairs.

Barbara Ward (1914–81), in later life Baroness Jackson of Lodsworth, was a British economist and writer concerned with the economic and ideological background of contemporary world politics. After studying economics at Oxford University, she became a writer and editor at *The Economist*. She was also a diplomatic correspondent of the *London Star* and an assistant editor of *The Dublin Review*. She was an early advocate of sustainable development and was an influential advisor to policy-makers in the U.K., the U.S., the Vatican, the UN, and the World Bank. She wrote numerous articles and books on the worldwide threat of poverty among less-developed countries and the importance of conservation. Her prolific written contributions to the development debate include *The International Share-Out*, *Defence of the West*, *Policy for the West*, *Faith and Freedom*, *Interplay of East and West*, *The Planet under Pressure*, *Nationalism and Ideology*, *Spaceship Earth*, and *Progress for a Small Planet* (1979).

The Image of Confederation is the text of the third annual series of Massey Lectures, broadcast on CBC Radio in the fall of 1963. The series was arranged by Robert McCormack and produced by Gordon Bruce of the CBC Department of Public Affairs.

Frank Underhill (1885–1971) was a Canadian historian, social critic, and political thinker. He studied at the University of Toronto and Oxford University. He taught at the University of Saskatchewan from 1914 to 1927, and from 1927 to 1955 he was a professor of History at the University of Toronto. He played a notable part in the political life of Canada as a founder of the Cooperative Commonwealth Federation and as a prominent member of the League for Social Reconstruction. His publications include *In Search of Canadian Liberalism*, a volume of essays for which he received the Governor General's Literary Award for Nonfiction in 1961. In 1967, he was made an Officer of the Order of Canada.

Time as History is the text of the ninth annual series of Massey Lectures, broadcast on CBC Radio in the fall of 1969. The series was arranged and produced by Janet Somerville, and organized by Lester Sugerman of the CBC Information Programs Department.

George Grant (1918–88) has been acknowledged as Canada's leading political philosopher. He taught religion and philosophy at McMaster University and Dalhousie University. His books include *Philosophy in the Mass Age, Lament for a Nation, English-Speaking Justice,* and *Technology and Justice.*

Myth and Meaning is the text of seventeenth annual series of Massey Lectures, broadcast on CBC Radio in December 1977. They were assembled from a series of lengthy conversations between Professor Lévi-Strauss and Carole Orr Jerome, producer in the Paris bureau of the CBC. The programs were organized by Geraldine Sherman, executive producer of *Ideas,* and produced by Bernie Lucht.

Claude Lévi-Strauss (1908–present) is a French social anthropologist who became a leading scholar in the structural approach to social anthropology. Lévi-Strauss was awarded the Wenner-Gren Foundation's Viking Fund Medal in 1966 and the Erasmus Prize in 1975. He has been awarded several honorary doctorate degrees from prestigious institutions such as Oxford, Yale, Harvard, and Columbia. He has also held several academic memberships including the National Academy of Sciences, the American Academy and Institute of Arts and Letters, the American Academy of Arts and Sciences, and the American Philosophical Society. His books include *A World on the Wane, Structural Anthropology, The Savage Mind, Anthropology and Myth,* and *Look, Listen, Read.*

Dangers & Options: The Matter of World Survival is the text of the twenty-first annual series of Massey Lectures, broadcast on CBC Radio in November and December 1981 as part of *Ideas*. The programs were recorded in Bonn by Doug Caldwell (CBC London), and produced by Executive Producer Geraldine Sherman.

Willy Brandt (1913–92) was a German statesman, leader of the German Social Democratic Party from 1964 to 1987, and chancellor of the Federal Republic of Germany from 1969 to 1974. He was awarded the Nobel Prize for Peace in 1971 for his efforts to achieve reconciliation between West Germany and the countries of the Soviet bloc. His books include *My Path to Berlin: An Autobiography*, *The Politics of Peace in Europe*, *Encounters and Insights 1960–75*, *Left and Free: My Path 1930–50*, *Organized Lunacy*, and *Memories*.